Poll Power

Poll Power

*The Voter Education Project
and the Movement for the Ballot
in the American South*

Evan Faulkenbury

The University of North Carolina Press CHAPEL HILL

© 2019 The University of North Carolina Press
All rights reserved
Set in MeropeBasic by Westchester Publishing Services
Manufactured in the United States of America

The University of North Carolina Press has been a member
of the Green Press Initiative since 2003.

Library of Congress Cataloging-in-Publication Data
Names: Faulkenbury, Evan, author.
Title: Poll power : the Voter Education Project and the movement for the ballot
   in the American South / Evan Faulkenbury.
Other titles: Voter Education Project and the movement for the ballot in the
   American South | Justice, power, and politics.
Description: Chapel Hill : University of North Carolina Press, [2019] |
   Series: Justice, power, and politics
Identifiers: LCCN 2018043542| ISBN 9781469651316 (cloth : alk. paper) |
   ISBN 9781469652009 (pbk : alk. paper) | ISBN 9781469651323 (ebook)
Subjects: LCSH: Voter Education Project (Southern Regional Council) |
   Voter registration—Southern States. | Civil rights movements—Southern States.
Classification: LCC JK2160 .F38 2019 | DDC 324.6/40975—dc23
   LC record available at https://lccn.loc.gov/2018043542

Cover illustration: Large crowd standing in line waiting to vote, circa
1960–1964. Voter Education Project Organizational Records, Atlanta University
Center Robert W. Woodruff Library.

Portions of this book were previously published in a different form as
"Preventing a Second Redemption: The Voter Education Project and Black
Elected Officials, 1966–1968," *Southern Historian* 36 (Spring 2015): 24–34.

For Alex and Clara

Contents

Abbreviations in the Text ix

Mapping the Voter Education Project xi

Introduction 1

CHAPTER ONE 8
Southern Disfranchisement and the Long Origins of the
Voter Education Project

CHAPTER TWO 29
Setting Up the Voter Education Project, 1959–1962

CHAPTER THREE 57
The Voter Education Project, 1962–1964

CHAPTER FOUR 90
The Second Voter Education Project, 1965–1969

CHAPTER FIVE 110
The Tax Reform Act of 1969 and the Undermining of the
Voter Education Project

Epilogue 135

Acknowledgments 137

Notes 141

Bibliography 181

Index 195

A gallery of images begins on p. 84.

Abbreviations in the Text

CIC	Commission on Interracial Cooperation
COFO	Council of Federated Organizations
CORE	Congress of Racial Equality
DOJ	U.S. Department of Justice
ICC	Interstate Commerce Commission
IRS	Internal Revenue Service
MFDP	Mississippi Freedom Democratic Party
MIA	Montgomery Improvement Association
NAACP	National Association for the Advancement of Colored People
NCVEP	North Carolina Voter Education Project
NUL	National Urban League
SCLC	Southern Christian Leadership Conference
SNCC	Student Nonviolent Coordinating Committee
SRC	Southern Regional Council
SVREP	Southwest Voter Registration Education Project
VEP	Voter Education Project
VOTE	Voters of Texas Enlist

Mapping the Voter Education Project

The Voter Education Project supported hundreds of projects across the American South, and most did not make it into this book. Instead of dozens of tables and graphs within these pages to identify each one, I decided to create an online map representing each VEP-backed campaign between 1962 and 1970. Designed by AUUT Studio, this digital public history map displays as much data as I could find. In ways that words cannot do alone, this map illustrates the scale and impact of the VEP on the southern black freedom movement. I hope this map will lead to additional research. Most local projects have yet to be explored and written about in depth. http://mappingthevep.evanfaulkenbury.com

Poll Power

Introduction

In 1962, James McPherson, a retired postmaster in his late seventies, helped start a registration movement in Orangeburg County, South Carolina. "It would be fair," wrote Randolph Blackwell, the field director for the Voter Education Project (VEP), "to say that Mr. McPherson is effective in what he is doing."[1] Under McPherson's leadership, hundreds of African Americans registered to vote between 1962 and 1964. Volunteers within the Orangeburg movement set up a headquarters, planned mass meetings at churches, purchased office supplies, cut radio commercials, printed flyers, paid utility bills, and bought advertisement space in newspapers. Leaders mobilized car owners to pick up rural residents and drive them to the registrar's office in the basement of Orangeburg County's courthouse. Men, women, and teenagers took off work to canvass neighborhoods across the city and county. Working in teams, they went door to door, rang doorbells, handed out pamphlets, and urged neighbors to register. Canvassers who brought the most people to the registrar's office even won small prizes. McPherson wrote notices imploring residents to register, writing with passion and urgency: "YOUR VOTE WILL SOLVE MOST OF THE RACE PROBLEMS! YOUR VOTE CAN CHANGE MANY THINGS! REGISTER! TAKE A FRIEND TO REGISTER!!"[2] But registering to vote was difficult for African Americans in Orangeburg. White supremacy infected the political system. Jim Crow laws stripped African Americans of their constitutional and human rights. Legal segregation and racist beliefs of black inferiority determined daily interactions on the streets, in schools, in politics, in neighborhoods, in restaurants, on jobs, in churches, and at the polls. The threat of violence remained constant. McPherson guided a movement to smash the racist order in Orangeburg by pursuing what the Fifteenth Amendment to the U.S. Constitution had promised: the right to vote regardless of race. White resistance to black freedom had increased over the last decade, McPherson noted, and that reality had "brought the Negro face-to-face with the bare fact that we must either hang together or be hanged together and that the ballot and our few dollars were our best weapons."[3]

Meanwhile, as the Orangeburg movement organized, VEP headquarters buzzed with activity. Within a small space on Forsyth Street in downtown Atlanta, Georgia, a handful of staff managed hundreds of thousands of dollars in grants from philanthropic foundations. The VEP collected and disbursed the money to voter registration projects across the American South. Inside the VEP's office, typewriters clacked while stacks of mail came in and out each day. A complex filing system tracked the finances and registration figures from community projects in almost a dozen states. The executive director oversaw a small team of researchers and office staff that solicited philanthropic funds, managed bank accounts, reviewed grant applications, mailed checks, visited projects, and compiled data on black disfranchisement. VEP staff regularly communicated with leaders from dozens of projects. To receive VEP money, organizers had to account for expenditures and report back to the VEP about how many people had registered or tried to register within a period. And grant recipients shared stories—narrative reports of their battles against registrars, police, politicians, vigilantes, and everyday white southerners who knew that black voting would fracture the racial caste system. Day after day, month after month, the VEP aided grassroots freedom movements, like in Orangeburg, and in return, the VEP compiled information about voting rights, white supremacist resistance, strategies that worked, and tactics that did not. If a visitor had walked into the VEP office in Atlanta on any given day, the view would have been unremarkable: an average, cramped office with desks, chairs, telephones, typewriters, filing cabinets, coffee pots, and stacks of paper covered with tables, numbers, and percentages. But within this office existed the behind-the-scenes engine of the southern freedom movement, an organization hidden from popular view in order to work efficiently without media attention, to finance as many voter registration projects as possible, to study the causes of black disfranchisement, to find remedies and strategies to fight Jim Crow at the ballot box, and to win back black political power.[4]

Dr. Charles H. Thomas Jr., an economics professor at South Carolina State College in Orangeburg, applied for his community's first VEP grant in the summer of 1962. He knew that the desire to vote was strong in his county, though few black citizens had been able to register. African Americans had limited resources to orchestrate a prolonged freedom movement. While churches passed offering plates and the local National Association for the Advancement of Colored People (NAACP) chapter held fund-raisers, sustaining a blitz on the registrar's office proved time consuming and costly. Fuel for vehicles required money. Paying bills, rent, speaker fees, and salaries added up. To implement a successful drive, one that could maintain the energy of Orangeburg's black community against the county's intractable white political structure, money was crucial. On August 19, Thomas received good news that the VEP had awarded $5,000 for a three-month registration operation in Orangeburg.⁵

With VEP support, a social movement for the ballot began in Orangeburg. "Because of the total unrest and the general disgust with existing unbearable conditions," McPherson wrote, "there was no time to form new organizations. We simply lined up what we had, closed the gaps and went to work. The Orangeburg Movement and a determined VOTER EDUCATION PROJECT was on."⁶ During those first three months, the county registrar's office opened only on September 2, October 7, and November 4. This was a common obstructionist tactic by registrar's offices across the South—open just one day per month. On September 2, the Orangeburg movement had barely started canvassing neighborhoods, and few attempted to register. But momentum grew, and on October 7, 220 African Americans registered to vote, 115 people were left waiting in line, and another 26 were rejected.⁷ On November 4, 161 people registered while 16 were rejected and 47 were left in line.⁸

Over the next year, the VEP supplied Orangeburg's movement with grants totaling $17,900.⁹ During that time, organizers expanded their campaign beyond Orangeburg into the state's Second Congressional District, covering areas within southwest South Carolina, and in the summer of 1964, they formed the South Carolina Voter Education Project (SCVEP). Where African Americans had once encountered difficulty registering, they began swarming registrar's offices throughout the state. Once, during the fall of 1963 in Orangeburg, "as a way of throwing the opposition off guard," movement activists took participating high school students "that assembled for downtown demonstrations and [instead] sent them on what they called 'Operation Door-Knock for Registration.' The cops were left downtown waiting and confused."¹⁰ VEP money allowed grassroots organizers to sustain this kind of activism. Other groups helped, such as the American Friends Service Committee, which found that "Orangeburg [was] highly organized voter education wise due to prior VEP support."¹¹ By the fall of 1964, 2,839 African Americans had registered in Orangeburg, and within two years, an estimated 40,000 had done so across the state through twelve other VEP projects.¹²

Orangeburg was one of many black freedom movements across the American South that thrived with VEP assistance. For nearly a century before the VEP, African Americans had fought for the right to vote, but segregationists had maintained control over local politics through poll taxes, literacy tests, intimidation, economic threats, violence, and political monopoly. In

South Carolina, according to McPherson, "each county had some type of organization to encourage persons to register," but "these organizations worked on their own, at their own expense," before the VEP.[13] Many communities like Orangeburg lacked a coordinated resistance movement—until the VEP launched in 1962.

The VEP discreetly supported nonpartisan registration campaigns across the eleven states of the former Confederacy. Formed in 1961 by civil rights leaders, U.S. Department of Justice (DOJ) officials, and liberal philanthropists, the VEP operated within the Atlanta-based Southern Regional Council (SRC), a research organization devoted to improving race relations, to finance local movements and collect data on African American disfranchisement. The first VEP operated from March 1962 through October 1964 with Wiley A. Branton as its leader, and in those two and a half years, the organization supported 129 projects, spent $855,836.59, and registered approximately 688,000 people.[14] Through this project, the VEP helped lay the foundation for the Voting Rights Act of 1965 by demonstrating both the magnitude of black disfranchisement and the desire for political participation. A second VEP under Vernon E. Jordan Jr. launched in 1966 and lasted through 1969. In 1970, the VEP separated from the SRC, formed VEP Incorporated, and under John Lewis's leadership amid financial difficulties, worked to expand black political power through 1976. The VEP closed its doors for good in 1992. Not every black registration movement in the American South drew on VEP funds during the 1960s and 1970s, but hundreds did. The VEP dispensed money for registration campaigns and, in the process, united civil rights groups around voting rights, sustained a southwide movement, documented the fight against disfranchisement, and fortified black political power.

The VEP was a unique organization within the movement. To earn a federal tax exemption from the Internal Revenue Service (IRS)—which philanthropic foundations required before donating money—VEP framers argued that it would be an educational body, working in a nonpartisan capacity to document the extent of black disfranchisement in the South. While it maintained the veneer of neutrality, in actuality, the VEP served as a one-of-a-kind action agency—an ally of local black freedom movements across the South—empowering grassroots activists with funding, advice, and data. The VEP did compile massive amounts of information, but, remembered Wiley Branton, "I felt that in order to accomplish the research goals of the Voter Education Project, that it was necessary that I conduct it pretty much as an action group. And therefore, from a day to day operational standpoint,

I treated it as an action group."[15] The VEP differed from the NAACP, the Congress of Racial Equality (CORE), the Southern Christian Leadership Conference (SCLC), and the Student Nonviolent Coordinating Committee (SNCC), but by equipping these agencies and many more with resources, the VEP fought white supremacy at the ballot box. It did so in semisecrecy, avoiding the limelight to stay out of segregationist crosshairs looking to undermine African American suffrage. The *Oxford English Dictionary* defines *engine* as "a machine with moving parts that converts power into motion."[16] That definition suits the VEP. The VEP did not oversee or manage the movement, but by working with local registration campaigns, it converted grassroots power into southwide motion.

The VEP is not a complete mystery to historians, but few have studied the organization in detail.[17] A common historiographical simplification classifies the VEP as a scheme of President John F. Kennedy's administration to pacify the civil rights movement's growing militancy.[18] Many local studies mention the VEP as a source for funds, and works on major leaders and the national struggle acknowledge the VEP.[19] And yet lost amid important debates over "top-down" versus "bottom-up," nonviolence or self-defense, whether or not the black power era represented a distinct period or if the bulk of the twentieth century ought to be viewed within the "long civil rights movement" was the understated narrative of how the VEP drove forward black voting power—a central civil rights issue that had been a priority since emancipation.[20]

Through the VEP, philanthropic foundations underwrote two of the southern movement's most notable achievements—its successful drive for the right to vote and the rise of African American political power. In 2000, the historian Charles W. Eagles wrote that, despite overburdened shelves of scholarship, "too little is known . . . about the non-activist patrons of the major protest organizations and how and why their support may have flowed and ebbed. In civil rights as in politics, historians might be wise to follow the money."[21] Following the money leads to the VEP and its philanthropic benefactors. With foundation money, the VEP empowered local campaigns, focused the struggle onto voting rights activism, and in the process, banded together a southwide social movement that fought Jim Crow at the ballot box.[22]

This history also reveals how opponents of the civil rights movement rewrote tax policies to undercut philanthropic support for the VEP—a successful strategy that has received scant attention. After African Americans won the right to vote and began competing for political power in the South, white opponents turned to a novel tactic: they wielded the federal tax code as a powerful defensive weapon. Through the Tax Reform Act of 1969, white conservatives in Congress, led by Senators Herman Talmadge and Russell Long, restricted tax-exempt contributions to nonpartisan voter registration campaigns, halting the VEP's momentum. Under the new law, organizations like the VEP could retain their charitable 501(c)(3) status only if they were active across five states at once and received no more than 25 percent of their funding from a single source. Violating the law would result in draconian penalties, such as organizations stripped of their federal tax exemption and executives personally fined. These two restrictions, especially the 25 percent rule, destabilized the VEP, and as a result, grassroots voter campaigns that had relied on the VEP for financial support received less. The VEP was no longer in a position to maintain black political activism across the entire American South, and slowly, the united movement for voting power ended.[23]

The VEP and its grantees focused on suffrage as the main objective within the movement. Since emancipation, African Americans understood the vote as a basic right, but after Reconstruction ended and Jim Crow laws made it nearly impossible for black southerners to register, the strain of going alone to the courthouse, risking humiliation, unemployment, assault, or death at the hands of a lynching mob kept progress at a glacial pace. Frank Edward DeLaughter, a sheriff's deputy in Concordia Parish, Louisiana, summed up how many white southerners felt about black political participation: "People in this town don't want to see no niggers voting."[24] African Americans saw voting as the gateway to full citizenship and, with it, a stronger position to advocate for better jobs, pay, public services, health care, education, housing, and everyday rights. "The ballot, while no longer conceived of as a magic key, is recognized as the indispensable weapon in a persistent fight for full citizenship," wrote Henry Lee Moon in 1948, a journalist, labor organizer, and public relations director for the NAACP. "In short, [the vote is] a tool to be used in the ultimate demolition of the whole outmoded structure of Jim Crow."[25] Moon had hoped black suffrage would increase as Republicans and Democrats competed for votes, but white southerners, such as DeLaughter, fought relentlessly to keep black southerners powerless. Moon helped create the VEP in 1961, recognizing it as a necessary program to arm local activists with materials needed to combat white supremacy across the South. White liberals, including philanthropists and DOJ officials, also believed that the movement should focus on voting rights, not only to fulfill the promise of the Fifteenth Amendment but to temper civil disobedience as it spread across the United States. And both black leaders and white liberals agreed that focusing the struggle on voting rights was a sound strategy to navigate Cold War politics by emphasizing the patriotic virtue of racial justice.

The story of the VEP also explains how hundreds of local movements broke out simultaneously during the 1960s. In towns, cities, and counties across Alabama, Arkansas, Florida, Georgia, Louisiana, Mississippi, North Carolina, South Carolina, Tennessee, Texas, and Virginia, the VEP empowered activists to intensify grassroots registration campaigns. Paying for fuel, booking rallies, hosting workshops, printing pamphlets, buying food, and giving a small stipend to people taking off work to canvass neighborhoods were requirements for a project spanning days, weeks, months, or years. Creating and sustaining a social movement cost money—a resource in short supply among southern African Americans. The VEP had a catalytic effect on the southern black freedom struggle, knitting together a massive social movement.[26]

With VEP support, similar movements to the one in Orangeburg became possible throughout the American South. In November 1963, the three-month project ended with 381 new registrants. Orangeburg's leaders applied for more VEP grants, and over the next year, over 2,000 more registered to vote. McPherson described their resolve: "When demonstrations were at their height and Negroes were being jailed by the hundreds and Negro pickets lined the streets, Negroes were standing in line outside of the registrar's office by the hundreds from one end of the courthouse to the other, quietly waiting to register."[27] Local power had long existed within Orangeburg. The VEP helped convert that power into political motion.

The movement spread. In 1969, Kathleen Knox, a student at Winthrop College, volunteered with the York County Voter Registration Project in South Carolina in connection with the SCVEP. Speaking with a journalist, Knox explained her involvement: "A lot of the people we have to reach have decided that voting will do them no good, that the white man controls everything and always will . . . It's up to us to convince our people that, because blacks for the most part lack economic power, they must compensate for it with power at the polls."[28]

CHAPTER ONE

Southern Disfranchisement and the Long Origins of the Voter Education Project

For a century, to register and vote as a black southerner meant to risk death. White southerners lost the Civil War, but they exacted their revenge on black southerners by keeping them politically powerless, often through violence and threats. After Reconstruction ended, southern states conceived insidious means to effectively nullify the Fifteenth Amendment of the United States. Southern states amended their constitutions and passed laws to erect barriers to stop African Americans from voting and holding office. For over seventy years spanning the Jim Crow era, white southerners enshrined political monopoly through legal and extralegal means, including the use of poll taxes, literacy tests, gerrymandering, registration slowdowns, voter roll purges, economic intimidation, all-white primaries, roving poll places, absent or uncooperative registrars, and outright violence. Yet these barriers failed to extinguish African Americans' drive to participate in a democracy.[1]

To overcome these hurdles required more than individual effort. No arc bent naturally toward justice, for voting became more difficult year by year for African Americans. Civil rights leaders perceived the need for a massive registration drive—an engine to convert the will to vote into a southwide movement. They believed that only a united movement could break the segregationist, one-party South. White supremacists constituted the majority, and their grip on political power neared absolute. Their hatred of black skin, obsession with interracial sex, fear of integrated schools, and paranoid belief that civil rights activists were communists anchored their resolve to fight. Black registration rose during the mid- to late 1940s on the heels of a progressive, left-labor movement, but rising anticommunist fervor wiped out the momentum by 1950. In 1954, the *Brown v. Board of Education* Supreme Court decision galvanized African Americans across the South, but it also reenergized the segregationist movement. Black voting became even more difficult as southern lawmakers tightened restrictions and violence surged.[2]

Between 1955 and 1958, white southerners attacked or murdered black southerners in 530 documented cases. The actual number was surely higher. In Brookhaven, Mississippi, Lamar Smith encouraged his neighbors to cast absentee ballots in the 1955 primary. Three white men gunned him down outside of the Lincoln County courthouse, and no one ever faced charges. In Prichard, Alabama, Joshua Barney, a sixty-eight-year-old reverend and carpenter, ran for city council in 1956. Barney lost, but he stayed in the race even after someone riddled his home with bullets. In Abbeville County, South Carolina, where only 15 out of 3,687 African Americans were registered in 1957, fear pervaded the community after a black man took a beating for voting. In Liberty County, Florida, where only a single African American was registered to vote in 1958, four made the attempt one day, including Reverend Dee Hawkins. Later that night, Hawkins was shot and his home bombed. On May 7, 1955, the Reverend George Washington Lee, the leader of the Belzoni branch of the NAACP, was assassinated after refusing to take his name off the polls and for working to register members of his community. The following year, Lee's successor as leader of the NAACP, Gus Courts, nearly died after being fired upon by a passing vehicle while working in his grocery store. Speaking to a reporter in his hospital bed, Courts said, "I've known for a long time it was coming, and I'd tried to get prepared in my mind for it. But that's a hard thing to do . . . I've never been a trouble maker and I've never had on handcuffs. I'm 65 years-old and I've never had the vote. That's all I wanted."[3]

Within this context, three key events laid the foundation for the VEP. The first was the emergence of the Southern Regional Council as a leading voice within the civil rights movement. A research agency in Atlanta, Georgia, with roots stretching back to 1919, the SRC turned increasingly outspoken against segregation during the 1950s and began compiling and publishing data on disfranchisement. Comprehensive research on black voting did not exist prior to the SRC, and its ability to document the severity of disfranchisement illuminated the issue and gave activists a cause around which to rally. The second event was the Prayer Pilgrimage for Freedom on May 17, 1957, the three-year anniversary of the *Brown* decision. Put together by A. Philip Randolph, Roy Wilkins, and Martin Luther King Jr., the Pilgrimage brought 25,000 people to the Washington, DC mall and directed the nation's attention toward the southern freedom movement in pursuit of black voting rights as a moral, religious, and patriotic imperative. The third was the Crusade for Citizenship in 1958. Following the Pilgrimage, the newly formed Southern Christian Leadership Conference launched the Crusade, an ambitious attempt to set in motion a voter registration campaign across the American South. The Crusade failed, but the idea took hold that a coordinated, interagency southwide movement for the ballot was possible.

IN ADDITION TO THE constant threat of violence, white southerners overrode the Fifteenth Amendment most successfully through poll taxes, literacy tests, voter purges, and the all-white primary, allowing county registrars wide latitude in overseeing each. Poll taxes—a class-based impediment as much as it was about race—charged American citizens money to cast ballots. Until the Twenty-Fourth Amendment outlawed poll taxes in federal elections in January 1964, five southern states still required the payment of poll taxes to vote—Alabama, Arkansas, Mississippi, Texas, and Virginia. For decades, anti–poll tax legislation had stalled in Congress after southern Senators voted against and filibustered any such proposals. Poll taxes usually consisted of an annual payment of between $1.00 and $2.00, an amount the poor could rarely spare. Local registration campaigns sometimes tried to raise poll tax money to distribute evenly to the community, but this annual requirement often drained energy as much as resources. In some states, poll taxes snowballed, meaning that failure to pay for five years where the annual poll tax was $1.50 would require $7.50 before receiving a ballot. Poll taxes raised little revenue for states but sowed resentment and confusion. Registrars would ensure payment had been received, sometimes by arbitrary dates well in advance of the election. Registrars would not always issue receipts, leaving black southerners with no proof that they had paid. Poll taxes helped keep elections white. In 1957, State Senator Sam Engelhardt of Macon County, Alabama, stated bluntly that poll taxes "serve as a deterrent to Negro voter registration."[4]

If they had the funds, black southerners could overcome the poll tax barrier, but they often could not pass literacy tests. These exams did not measure the ability to read or write, but they provided registrars with a tangible reason to deny the franchise. Most often, state literacy tests asked prospective voters to write from memory and interpret portions of the state or federal constitution. No matter how reasonable the responses, registrars could fail according to their whim. As part of the tests, applicants had to fill out forms and questionnaires about themselves, often having to list the names of their employers or properties owned. Placing on record personal information left black registrants vulnerable and exposed their families to possible reprisal. By the time the Voting Rights Act of 1965 outlawed literacy tests, seven southern states had continued to use them—Alabama, Georgia, Louisiana, Mississippi, North Carolina, South Carolina, and Virginia. In Ouachita Parish, Louisiana, for example, the registrar, Mae Lucky, developed a reputation for intimidating black registrants by distracting them while they worked on literacy tests, slowing down the lines, requiring three forms of identification, and openly mocking applicants as they filled out paperwork. On July 29, 1964, Ella Lee White tried to register in Ouachita Parish, but on her test, Lucky accused her of misspelling the word *democratic* and failed her.[5]

In addition to literacy tests and poll taxes, counties could purge their rolls to disqualify as many black voters as possible in a single stroke. Under the guise of electoral integrity to ensure accuracy, implement new technology, or take off deceased and former residents, segregationists learned that purges could preserve white political power. In 1948, the registrar of Laurens County, Georgia, sent notices to all black registered voters instructing them to appear at the courthouse for a literacy test. Failure to appear within a certain time meant automatic disqualification. White registrants received no such notices. In McCormick County, South Carolina, every black voter was purged in 1948. Louisiana began a wholesale purge of its northern parishes in 1958, lowering black registration in Ouachita Parish from 5,700 to 776, Morehouse Parish from 935 to 200, and Natchitoches Parish from 2,800 to 1,300. African Americans had few options to combat purges, and disillusionment in the democratic process often followed. White supremacists took notice and advocated more purges. In a 1958 tract for the Jefferson County Citizens Council, Grover S. McLeod wrote that in response to growing black political power, "the answer is simply this, that we must purge the polls."[6]

As efficient as poll taxes, literacy tests, and purges later proved in keeping black southerners away from the polls, before 1944, the all-white primary functioned as the main barrier. Southern states argued that the Fifteenth Amendment stated nothing about primaries. In the South after Reconstruction, the Democratic Party rose to dominance, meaning that in most cases, the primaries were the only elections that mattered. Barring African Americans from primaries cut off their political influence at the root. In 1944, the Supreme Court struck down the white primary in *Smith v. Allwright*. The NAACP had fought the all-white primary in court, and the decision culminated a half-century fight for black voting rights. Middle-class black leaders began battling disfranchisement in the courts back in 1890, but in all twelve cases that reached the Supreme Court between then and 1908, the justices allowed southern states the freedom to discriminate at the polls.[7] In 1909, activists founded the NAACP and, with it, developed a goal of reclaiming black voting rights across the United States. At the NAACP's seventeenth annual conference, Moorfield Storey outlined the objectives of African Americans nationwide, which "above all" included "the right to vote."[8] During the 1920s and 1930s, the NAACP aided its southern branches working to register voters, but the case-by-case approach drained resources and remained tedious. The NAACP continued to fight in court, and amid the height of World War II and the Double V campaign to fight for democracy at home and abroad, the victory of *Smith v. Allwright* promised easier access to the franchise for African Americans.[9]

Following the *Smith v. Allwright* decision, black registration grew amid a left-wing political movement, but it did not last. Looking ahead to the 1946 midterm elections, interagency coordination between the NAACP, the Progressive Democratic Party of South Carolina, the Congress of Industrial Organizations (CIO), the Southern Conference for Human Welfare (SCHW), and the Southern Negro Youth Congress (SNYC) worked to break the one-party South and register African Americans. Although more black southerners registered, especially in such cities as Memphis, Tennessee, and Richmond, Virginia, white supremacists continued their electoral dominance in the South. During his presidential campaign of 1948 on the Progressive Party ticket, Henry A. Wallace courted southern black voters and promised to fight segregation, but his support among communists doomed his chances of winning. Accusations linking civil rights organizations and alleged communist sympathizers undercut the momentum of *Smith v. Allwright*, and a long-term, southwide movement for the ballot never materialized.[10]

The Southern Regional Council was an unlikely organization to reignite interest in southern black disfranchisement during the mid-1950s. The SRC's origins stretch back to 1919 with the founding of the Commission on Interracial Cooperation (CIC). The Methodist minister Will W. Alexander and one of his parishioners, Willis Weatherford, established the CIC in Atlanta to be "a meeting ground where the best people of both races could work together to dispel prejudice, tensions, and violence."[11] The CIC included moderate ministers and businessmen in a church-based, mostly white, middle-class association that advocated for better race relations, but not to end segregation. Under Alexander, the CIC supported affiliates throughout the South that organized moderate leaders to address local issues. Above all, the CIC wanted to educate white and black community leaders about the dangers of racial violence and promote interracial harmony. The CIC did so by cultivating relationships with newspapers and by appealing to the white upper middle class, asserting that racial strife was bad for business. After the Great Depression set in, CIC leadership scaled back their operations to concentrate on publishing and education, primarily on antilynching. In 1929, Jesse Daniel Ames, a suffragist and antilynching advocate, joined the CIC as leader of the Women's Committee, and along with her management of the Association of Southern Women for the Prevention of Lynching, Ames kept the CIC afloat during the 1930s. Alexander and Howard Odum, a sociologist at the University of North Carolina, were unhappy with the decline of the CIC, and after a series of conventions in 1942 and 1943, they wrested control away from Ames and consolidated the CIC into a new organization: the Southern Regional Council. The old CIC had grown stagnant, and its male-dominated leadership wanted to refocus its mission on the academic study of southern racial and economic problems. Organizers chartered the SRC on January 6, 1944, in Atlanta.[12]

The SRC at first mirrored the racial timidity inherited from the former CIC, but beginning in 1947, SRC leaders began denouncing segregation. Testifying before the President's Committee on Civil Rights on May 14, 1947, Guy B. Johnson, a sociologist at the University of North Carolina and the SRC's first executive director, outlined obstacles to black voting. He called for "a wide campaign of popular education which will inform Negroes as to their suffrage rights and instruct them as to the procedures they should follow in trying to exercise those rights."[13] In 1951, the SRC "formally committed itself to the aim of an unsegregated society."[14] Under the leadership of Paul Williams, a Richmond publisher, and George S. Mitchell, an economist who came to the SRC to lead its Negro Veterans Program, the SRC began publicly criticizing Jim Crow. They believed white southern liberals could no longer advocate for progressive change while accepting the segregationist order. While the SRC lost members who disagreed with its new direction, it evolved into a comprehensive research agency to battle Jim Crow. To widen its scope, the SRC established councils in twelve southern states as independent, though affiliated, subgroups to study and publish reports about local issues. SRC membership remained small, but its influence grew. In 1955, the SRC stated its purpose: "The Council works through the sound methods of education, fact-finding, and persuasion. It seeks no legislation, it carries on no court action, and it uses no 'pressure group' tactics. It collects the facts about racial problems and progress in the South and makes these facts available."[15]

As the SRC criticized segregation, red-baiters attacked. The harassment began in December 1950 when Roy Harris, editor of the right-wing *Augusta Courier*, criticized Benjamin Mays for an article published in *New South*, the SRC's main publication. Mays, the president of Morehouse College, supported the desegregation of Atlanta's public schools, ending his article with the question, "Can there be equality in segregation?"[16] Harris thought so, and throughout the 1950s, he and other segregationists charged the SRC as being a communist front. In 1951, Governor Herman Talmadge of Georgia lashed out at "foreign agitators," including the NAACP, the Communist Party, "and the Race-Mixing Southern Regional Council."[17] In 1954, the Fund for the Republic, a think tank sponsored by the Ford Foundation known to criticize reactionary anticommunism, raised Harris's suspicions further. After the Fund for the Republic donated to the SRC, Harris accused the SRC as being "a haven for known communist fronters [that] could well become the Communist Party apparatus in the South."[18] Other newspapers followed suit, including the Charleston *News and Courier*, whose editorial staff compared the Fund for the Republic's support of the SRC to John Brown's northern allies before his raid on Harper's Ferry.[19] George Mitchell and SRC staff fought back by publishing editorials and sending corrections to newspapers, but the stories kept coming. In 1956, Georgia's attorney general, Eugene Cook, condemned the SRC and its state affiliate, the Georgia Committee on Interracial Cooperation, as "both dominated by individuals who, like the officials of the NAACP, have long records of affinity for and participation in Communist, Communist-front, fellow-traveling, left-wing and subversive organizations and activities."[20]

Red-baiting against the SRC increased alongside its support for school desegregation. Beginning with Benjamin Mays's 1950 article, the SRC fought segregated public schooling. Segregationists not only linked this position with communism, but they feared the SRC promoted race mixing. Reactionaries believed that communists within the SRC wanted "to explore relationships between white and Negro in the South," especially regarding schoolchildren and sex.[21] When the Supreme Court handed down *Brown v. Board of Education* in May 1954, SRC members rejoiced. But over the next three years as the SRC studied local reactions to *Brown*, it became clear that southern school districts would only allow token desegregation, if that. Massive resistance became the new reality as white citizens' councils gained strength and formed a movement against integration. According to SRC research, within two years of *Brown*, citizens' councils had covered the South, included over 300,000 members, and had raised nearly one million dollars in its militant opposition to school desegregation. Responding to *Brown*, in addition to preserving school segregation, southern legislatures "directed their attention to other means of continuing the status quo or even turning back the clock for the Negro citizen . . . Voting laws were tightened in some states, making it even more difficult for Negroes to register."[22] Since addressing school desegregation appeared futile for the time being, the SRC decided to shift strategies and concentrate on black voting rights.[23]

In 1956 and 1957, the SRC undertook a major research project to document African American voter registration and, with its final report, revealed the pervasiveness of disfranchisement across the South. The SRC had kept watch over black registration since the late 1940s, but it had not studied the problem in depth. *Smith v. Allwright* allowed for more African Americans to register, but since 1947, the number of black voters had steadily decreased as local registrars purged rolls and state legislatures implemented new barriers. "Those who rejoiced in the recent series of court decisions upholding a free ballot unhampered by racial restrictions have been sobered by the vexing problems which have persisted," the SRC wrote in a 1953 report.[24] Amid the Montgomery bus boycott when the injustices of the Jim Crow system were on full display to the nation, the SRC launched its registration study.

With a grant from the Fund for the Republic, the SRC commissioned twelve social scientists to visit counties, interview residents, make observations, and, where possible, look through official rolls to inspect black registration figures. After accumulating the data, Margaret Price, a researcher for the SRC, wrote the final report, entitled *The Negro Voter in the South*. In many places, Price found, violence against African Americans had risen, but more common were the "legal weapons" that served as "successor to the white primary," including poll taxes, literacy tests, purges, and intractable registrars. Price estimated that around a quarter of the eligible southern black population had registered—an optimistic tally. But she admitted the results were imprecise, complicated by poor records and white registrars who impeded the process. The SRC also documented hesitancy among African Americans to attempt to register. In Dallas County, Alabama, after visiting people in barber shops and pool halls, many "would not even talk about voting" and when pressed, responded, "I don't want nothing to do with it . . . If they don't want me to vote, I don't want to." But rather than blame that hesitation on apathy, the SRC noted the level of oppression, the difficulty of going to the registrar's office alone, the ease at which local governments purged black voters, and the segregationist system that surrounded their lives. "It is difficult to arouse a motivation to vote when there is little concrete evidence of benefits to compensate for the trouble of qualifying," Price wrote.[25]

And yet black communities throughout the South, like in Laurens County, Georgia, tried to register, vote, and exercise political power. As part of the

SRC study, Dr. Brailsford R. Brazeal, a dean and professor of economics at Morehouse College, went to Laurens County in August 1956. A large county in size and population, Laurens County rested in the middle of Georgia with a total population of 53,606. African Americans made up about 40 percent, yet white registrants outnumbered them by almost six to one. A purge in 1948 had "lowered the morale" of the black community, Brazeal wrote. In Dublin, the county seat, the registrar even segregated registration systems, with white residents registering and voting at the courthouse and black residents at city hall. Without a political voice, few black neighborhoods had sewage or running water, and none had streetlights. The sheriff held "complete authority" and crafted a reputation as the "baddest man" in the county. The local NAACP chapter kept a low profile. But recently before Brazeal's 1956 visit, local leaders had organized the All Citizens Voters League of Laurens County in hopes of winning political influence by taking advantage of factional splits. They held mass meetings on Monday nights, and they organized a voter registration campaign. Black citizens were determined to vote, even though white officials had put the word out that "we got to stop these niggers from registering." Newspaper editorials expressed worry for rising black political power and called for more purges. Speaking with Brazeal, one local black leader expressed little concern: "I have already overlived my time on earth and will meet whatever they bring . . . If they assassinate me it would set off one of the finest race riots imaginable."[26]

The SRC researched, published, and highlighted disfranchisement in Laurens County and throughout the South, but it did not take action. The SRC saw itself only as an ally to civil rights agencies. It made the decision not out of indecisiveness or conservatism but to protect its federal tax exemption. To continue receiving funding from sources like the Fund for the Republic, it had to remain nonpartisan and educational. To become an advocacy group would risk the ire of the IRS. The SRC relied on philanthropic donations, and those foundations made their gifts on condition of their grantees maintaining tax exemption. To lose tax exemption meant a loss of funds and reputation. The SRC also saw itself as the only organization providing robust, academic-quality research on segregation and disfranchisement. Since July 28, 1947, the SRC had existed as a 501(c)(3) under the IRS, at once protecting its status while limiting it from expanding into an action-oriented, grassroots agency.[27]

While the SRC conducted its disfranchisement study, the bus boycott in Montgomery, Alabama, shook the segregationist order and captured the nation's attention. Martin Luther King Jr., who rose in leadership within the Montgomery Improvement Association (MIA), connected with the SRC soon after becoming pastor of the Dexter Avenue Baptist Church. King joined the local chapters of both the NAACP and the Alabama Council on Human Relations—the SRC's state affiliate. The Montgomery chapter of the Alabama Council met in the basement of King's church. King served for a time as the Alabama Council's vice president. He later described the Alabama Council as "the only truly interracial group in Montgomery."[28] Serving with the Alabama Council put King in conversation with SRC members, such as progressive white ministers and academics. The SRC's point person for researching disfranchisement in Alabama for its 1956–57 report was Dr. James E. Pierce from Alabama State College, who also participated in the MIA. Along with the SRC's research, the bus boycott exposed how deeply embedded segregation was in both public services and at registrar's offices. During the boycott, the MIA formed a registration and voting committee, and King saw firsthand how a mass movement could incorporate the deliberate pursuit of voting rights.[29]

Soon after the bus boycott ended in January 1957, King and around sixty ministers met in Atlanta to form an organization to make the African American church the epicenter of a nonviolent revolution. To them, the boycott was just the beginning. They thought that a handful of southern ministers could initiate a voting rights movement spanning the South. During a conference at Ebenezer Baptist Church, the pastors asked themselves, "How can we utilize the bus protest to stimulate interest in voting?" and "What broad campaign in the South should be carried on to stimulate interest in and educate Negroes to see the basic significance of voting?" They did not have answers, but they were convinced that the time had come "to broaden the struggle for Negroes to register and to vote."[30] After more meetings and two name changes, the Southern Christian Leadership Conference formed with the goal to achieve "full citizenship rights, equality, and the integration of the Negro in all aspects of American life."[31]

From its inception, the SCLC tried to channel the energy of the bus boycott into a southwide movement for the ballot, but King and his allies were unsure how to turn their idea into reality. They also faced criticism from the NAACP's national leadership, who believed the upstart SCLC would drain resources from local branches better equipped to register voters. But King believed that the church could inspire more African Americans to register, especially those who were uninvolved in the largely middle- to upper-class leadership of the NAACP. On the national scene, the opportunity to concentrate on the ballot seemed more likely as Congress deliberated a new civil rights law. Since January 1956, Congress had considered legislation to expand federal government oversight of civil rights violations, but it stalled by the end of the year. After reelection, President Dwight Eisenhower encouraged both parties to begin anew, focusing on civil and voting rights rather than school integration. But the legislation crawled through Congress, held up by southerners who opposed expanding citizenship rights to African Americans. Still, hope for federal legislation motivated King and the SCLC to plan a demonstration that tied together Christianity, nonviolence, and voting rights.[32]

On February 22, 1957, King announced a "Prayer Pilgrimage" to Washington, DC. "This will not be a political march," he told journalists. "It will be rooted in deep spiritual faith."[33] With possibilities for the Pilgrimage fresh on his mind, King visited Ghana in March at the invitation of President Kwame Nkrumah to witness the nation's independence. Motivated by what he saw, King returned to the United States excited for the potential of nonviolent revolution. King found further inspiration in Billy Graham, whose evangelical crusades filled arenas across the country. With Graham's crusade rhetoric as his model, King had the idea to merge civil rights with spiritual renewal. White supremacy could be defeated, but the solution had to come from mass action rooted in Christian faith. With this focus, planners of the Prayer Pilgrimage for Freedom articulated five goals: to inspire nationwide black unity, to connect the North to the growing movement in the South, to protest racist violence, to oppose state attacks on the NAACP, and to press Congress to pass a civil rights bill.[34]

The Prayer Pilgrimage for Freedom drew inspiration from the March on Washington Movement (MOWM). Organized by A. Phillip Randolph in 1941, the MOWM criticized federal economic policies that discriminated against African American laborers during World War II. Randolph and his supporters, especially the NAACP, National Urban League, and labor unions, including his own Brotherhood of Sleeping Car Porters, demanded federal protections to ensure greater job security for black men. During the first half of 1941, President Franklin D. Roosevelt hesitated to intervene, prompting Randolph to launch the MOWM. Chapters formed throughout the country, and organizers prepared for a massive protest in Washington, DC to demand action on behalf of black workers. As pressure mounted, Roosevelt acquiesced, and a week before the march, he signed Executive Order 8802 establishing the Fair Employment Practices Committee and ending employment discrimination for federal jobs and defense contracts. With this victory, Randolph called off the march. The MOWM continued until 1947, and although it never recaptured the enthusiasm of 1941, it served as a reminder of the potential for mass action in Washington, DC.[35]

Unlike the MOWM, King, Randolph, and Wilkins planned the Prayer Pilgrimage to focus on the moral necessity of political enfranchisement. Responding to criticism that communism would infiltrate the demonstration, Wilkins told reporters that the Pilgrimage would be a "spiritual assembly" where "there will be no place for the irreligious." Furthermore, he answered, "No Communist has been or will be invited to participate in the program either as a speaker, singer, prayer leader, or scripture reader."[36] To assuage doubters, the group declared three days before the event, "We wish to state emphatically that the Prayer Pilgrimage for Freedom is dedicated to the assurance that full freedom for all Americans is possible with the help of God under the democratic process."[37] As the Cold War raged and segregationists equated civil rights activists to radical subversives, Pilgrimage organizers painted white southerners fighting equality as the real enemies of the United States. "How foolish is the Southern white man to think that he can bomb us into accepting segregation," stated Ralph Abernathy, King's second in command of the SCLC. "He may as well try to bomb world opinion, the Constitution and the Bill of Rights."[38]

Behind the scenes, Bayard Rustin, a labor organizer and adviser to both King and Randolph, crafted the message for the Prayer Pilgrimage for Freedom. Rosa Parks agreed to drum up support for the Pilgrimage through speaking engagements. Rustin wrote Parks with suggestions: "You might indicate that for hundreds of thousands of Negroes in the South who cannot vote, the only political action left to them is to bring their bodies to the nation's capitol. In this way they cast their total vote by placing their physical and spiritual being in prayer at the seat of government 'to arouse the conscience of the nation' since they have no ballot with which to influence the nation's affairs."[39] Rustin also counseled King on his keynote address. He suggested that King be more insistent about the need for nonviolence alongside the pursuit of the ballot. In addition to coordinating with labor unions, Rustin advised King that voting rights was "where action [was] demanded and where action [was] possible in the wide struggle of community organization."[40] King agreed, for if the movement was to stretch across the South, people needed to believe that it was their moral right and American duty to register and vote—shielded against any charge of radicalism.

The Prayer Pilgrimage amounted to part church service, part anticommunist voter rally. Septima Clark was one of many pilgrims who attended. Early on the morning of May 17, Clark, an organizer and teacher with

Highlander Folk School, boarded a train in Newark, New Jersey. Clark wrote Randolph of her experience after she arrived at the Pilgrimage: "As a sufferer in the cause of real freedom I wept tears of joy to see those people of all nationalities and backgrounds with banners waving marching across that green turf to stand in front of the Lincoln Memorial."[41] Along with 25,000 others, Clark heard Mahalia Jackson sing, Representative Adam Clayton Powell and Senator Jacob K. Javits speak, and Randolph, Wilkins, and King urge the United States to end black disfranchisement. Keeping with the theme of anticommunism, Randolph told the crowd, "We know that Communists have no genuine interest in the solution of problems of racial discrimination, but seek only to use this issue to strengthen the foreign policy of the Soviet Union." To combat the reds and bring every African American into the political process, Randolph stated, "I suggest no party to vote for, but call upon every Negro to register and vote. Be a missionary, and have every neighbor in your house, block, neighborhood, hamlet, village, city, and state to register and vote."[42]

After three hours of singing, speeches, and testimony, King went to the podium to offer final remarks. Wearing a minister's robe, he called on the federal government to guarantee the right to vote for black southerners. Rather than bring about equality on its own, the *Brown* decision had ignited fierce opposition. With states crafting new laws to deny the franchise and violence on the rise, King outlined how African Americans wanted to participate in American democracy, but they could not do so without help. He called on the federal government to intervene: "Give us the ballot and we will no longer have to worry the Federal Government about our basic rights . . . Give us the ballot and we will transform the salient misdeeds of bloodthirsty mobs into the abiding good deeds of ordinary citizens . . . Give us the ballot and we will quickly and non-violently, without rancor or bitterness, implement the Supreme Court's decision of May 17, 1954."[43] King's "Give Us the Ballot" speech before the Lincoln Memorial did not garner the attention his "I Have a Dream" speech would six years later, but it illuminated the problem of disfranchisement to the nation. Since organizers billed the Pilgrimage as a religious service, the crowd did not applaud, but "frequent showers of handkerchief and pennant waiving as expressions of approval" greeted King's words.[44] His sermon was "a fiery speech delivered calmly," one journalist wrote, words that "awakened the Negro people to a new and more effective utilization of their ballots."[45] The Prayer Pilgrimage introduced King to the nation, and with this address, he focused on voting rights as the key to ending Jim Crow.[46]

Journalists pointed out that while King's message inspired, the path ahead remained unclear. Writing for the Associated Negro Press, Hamilton T. Boswell concluded, "After all that great emotional outpouring, the one thing lacking was an effective program to harness it."[47] Similarly, Earl Brown with the *New York Amsterdam News* wrote that while the day was successful, more than prayers were needed to fix society: "The Pilgrimage will become only another meeting if we don't roll up our sleeves and give the Lord a little help in our battle for civil rights."[48] But the Pilgrimage symbolized an important step, acknowledged the *Chicago Daily Defender*: "The pilgrimage is a warning under the guise of religious fervor that black America is ready for the ultimate test—that is the Negro is either a full citizen in the context of democracy or he is not."[49] The Pilgrimage helped spark the idea for a south-wide voter campaign, but without funding, organization, federal backing, or a unified plan, skepticism endured.

The urgent issue immediately following the Prayer Pilgrimage was the pending civil rights legislation held up in Congress. On June 13, King and Abernathy met with Vice President Richard Nixon and Secretary of Labor James P. Mitchell at the White House to discuss the bill. King had met Nixon previously during his trip to Ghana, and during their second meeting, King "pointed out the few number of Negroes in the South who had any voting rights in most, if not all, of the states in the South."[50] Nixon and Mitchell listened, and they assured King and Abernathy that on behalf of the president, they would push for Congress to pass the legislation.[51]

On September 9, after months of delays and a record filibuster by Senator Strom Thurmond, President Eisenhower signed the Civil Rights Act of 1957 into law. The first federal legislation that addressed African American civil rights since Reconstruction, the bill established a six-member Commission on Civil Rights to serve within the executive branch to study and report on major issues. It also created a new assistant attorney general position, paving the way for a Civil Rights Division within the Department of Justice. Ignoring the issue of school desegregation, the Eisenhower administration had urged Congress to focus the legislation on voting rights. But southerners in Congress still fought against the bill, and while the final version barred any attempt to "intimidate, threaten, [or] coerce . . . for the purpose of interfering with the right of such other person to vote," consequences were vague, and no policies were set up to monitor disfranchisement by southern states. Instead, the attorney general could bring a "civil action" in individual cases, but each trial would be decided by a local jury, all but guaranteeing maintenance of the Jim Crow system. The bill passed, but it lacked potency. While the Civil Rights Act of 1957 did little to empower the federal government to stop disfranchisement, it did help cement voting rights as the centerpiece of the expanding civil rights movement, and it gave the SCLC a stronger platform on which to organize.[52]

King criticized the Civil Rights Act of 1957, but he felt it offered the opportunity to inspire a southwide movement. Soon after the Senate approved the legislation, King wrote Vice President Nixon, "History has demonstrated that inadequate legislation supported by mass action can accomplish more than adequate legislation which remains unenforced for the lack of a determined mass movement." While the law contained flaws, the SCLC would use it as an organizing tool. "I am initiating in the South a crusade for citizenship in which we will seek to get at least two million Negroes registered in the south for the 1960 elections," King promised Nixon.[53] The Crusade for Citizenship would fall far short of this goal, but it would build the foundation for a mass movement around voting rights and set the stage for the VEP.

Like the Prayer Pilgrimage, the Crusade for Citizenship blended religion and civic duty to guard against charges of communism while making equal access to the ballot the ultimate goal. Two weeks after the Prayer Pilgrimage, A. Phillip Randolph spoke to the Ladies Auxiliary of the Brotherhood of Sleeping Car Porters in Pittsburgh: "We need a crusade in the interest of the right to register and vote so that every door of every house in every city and hamlet of this nation will be knocked on."[54] The idea to label this strategy a "crusade" came from Billy Graham's popular religious rallies. On July 18, in the midst of a summer-long program at Madison Square Garden in New York City, King delivered the invocation for the Billy Graham Evangelistic Association Crusade. King felt drawn to Graham's enthusiasm, his ability to connect to people, and his mild yet increasing outspokenness against racism. While Graham pushed a nonpolitical revolution of the soul, King's crusade hoped to enfranchise all southern African Americans.[55]

In August 1957, the SCLC announced a massive voter registration drive that would span the American South. The idea took hold, but the SCLC lacked staff, offices, money, and strategy. The SCLC picked a budget of $200,000 seemingly at random, with no idea how it would raise money. Not until November 5 at a board meeting in Memphis did SCLC staff begin planning for the Crusade. Less than two months had passed since the events surrounding the Little Rock Nine in Arkansas, calling further attention to the intransigence of the white South to black civil rights. Something needed to be done. King released a statement that was short on specifics but grand in scale: "We are now embarking upon an historic campaign—the Crusade for Citizenship. We intend to encourage every Negro in the South to register and to vote" and "to restore the honor and integrity of our nation as a whole."[56]

While King and other ministers were enraptured with the idea for the Crusade for Citizenship, two of King's advisers, Stanley Levison and Bayard Rustin, realized they had a problem. Without someone who knew how to coordinate an organization from the top while working with the grassroots, the Crusade had little chance of success. Levison and Rustin believed the only person who could help was Ella Baker. An NAACP leader with connections to many grassroots organizations after decades of activism, Baker had a reputation for effective leadership and organization while remaining outside the spotlight. But she was a woman, and a woman occupying a leadership position within the patriarchal, minister-led SCLC promised dissent. Levison and Rustin met King at an airport, where they pressed him to ignore her gender and hire her to organize the Crusade. King relented, and Levison and Rustin moved quickly to get Baker in Atlanta to set up the SCLC office and manage the Crusade.[57]

Levison and Rustin did not ask Ella Baker if she wanted to head up the Crusade for Citizenship, but they drafted her without asking. They met Baker and told her that they had committed her to Atlanta and the SCLC. "I suppose this is one of the few times in my life that I accepted being used by people," Baker later remembered. "And this, of course, irritated me because I don't like anyone to commit me. But, my sense of values carries with it something to this effect: that the welfare of the whole, of the people or a group of people, is much more important than the ego satisfaction of the individual."[58] The historian Barbara Ransby attributed Baker's acceptance to her belief that the civil rights movement was at a "critical crossroads," one that bridged direct action militancy with voting rights.[59] Even though Baker had little respect for the condescending attitude of southern black ministers, she hoped to influence the direction of the SCLC toward grassroots organizing. She agreed to move to Atlanta, piece together the SCLC, and plan the Crusade for Citizenship.

When Ella Baker arrived in Atlanta on January 9, 1958, she discovered that the SCLC existed only in the minds of King and his colleagues. No one had prepared for her arrival, and she had no office space. On Auburn Avenue, one of the centers of black Atlanta, Baker rented a room in the Hotel Savoy, and for about a week, she used pay phones and borrowed office phones in Ebenezer Baptist Church to coordinate the February 12 launch of the Crusade. She eventually secured her own office and an assistant, but by that time, she had realized the state of the SCLC's unpreparedness. She had planned to stay no more than two weeks, but no one could take over her responsibilities. Baker recalled having no contact with King during this period. King spoke with the media but not to her about coordination. King told the *Atlanta Daily World* that the purpose of the Crusade was "to see that the Negro masses give meaning to the recently enacted Civil Rights Bill by using it to the fullest possible extent."[60] While King broadcasted his ambitions, Baker sat in her office trying to make them come true. She spoke with ministers in Miami, Durham, Hattiesburg, and eighteen other cities to plan the February 12 rallies. She encouraged journalists to cover the story, and she invited members of the newly formed U.S. Commission on Civil Rights to participate. Without direction, Baker worked twelve or more hours per day to cobble together the "great registration movement" that King envisioned.[61]

On January 30, after weeks of Baker's labor, the SCLC executive committee convened at Ebenezer Baptist Church to sketch out the Crusade's aims for a southwide movement. After the meeting, King circulated a report to allies across the South. The Crusade had two goals: to double the number of black voters by 1960 and "to help liberate all Southerners, Negro and white, to extend democracy" so that "the South can have a real two party system—a necessity for real democracy." King emphasized that the Crusade was a southwide movement—the "opening step in a long and hard, but necessary and glorious struggle"—one that was nonpartisan and spiritually focused. He encouraged mass participation and advocated for the ballot as the solution to fix society: "Negroes must vote because every problem we face can be, in large part, overcome by a short walk—a few steps into the Ballot Box."[62] King also had to assuage doubt from Roy Wilkins and NAACP leadership that the Crusade would work in partnership with other organizations. Without specifics, King promised to fund the Crusade through church offerings and donations, yet he provided no instructions for local leaders to harness the February 12 rallies into a long-term registration movement. But the Crusade "*must succeed for God* has promised his children that the loving and the meek (the non-violent) shall inherit the earth."[63]

As February 12 neared, Baker worked with ministers to plan twenty-one simultaneous meetings in such cities as Memphis, Nashville, Atlanta, and New Orleans. Meanwhile, King finally devoted his attention to the Crusade. The two came together, invested in the idea that a southwide movement for the ballot was possible. After Baker confirmed Congressman Adam Clayton

Powell to speak at the Houston rally, King thanked Powell for participating, noting that Baker "has worked so selflessly in the Atlanta Crusade office for the past few weeks."[64] As Baker organized outside the limelight, King issued press statements and drummed up support for the Crusade. Deciding on the theme, "The Franchise Is a Citizen's Right—Not a Privilege," King declared that the SCLC would "function as a service agency to help further registration and voting in communities where such efforts are already underway, and to stimulate other communities into action."[65] King also outlined the SCLC's long-term strategy "to facilitate joint [civil rights] activities and avoid wasteful duplication, give strength to movements by united actions, and . . . assess areas of major concentration to achieve maximum effectiveness."[66] It had never been done before, but King, Baker, and the SCLC were trying to ignite a social movement that stretched across the South.

The Crusade for Citizenship began on schedule in all twenty-one cities with ministers coaxing audiences to register, vote, and pray. In Nashville, King's father was the main speaker. In Shreveport, Fred Shuttlesworth spoke to 450 people. In Montgomery, the headliner was Kelley M. Smith, a Baptist minister from Nashville, who spoke to an audience of 1,000 at Holt Street Baptist Church—the site of the first mass meeting for the bus boycott. And in the other eighteen cities, ministers called on their audiences to take part in their local registration campaign. In Miami, King spoke at the Greater Bethel AME Church on why voting mattered. He opened with a civics lesson: "The history of our nation is the history of a long and tireless effort to broaden and to increase the franchise of American citizens." King went on to describe how white men and women eventually won the right to vote. Soon, King said, African Americans would gain that same right, no matter how brutal the resistance. Southern disfranchisement was "a very real embarrassment to our nation which we love and must protect." Evoking the Cold War, King warned, "If a tragic global crisis is to be avoided, if America is to meet the challenge of our atomic age—then millions of our people, Negro and white, must be given the right freely to participate in the political life of our nation."[67]

The SCLC had meant for February 12 to be the start of a movement, but the Crusade for Citizenship collapsed almost as soon as it began. Ella Baker put together the initial programs of February 12, but she could not guarantee long-term success in any location. Baker, King, and the SCLC hoped the coordinated drive would inspire registration movements across the South, but without money, organization, or stronger collaboration with other civil rights groups, the Crusade never had much opportunity for success. The SCLC never came close to its goal of $200,000. Yet Baker stayed on the job until a replacement could be found, trying without success to motivate local leaders to orchestrate registration drives and file reports to her office. She encouraged Reverend J. E. Lowry of Mobile to continue with the Crusade, and she asked Reverend Edward T. Graham of Miami to report on any registration activity that came after February 12. Graham wrote of vague plans to continue the effort to register black Miamians, but he never sent a full report. Neither did anyone else. Baker tried to remain positive, knowing that "it was most unreasonable to imply failure because no record-breaking increase in Negro registration immediately followed the February 12 meetings."[68]

The Crusade faded from the minds of SCLC leaders once it became clear that it had failed. Ralph Abernathy responded to Edward Graham's request for results by writing that Baker was out of town, implying that he did not know or care.[69] King was also quiet about the Crusade's collapse. On March 13, Congressman Charles Diggs wrote King of his disappointment: "Even in Montgomery, Negro voter applicants have dropped below normal . . . Rallies and speeches are fine for inspirational purposes but a successful registration campaign demands skillful follow up in the field."[70] Besides Baker, no one in the SCLC possessed the ability to manage the grassroots. *U.S. News and World Report* published a story on southern African American registration, and while it did not mention the SCLC specifically, according to the authors, the "Civil Rights law isn't bringing out the masses of Negro voters in the South . . . There is no stampede among Negroes to qualify as voters. 'Get out the Vote' campaigns have flopped so far."[71]

In May, the SCLC replaced Baker with Reverend John Tilley from Baltimore, but by this time, the Crusade no longer had priority. Tilley had no experience organizing grassroots movements, and King later fired him in April 1959. During his and Baker's tenures, the Crusade failed to raise much money. "Because they didn't have any money," Baker recalled, she relied on phone calls and resorted to clipping and pasting flyers together to organize the Crusade.[72] She put some distance between herself and the SCLC, annoyed by its leadership, who had thought rallies and sermons would inaugurate a movement without bottom-up organization and fund-raising. Yet she stayed in touch with King and the SCLC, and the following year, she told King of a new potential source of funding. She cited a "need for developing a tax exempt 'arm' of SCLC," Baker wrote. "I understand that the Marshall

Field Foundation has some special interest in leadership training among religious leaders."[73] Under the leadership of its executive director, Maxwell Hahn, the Field Foundation had recently emerged as a committed financier of civil rights organizations, especially the SRC, rooted in Marshall Field III's prior support of the Chicago-based American Council on Race Relations during the 1940s. Baker heard about the Field Foundation's interests, and because of her tip, King and his SCLC staff began considering the possibility of philanthropic support for their voter registration fieldwork.[74]

As the need for a mass voter campaign became more evident into the late 1950s, disfranchisement seeped deeper into the South. To update its 1957 report, the SRC conducted another comprehensive survey of black southern voting. With a grant from the Field Foundation, the SRC commissioned social scientists to compile data in 1958, and in August 1959, the SRC released "The Negro and the Ballot in the South" by Margaret Price. In two years, rather than getting any easier, voting had become even more difficult. In Arkansas, over 5,000 fewer African Americans were registered in 1959 than in 1957. Georgia and Florida both decreased by several thousand. Louisiana and South Carolina shrank the most, with Louisiana dropping by 30,000 and South Carolina by 42,000. Mississippi remained stagnant at 20,000. Through purges, violence, slowdowns, literacy tests, and poll taxes, segregationists fought black political participation. The Civil Rights Act of 1957 had accomplished little to aid black voters. According to Price, "there seems to be no reason to expect a sudden dramatic rise in the number of Negro voters in the South, for the obstacles which have restricted Negro voting in the recent past are still strong."[75]

"The Negro and the Ballot in the South" expressed a grim outlook. As the federal government looked the other way, southern states implemented roadblocks. The SRC discovered that opposition had swelled since *Brown*, where a "strained atmosphere created by resistance to school desegregation has slowed the pace of Negro voter registration in the South."[76] At the same time, violence surged after *Brown*, and even in places that appeared peaceful, Price wrote, "an instance of racial violence in the South is rarely an isolated event—it serves as a reminder to Negroes that what has happened can happen again."[77] The SRC documented problems but prescribed no solutions. The Prayer Pilgrimage called national attention to the problem of black disfranchisement, and the Crusade for Citizenship tried and failed to fight back. Elston Roady, a political scientist at Florida State University who helped with the report, told Price, "We may well have reached that plateau in the development of greater Negro participation in politics . . . The successful assault on the next mountain seems to rest largely in the hands of the Negro citizen."[78]

Black southerners needed an engine to power a movement for the ballot. Soon after the Crusade for Citizenship ended, James M. Nabrit Jr., a civil rights attorney and dean of the Howard University law school, called for a "south-wide state by state campaign to get Negroes to register" and an "educational campaign to instruct Negroes in the value of the vote, the use of the ballot, how to register, how to vote, and that voting is a federal right."[79] Black southerners wanted to vote, as the SRC had documented at length, but violence, poll taxes, literacy tests, and segregationist obstinacy prevailed. Individually, registering remained difficult, but if a movement could organize around the franchise, the one-party, white supremacist South could be broken. Nabrit saw "an immediate need for the registration of a number of Negroes so as to furnish a reservoir out of which actual voters may come. The very existence of a vast number of registered Negroes may have an astonishing result."[80] The VEP would fill this reservoir.

CHAPTER TWO

Setting Up the Voter Education Project, 1959–1962

On June 16, 1961, Attorney General Robert F. Kennedy hosted the Freedom Ride Coordinating Committee in his office. For seven weeks, Freedom Riders—young activists affiliated with SNCC and CORE—had boarded Greyhound and Trailways buses to test the Supreme Court's 1960 *Boynton v. Virginia* decision outlawing segregated bus terminals. After weeks of bus bombings, white mob violence, and dozens of activists imprisoned in Mississippi, Diane Nash of SNCC wrote President John F. Kennedy requesting a White House meeting to discuss "the possibilities of action on the part of the federal government" to assist the Freedom Riders.[1] Instead, the attorney general accepted Nash's request. He hoped to persuade the Freedom Riders to drop the protests and make black voter registration their primary objective.

For weeks, Robert Kennedy and his DOJ staff had been in conversation with philanthropists and black leaders to create a collaborative project that promoted voter registration as the main avenue of civil rights activism. SNCC had not yet been involved in the discussions. When Diane Nash, accompanied by Charles Sherrod, Charles Jones, and Charles McDew—the three Charlies, as they were known within SNCC—met Robert Kennedy, they demanded that the federal government do more to protect Freedom Riders. Kennedy heard them out; then he suggested the time had come to switch tactics. Kennedy let them know about the DOJ's ongoing conversations with philanthropic and civil rights leaders about forming a project that would fund registration fieldwork throughout the South. The plans were still confidential, but Kennedy broached the subject with the SNCC activists to let them know about the possibility of generous, tax-free funding to help register southern African Americans.[2]

Charles Sherrod reacted angrily. Along with the others, he believed that Kennedy's offer bordered on bribery. "That's where I jumped in," Sherrod later remembered. He stood up to confront Kennedy. Wyatt Tee Walker, the SCLC executive director, held Sherrod back by his coattails. Sherrod told Kennedy "that he was a public official who was supposed to . . . keep people who made trouble for us off our backs" and that it was not Kennedy's "responsibility to tell us how to honor our constitutional rights."[3] Tensions cooled, and Kennedy continued on, arguing that registering voters might not be as attention-grabbing as the Freedom Rides, but it had the potential to undo Jim Crow voting practices.[4]

The meeting between Robert Kennedy and the Freedom Riders signified an unprecedented partnership between civil rights activists, the DOJ, and philanthropy—one that would spark conflict but one that would also influence the civil rights movement to embrace a focus on voter registration. Since the mid-1950s, the southern black freedom struggle had been an ill-defined movement. The widely shared goal had been to end segregation and achieve equal rights, but no coordinated strategy existed. Activists in local communities organized marches, protests, boycotts, sit-ins, and Freedom Rides, and while each chipped away at segregation, white supremacy remained as long as black disfranchisement continued. A stronger realization took hold that without poll power, victories would be short-lived. Leaders in the NAACP, SCLC, SRC, and other organizations sensed that voter registration would be the future of the fight, and philanthropists wanted to help pay for it. The Kennedys encouraged this partnership between foundations and civil rights groups because they believed black supporters for the Democratic Party would increase, and at the same time, the Kennedy administration could bypass intransigent southern Democrats in Congress. Together, civil rights leaders, philanthropists, and DOJ officials created the Voter Education Project.

DOJ officials, foundation executives, and civil rights leaders each had separate motives, but all agreed that the black freedom struggle should concentrate on voting rights activism. Activists were already interested in registration, but they lacked the finances to manage a southwide voter campaign. The SCLC's Crusade for Citizenship in 1958 had proved that such a project might be possible if it had widespread support. The VEP would be that support, but establishing the VEP was not a foregone conclusion. For over a year between 1961 and 1962, those who believed in the idea of the VEP labored behind the scenes to convince others that the plan would work. In the process, they began to concentrate the civil rights movement as a battle for the ballot.

STEPHEN CURRIER REMAINS an unheralded character within the story of civil rights, but he played a vital role in the formation of the VEP. Born on August 24, 1930, Currier grew up in privilege, groomed by his family for upper-class life in New York City. His mother, Mary Whelan Prue, left her family ranch in New Mexico for New York sometime during the early 1920s to pursue a modeling career, where she found work as an assistant fashion editor at *Vogue* magazine. Soon after, she met Richard Currier, a painter who spent much of his career in Europe. Richard and Mary married at a young age, had one child, Stephen, and divorced after several years. Stephen spent much of his early childhood in Italy alongside his father, but he returned to the United States for boarding school once he reached adolescence. In 1939, his mother married Edward M. M. Warburg, a decision that launched Stephen into a life of greater opportunity. Warburg came from a prestigious family with links to New York financial markets and philanthropy. His grandfather was Jacob Schiff, a Jewish German immigrant who became an influential investment banker and corporate executive from the mid-1870s until his death in 1920. His son-in-law, Felix Warburg, grew the family fortune as a partner with the investment bank Kuhn, Loeb and Company. Felix's son, Edward, continued the financial dynasty. Fine arts captured his imagination, and during the 1930s, Warburg helped establish the American Ballet and supported the Museum of Modern Art. Edward Warburg valued philanthropy as a public good. In New York City, however, Stephen never quite fit in. "He'd had a difficult upbringing, always in that sort of no-man's land on the edge of the rich New York world," according to a friend, Harold Fleming.[5] Stephen Currier went to Harvard, where he would meet one of the wealthiest heiresses in the United States.[6]

Audrey Bruce was born in 1933 into the Mellon clan, the richest family in the United States. Her grandfather was Andrew W. Mellon, former secretary of the Treasury, entrepreneur, banker, diplomat, and philanthropist. His firstborn daughter, Ailsa, married David K. E. Bruce, a lawyer and state representative in Maryland who later became an officer with the Office of Strategic Services and served as U.S. ambassador to France, West Germany, and Great Britain. Their marriage was turbulent, and they separated around the time of Andrew Mellon's death in 1937 when Audrey was four years old. Ailsa inherited a vast fortune, becoming one of the richest women in the country overnight. Like her father, Ailsa turned to philanthropy primarily as a tax haven, establishing the Avalon Foundation in 1940 but distancing herself from its operations. Bruce finally convinced Ailsa to divorce in 1945, agreeing that Audrey would stay with her mother. Growing up, Audrey was a reserved child who enjoyed the privacy of her family estates. But Ailsa was restless, and she moved Audrey with her from mansion to mansion. Audrey later attended boarding schools in New York and Virginia, and in 1952, she enrolled at Radcliffe College.[7]

Although Audrey knew of her family's wealth, her parents did not explain the extent of it until well into her college career. By that time, she had met Stephen Currier. College bored Currier, and he found work as an art consultant in Boston after dropping out of Harvard. Higher education exhilarated Audrey, yet she found herself drawn to Currier, whose unstable, affluent family mirrored her own. Currier later confided to friends that he did not know about Audrey's family fortune until after they married. Whether or not that was true, Audrey's family and their close friends despised Currier. They thought he took advantage of Audrey to gain access to the Mellon coffers. Lauder Greenway, a close friend to Ailsa, believed Audrey chose Currier because she knew that the family would not approve and therefore would not have to worry about the Mellons corrupting him. Audrey had little patience for family drama, and she gravitated toward Currier because she saw her life with him as separate from her upbringing. Knowing that neither the Mellons nor the Bruces would approve the match, Audrey and Stephen eloped on November 15, 1955, in Fairfield, Connecticut. They did not publicly announce their union until the following April, enough time for Audrey to graduate from Radcliffe without distractions. After marriage, they began to consider philanthropy as their future career.[8]

Two friends motivated Stephen Currier to consider southern African American inequality as a philanthropic opportunity. The first was Marshall Field III. Field had inherited his family's empire of department stores in Chicago, and he later purchased and ran two newspapers. In 1940, he and his wife, Ruth Pruyn Phipps, founded the Field Foundation. Currier often visited the Field family, and Marshall urged Stephen to look to philanthropy as a way to put his fortune to good use. Unlike many of their rich peers in the Midwest, the Fields supported the Democratic Party, the New Deal, and civil rights for African Americans. Inspired by the philanthropic legacy of Julius Rosenwald, whose Rosenwald Fund sponsored the construction of thousands of one-room schoolhouses for southern African American communities, Field in turn inspired Currier, who began following the events of the civil rights movement.[9]

The second major influence on Currier was financial expert Lloyd K. Garrison, the great-grandson of the abolitionist. In his unpublished memoir, Garrison remembered that the Curriers arrived at his office with a problem concerning Audrey's inheritance. The Mellons were pressuring Audrey to sign a document neither she nor Stephen fully understood, "which would effectively have turned over her vast fortune to the management of the Mellon bank in Pittsburgh and have placed restrictions on the free use of her income."[10] With Garrison's help, the Curriers retained control of Audrey's inheritance. After settling the matter, they "talked about what Stephen should do with his life."[11] Garrison encouraged the Curriers to become philanthropists. The Curriers and Garrison discovered they had a mutual interest in race problems. Garrison had served as president of the National Urban League from 1947 to 1952, and he promised to introduce Currier to civil rights activists. The two became close friends, and as Stephen and Audrey considered starting their own foundation, Garrison urged them to concentrate on racial inequality. The Curriers took Garrison's advice.[12]

In 1958, Stephen and Audrey launched the Taconic Foundation. Named for the mountain range where the couple often vacationed, the Curriers had a novel vision for Taconic: enact progressive change with a personal touch. They set up their office on the thirty-fifth floor of a Manhattan tower at 666 Fifth Avenue, and there, Stephen and Audrey worked together with a small staff to channel funds to groups working to advance civil rights, mental health, and child welfare. In their view, the arts, sciences, and medicine had an overabundance of benefactors, and they wanted to finance unorthodox ventures. A favorite term of theirs was "enablement," meaning, to them, a commitment to partner with "those with the fewest options."[13] Building on the long history of philanthropy in the United States, the Taconic Foundation's goal was to make incremental improvements toward "equality of opportunity."[14] According to the journalist John Egerton, the Curriers believed "that a foundation could be a *participant*, not merely a money dispenser."[15] Among dozens of grantees, Taconic sponsored the Child Welfare League of America, the NAACP, the National Urban League, the Northside Center for Child Development, the Morningside Community Center, and an innovative program in Harlem that later became the inspiration for Project Head Start. According to a family friend and adviser Victor Weingarten, "They never gave a dime for a building [to be named for them], no bricks, no mortar, only programs and people. They were pioneers who spent an enormous amount of time finding out for themselves what they wanted to support."[16]

The Mellons were aghast that Audrey spent family money on "distastefully radical political causes."[17] A cousin of Audrey's recalled, "My family disapproved of the things they [Stephen and Audrey] were working on. Something having to do with the colored. We felt they were on the wrong side."[18] Members of the Mellon clan, along with Audrey's father, believed that Stephen controlled Audrey and her money. The family was further annoyed that Audrey had not entrusted her inheritance to Mellon banks. Throughout her adolescence, the family had infantilized Audrey, viewing her as sensitive and naive. The family's fears were confirmed when Audrey appeared unhappy, at one point even asking her father for divorce advice. But to their disappointment, Audrey stayed with Stephen. She attended Taconic board meetings, and she also volunteered as a nurse at Lenox Hill Hospital, where she kept her identity secret from her colleagues. The couple purchased a 1,600-acre estate near The Plains, Virginia, where they spent much of their time when not in New York City. Stephen was sensitive to the Mellons' dislike of him and charges of opportunism, but he valued Audrey in a way the Mellons never did, and together they grew the Taconic Foundation.[19]

Soon after launching, the Taconic Foundation began sponsoring the SRC, and the Curriers became friends with its executive director, Harold C. Fleming. Having worked with the South's foremost interracial organization since 1944, Fleming was a "self-effacing southerner . . . with an instinctive empathy for people in need."[20] Since the late 1950s, the SRC had functioned as a mediator between multiple civil rights groups. On November 5 and 6, 1957, the SRC hosted a southern interagency meeting in Atlanta to discuss a "joint fact-finding project" on black disfranchisement, employment discrimination, and school segregation. Many groups joined the SRC, including the NAACP, the Anti-Defamation League, the American Friends Service Committee, and Martin Luther King Jr.'s new Southern Leadership Conference. Attempting to link multiple groups involved in the growing "resistance movement" in the South, the SRC became a central meeting place for leaders and organizations.[21]

On October 19, 1959, Harold Fleming circulated a short essay entitled "Some Observations on Foundation Giving in the Field of Race Relations" reflecting on the dearth of philanthropic support to southern groups fighting Jim Crow. The major foundations—Carnegie, Ford, and Rockefeller—had "shunned direct efforts in this field like the plague," not wanting to support controversial organizations for fear of bad publicity or inviting charges of communism. But he began to notice "a slight, but encouraging, trend toward more interaction between Southern race-relationists and foundation persons."[22] Midsized and smaller foundations—such as the Taconic Foundation, the Field Foundation, the New World Foundation, and the Christopher Reynolds Foundation—had supported the SRC over the past few years because Fleming developed personal relationships with those who oversaw donations. Fleming and the Curriers, for example, had become friends, and the Taconic Foundation granted $95,000 to the SRC for programs in 1959 and 1960.[23] Not wanting to create "undue dependence," the Taconic Foundation's grants to the SRC were not exorbitant, but they were consistent.[24] Fleming tried to convince other wealthy donors that supporting the SRC and similar organizations battling Jim Crow was a worthwhile cause. These budding relationships brought various philanthropists into the SRC's orbit.

Impressed with the SRC's work, Currier approached Fleming about a new idea: do something unorthodox as a foundation and lobby the federal government to ensure the rights of African Americans. Soon after John F. Kennedy became president in November 1960, Currier and Lloyd Garrison flew to Georgia to discuss with Fleming the idea for a philanthropic hub based in Washington, DC, and devoted to public policy and racial issues. They toured parts of rural Georgia and talked about racism. They also attended a Sunday morning service at Ebenezer Baptist Church, where they heard a young Martin Luther King Jr. preach from his father's pulpit.[25] Fleming had second thoughts about leaving the SRC, but after talking with Currier, he agreed to lead the effort. Currier had big ideas, but, at only twenty-nine years old, he was unsure how to move forward. The seasoned Fleming did, and with his enormous contact list, they established the Potomac Institute as an "off-shoot or subsidiary of Taconic."[26] The Curriers had conditions, though. As with their earlier work, they wished to remain out of the limelight. Fleming remembered, "They insisted that their personal benefactions be given no publicity and that their privacy be respected."[27] As executive vice president, Fleming put together a small staff in an office on 18th Street, meeting Currier's wish that the organization remain "quiet" and "unpretentious."[28] Currier and Fleming sensed they were in the midst of a political shift incorporating civil rights issues into the national legislative agenda. They wanted to be at the forefront, and the Potomac Institute became an influential research and lobbying firm in Washington, DC. According to Fleming, "No other organization was so linked both to government offices and the southern civil rights movement, and so trusted by both."[29]

Stephen Currier's creation of the Potomac Institute was important because it challenged an old precedent within the world of philanthropy, one that the VEP would shatter a year later. Since major foundations first emerged a half century earlier, philanthropists like Currier had wanted to get involved with politics, but interpretations of the law prevented them from doing so. At stake was federal tax exemption. Educational pursuits counted as tax-exempt, but political advocacy did not. After the Sixteenth Amendment established the federal income tax in 1913, the Treasury Department created policies by which charitable gifts could be tax-exempt. But the rules were murky, especially since so few major foundations existed at the time. For years, the Treasury Department relied on a mixture of court rulings and state laws to clarify the terms, approving most charitable gifts as long as they somehow benefitted society and were not overtly political. Treasury allowed tax exemptions for educational initiatives, but over time, the difference between education and political advocacy blurred as more people applied for exemptions and foundations increased in number. In 1919, Treasury regulators updated their policies by "drawing a line in the sand" between advocacy and education because they "wanted to make sure beneficiaries of tax exemption did not engage in politics under the cover of educational activity," according to the historian Olivier Zunz.[30]

Although regulators designed the Revenue Act of 1934 to clarify tax exemption, it only added to the confusion. The main reason for the 1934 law was to close loopholes and raise tax revenue amid the Great Depression, but buried in one article was the root cause of philanthropy's boom over the next three decades. After some debate in Congress regarding the language, members compromised with this clause: as long as "no substantial part of the activities" were political in nature, foundations and other organizations could be tax-exempt if "organized and operated exclusively for religious, charitable, scientific, literary, or educational purposes." But the law forbade them from engaging in "propaganda, or otherwise attempting, to influence legislation."[31] With parameters set, foundations concentrated on education, medicine, public health, poverty, and fine arts. Hundreds of small to midsized family foundations joined Carnegie, Ford, and Rockefeller, looking to spend their wealth for the public good on their own terms. But while the law appeared explicit, the word "substantial" left plenty of ambiguity in place. Foundations avoided outright partisanship, but as they funded more and more projects, the difference between education and advocacy remained hazy.[32]

Philanthropy relied on tax exemption. Through tax exemptions, charitable giving became an American institution, practiced by the middle class and the wealthy alike. The Revenue Act of 1934 ushered in a new era of giving, one not wholly motivated by altruism. Donors found a way to avoid taxation by giving through family foundations. Writing about the law's effect five years after implementation, the economist C. Lowell Harriss realized, "The exemption acts in effect as a government subsidy to institutions qualifying for the benefit under the law."[33] The federal government picked up the tab in lost tax revenue by providing generous terms for tax exemption, and America's wealthy class took advantage. Tax lawyers perceived the implications, and they advised their rich clients to set up family foundations to serve as tax shelters where they could protect their family assets from the government, maintain control of their holdings, and spend on public causes, or not. Studying these effects in 1949, the researcher B. W. Patch found, "With tax rates at high levels and with charitable contributions exempt from income tax . . . large contributors in the top tax brackets sometimes may make up in tax savings, for themselves or their estates, more than one-half of the amount of their contributions."[34] Over the years, foundations fiercely guarded their tax-exempt status, creating a culture within big philanthropy dependent on tax breaks. This idea remained paramount during the late 1950s and early 1960s as the Curriers managed the Taconic Foundation, established the Potomac Institute, and looked ahead to supporting civil rights activists in the South.

While the Curriers concentrated on the Taconic Foundation and the Potomac Institute between 1958 and 1961, the election of John F. Kennedy on November 8, 1960 suggested a new focus on civil rights within the federal government. Running on a campaign that included greater, albeit vague, plans for federal action, Kennedy appeared to many African Americans as sympathetic on race. Unlike his Republican opponent, Richard Nixon, Kennedy promoted equal rights during his campaign, although he never offered specific policies for fear of upsetting southern Democrats. Kennedy called Coretta Scott King while her husband sat in jail to offer some comfort, and his staff made sure his display of sensitivity reached the media. Several months after the sit-in movement began, Kennedy praised the demonstrators: "It is in the American tradition to stand up for one's rights — even if the new way to stand up for one's rights is to sit down."[35]

After Kennedy won the presidency, the SRC sensed a positive shift toward improved race relations. Harold Fleming and his research director, Leslie W. Dunbar, wanted to create an ally in Kennedy. Following the election, the SRC invited incoming Kennedy administration staff to attend their annual meeting. Several came, and suddenly SRC staff felt like they "were on the same side as the people running the country."[36] With segregationists dominant in the Senate, effective legislation to address civil rights stood little chance of passing, but many believed the president could issue executive orders. A few weeks before the election took place, with help from a Rockefeller Brothers Fund grant, the SRC commissioned Daniel H. Pollitt, a law professor at the University of North Carolina, to draft a paper detailing the possibilities of executive action on civil rights. Explaining the assignment to his mother, Pollitt wrote that he was preparing a "study on what a strong and willing President could do within existing powers to alleviate the racial problems in as many areas as I can think of."[37] After Pollitt completed the first draft and Kennedy won the election, the SRC coordinated with dozens of other civil rights activists to make sure the report was comprehensive, incorporating recommendations from the NAACP, the National Urban League, and the U.S. Commission on Civil Rights. After revisions, Dunbar and about a dozen others met in Washington, DC with Kennedy staff to scrutinize the document. Before sending it to the president-elect, those involved wanted to make sure the report's recommendations were achievable and legally sound.[38]

In January 1961, Harold Fleming sent the completed forty-eight-page report to Kennedy in hopes of persuading the president-elect to act on civil rights. Entitled "The Federal Executive and Civil Rights," the paper made eighteen recommendations for ways the president could use the power of his office to end racial inequality in the South. Among the proposals, the SRC encouraged the president to take executive action to affirm the *Brown v. Board of Education* Supreme Court decision, push the DOJ to enforce civil rights laws, increase the staff of the Civil Rights Division, end housing and employment discrimination, and accurately represent the country's racial problems to the international press. In what would later read as a prelude to the VEP, it called on the president to promote African American voting participation by organizing a "national campaign to educate people in their voting rights and to encourage them to vote."[39] The SRC also circulated the report to the national press. The report introduced the Kennedys and members of his administration to the SRC, an important factor that later brought movement activists and DOJ officials together to form the VEP.[40]

Kennedy had met African American leaders during his senatorial career and early presidential campaign, and he began assembling a team sympathetic to the movement, including Harris Wofford. An advocate of Gandhian nonviolence, Wofford earned law degrees from Howard University and Yale University before serving as an attorney with the U.S. Civil Rights Commission under the Eisenhower administration. During his time with the Commission, he became friends with Martin Luther King Jr. and sent him literature on nonviolence. While teaching at the University of Notre Dame Law School in 1959, Wofford became interested in Kennedy's presidential aspirations. Wanting to push Kennedy on civil rights, Wofford mailed the Kennedy brothers an opinion paper in which he suggested that "a shift of focus to the clear-cut issue of voting rights would be 'politically right and psychologically healthy.'"[41] Wofford's paper made an impression, and the following year, the Kennedys brought him on board their campaign as an adviser on civil rights.[42]

The Kennedy brothers began promoting voting rights as their primary intervention into the civil rights movement. To them, focusing on access to the polls seemed the best way to address civil rights without inflaming southern conservatives over the prospects of integrated schooling. According to Arthur M. Schlesinger Jr., the Kennedys believed "Negro voting did not incite social and sexual anxieties; and white southerners could not argue against suffrage for their fellow Negro citizens with quite the same moral fervor they applied to the mingling of the races in schools."[43] After the election, Robert Kennedy noticed an anomaly in Fayette County, Tennessee that signaled the rising power of the black vote. Under Eisenhower, John Doar with the DOJ had investigated economic reprisals in Fayette and Haywood Counties, where evidence indicated that white landowners punished and removed black tenants for political participation. In the 1960 election, demonstrating some Republican loyalty for investigating these acts, African Americans voted overwhelmingly for Nixon in Fayette County. Whereas Kennedy captured a much higher percentage of the black vote elsewhere in the country, the numbers in Fayette County suggested that black voters were not locked in for the Democrats. Fayette County's example cemented in Robert Kennedy's mind the need to increase black registration and hopefully win over more Democratic voters.[44]

Harris Wofford became the special assistant on civil rights within the DOJ after Kennedy's victory, and soon after his appointment, he recommended executive actions to the president-elect. Familiar with "The Federal Executive and Civil Rights," Wofford echoed its message and laid out a plan for translating ideas into action. He argued that Kennedy should welcome the opportunity to skirt an unhelpful Congress. This route offered the greatest number of possibilities to do good, Wofford suggested, because the executive branch could do more than any piece of watered-down legislation, such as the Civil Rights Acts of 1957 and 1960. Wofford advised Kennedy to support the anti-poll-tax amendment clogged in Congress, strengthen the Civil Rights Division within the DOJ, compel southern leaders to fully desegregate schools, end federal housing discrimination, renew the U.S. Commission on Civil Rights, and host public meetings with civil rights leaders to demonstrate empathy. According to Wofford, "you [Kennedy] can do without any substantial civil rights legislation this session of Congress *if* you go ahead with a substantial executive action program."[45]

In the same memorandum, Wofford counseled Kennedy to prioritize black voter registration. Taking stock of the civil rights movement, Wofford wrote, "It would probably help now to shift the spotlight from lunch counter sit-ins and school desegregation to Negro enfranchisement."[46] Citing his belief that registration offered the greatest potential for concrete progress with less chance of conservative resistance, Wofford envisioned African Americans registering en masse if only given federal support. He also explained that focusing on black registration could be a boon for the Democratic Party:

"It would be a dramatic and good thing for the national Democratic Party to announce and launch such a drive, instead of leaving it to the NAACP and King's movement."[47] With more black votes, Democrats would secure the South while evolving beyond a whites-only party in the region. If the national Democratic Party did nothing to wrench the segregationist wing out of power in the South, Wofford feared African Americans would turn to the Republican Party. To make sure this did not happen, Wofford suggested state parties pursue black registration while national leaders supported greater enfranchisement. "The southern Negro temper is changing fast and these state Democratic parties will need to adjust or risk losing the Negro vote," Wofford warned.[48] Robert Kennedy was convinced, later telling DOJ lawyer John Doar, "I want to move on voting."[49] In May during a speech at the University of Georgia, he promised students that the DOJ would protect voting rights: "An integral part of all this is that we make a total effort to guarantee the ballot for every American of voting age . . . The right to vote is the easiest of all rights to grant."[50]

During the transition from Eisenhower to Kennedy, the search to find a new leader for the Civil Rights Division became crucial to the DOJ. President Kennedy's brother-in-law and campaign manager Sargent Shriver wanted Wofford, but others within the DOJ worried over his politics and friendship with King, not wanting to unnerve allies among southern Democrats. Burke Marshall came up as an alternative. Wofford and Marshall had attended law school together at Yale and had been law partners. Unlike Wofford, Marshall was a corporate antitrust lawyer with no apparent opinions on racial matters or personal ties to civil rights leaders. His lack of knowledge worked in his favor, and after an awkward interview with Robert Kennedy in which the two men reportedly sat in silence for several minutes staring at each other, Marshall became the new head of the Civil Rights Division. Robert Kennedy thought Marshall was sympathetic to improved race relations but uninformed enough not to alarm conservatives. On February 8, 1961, Fleming wrote Currier with the disappointing news that their friend Harris Wofford would not be appointed to lead the Civil Rights Division. Fleming heard from a source that "Bobby Kennedy decided Harris was too hot for the Assistant Attorney General spot." Wofford approved the selection of his old partner, although Fleming heard "a dismal picture of the prospects for vigorous action generally in civil rights" from his informant.[51]

On March 6, Robert Kennedy and Burke Marshall met with the SRC and civil rights leaders to argue that agencies should pursue voter registration above all else. Martin Luther King Jr. was conspicuously absent. A month earlier, *The Nation* had printed an editorial by King calling on the Kennedy administration to support the civil rights movement by issuing executive orders, bucking tradition that incoming presidents be given a grace period in the media. King based much of his material on "The Federal Executive and Civil Rights."[52] Feeling shut out, King wrote the White House requesting a private meeting. Busy with foreign policy matters, the president's staff declined, but DOJ officials weighed the merits of engaging King. Louis Martin, assistant chairman of the Democratic National Committee, suggested bringing King in for a private meeting to gauge how well he could work with the new administration. A month later, they met for lunch at the Mayflower Hotel in Washington, DC. Accompanied by his trusted friend Stanley Levison, King met Robert Kennedy, Marshall, Wofford, and others from the DOJ. At the meeting, the Civil Rights Division laid out their vision for the future of the movement. Marshall said that the SCLC and other race organizations ought to concentrate on voter registration, a pressing issue throughout the Jim Crow South. Marshall explained the DOJ could be most effective by filing lawsuits and pressuring local officials to stop harassing African Americans if they were trying to register. Militant demonstrations exacerbated tensions and conflicts the DOJ might not be able to resolve. According to John Seigenthaler, a DOJ aide, Kennedy told King, "Put on drives in these areas . . . I think some funds can be found from some of the foundations who are interested in this sort of thing."[53] King listened and did not say much. He agreed with the DOJ's opinion, but King made sure the DOJ understood his belief that meaningful demonstrations should include much more than voting campaigns. Kennedy and his colleagues were relieved to find King amenable to their ideas on registration. As a show of good faith, Marshall gave King his personal phone number with instructions to call him if trouble arose.[54]

On May 4, 1961, the first Freedom Rides set out from Washington, DC toward New Orleans. The passengers made it through Virginia and North Carolina largely unscathed, but in Rock Hill, South Carolina, locals attacked Freedom Riders at the terminal. The worst violence occurred on May 14 outside Anniston, Alabama, when police coordinated with the Ku Klux Klan. The attackers bombed the bus and beat passengers as they fled the smoke-filled cabin. Images of bloodied Freedom Riders and a smoking bus filled the nation's newspapers. Robert Kennedy tried to negotiate a peaceful solution. James Farmer of CORE called off the journey to New Orleans after "mobs and official hostility broke the back of the first Freedom Ride," but SNCC organized more passengers to take their place.[55] Recognizing the students' determination and the callousness of Alabama's governor John Patterson, Robert Kennedy directed DOJ officials to arrange protection for the Freedom Rides to avoid more violence. Once activists crossed into Mississippi, officials arrested the passengers and put them into Parchman, Mississippi's infamous penitentiary. But the Freedom Rides continued, ignoring Kennedy's criticism.[56]

Behind the scenes, Robert Kennedy worked to resolve the crisis. Before the Freedom Rides began, King suggested that Kennedy pressure the Interstate Commerce Commission (ICC) to act on the *Boynton v. Virginia* ruling and desegregate bus terminals. Kennedy declined, citing the slow-moving reputation of the ICC, not to mention that it was an independent body unaccustomed to arm-twisting from the DOJ. By May 29, Kennedy had changed his mind. He pressured the ICC to desegregate bus terminals in line with the goals of the Freedom Riders. Kennedy's staff at the DOJ petitioned the ICC, an unprecedented move and breach of traditional executive procedure. For months, DOJ officials urged the ICC to rule for desegregation, and on September 22, 1961, the ICC issued the official order. Marshall remembered the ICC ruling "was really a remarkable administrative law achievement" that prevailed on a "conservative, very difficult administrative body."[57] According to Taylor Branch, Kennedy "telescoped a process that normally took years" and pulled off a "bureaucratic miracle."[58] This example of strong-arm lobbying established a new precedent within the DOJ, one that would reverberate when it assisted the VEP months later.

While the DOJ dealt with the Freedom Rides, the SCLC happened on a fortunate break. Myles Horton of the Highlander Folk School, an interracial training institute for labor and civil rights activism in Tennessee, suggested the SCLC take over its citizenship schools as it faced legal battles regarding its tax exemption. Directed by Septima Clark, a longtime NAACP activist, educator, and Highlander workshop organizer, the citizenship schools had trained hundreds of men and women through weeklong courses on how to register, circumvent uncooperative registrars, and mobilize communities. Recalling the failure of the Crusade for Citizenship in 1958, Martin Luther King Jr. and Wyatt Tee Walker leaped at the chance to absorb an already functional voter registration organization into the SCLC. Clark expressed dismay because she was not consulted about the transfer, but she agreed to continue working under the SCLC banner and the renamed Citizenship Education Program (CEP). The CEP continued well into the 1960s in Dorchester, South Carolina, training activists in grassroots methods of voter registration. The Field Foundation donated $26,500, which the United

Church of Christ administered to avoid tax liabilities. With this grant, King's and Walker's eyes opened to a vast new source: big philanthropy. Walker knew that to expand the SCLC's reach, it needed money. After the Field Foundation's donation, he began to notice other foundations that seemed willing to assist. Together, King and Walker "learned a whole new vocabulary: grant proposals, funding conduits, advance budgeting, program reviews."[59]

While King and Walker sought foundation sponsors, Harold Fleming and Burke Marshall began discussing how to win IRS approval for a major philanthropic-backed registration project. In his memoir, Fleming remembered that in their frequent conversations, Marshall cited the need for black southerners to devote themselves to voter registration rather than sit-in demonstrations because he believed the DOJ could only get involved when local authorities discriminated against registrants. While scattered voter leagues had organized for years and NAACP chapters had mounted registration drives in the South, no coordinated, intergroup effort existed. Marshall realized the main impediment to mass registration was financial. He knew foundations were interested in donating money to voter registration, but murky tax rules restricted assistance. Marshall told Fleming that it might be possible to maintain tax exemption for foundations engaged in voter registration if it could be framed in a way that would not alarm the IRS. Fleming suggested the SRC, as a tax-exempt and research-based organization, could serve as base. If a project "included a significant research component and adequate safeguards against political partisanship," Fleming recalled Marshall saying, it might be possible to link philanthropy and African American registration activism.[60]

While Currier, Fleming, Marshall, Kennedy, King, and Wofford pursued the idea, they believed that all of the major civil rights organizations needed to commit as partners. Tensions between leadership of the NAACP, SCLC, CORE, and SNCC sometimes boiled over. Another challenge would be to get everyone to see eye to eye on the primary importance of voter registration. On a diplomatic mission, Burke Marshall traveled to Capahosic, Virginia in June 1961 to meet with CORE and SNCC leaders not locked up in Parchman. From the DOJ's perspective, he explained why voter registration offered the best strategy moving forward. Timothy Jenkins, a young SNCC member and former student body president at Howard University, listened with particular interest. Unlike some of his SNCC colleagues, he put little faith in the long-term goals of sit-ins and Freedom Rides. Marshall's presentation intrigued him, and he left the meeting committed to influencing others within SNCC to work with the Kennedy administration and pursue voter registration.[61]

After the June 16, 1961 meeting with the Freedom Riders, Robert Kennedy and Marshall aggressively lobbied SNCC to accept their plan. To them, if SNCC maintained its focus on nonviolent demonstrations instead of voter registration, the philanthropy-backed plan could fall apart. Kennedy and Marshall arranged for a *New York Times* front-page story by the journalist Anthony Lewis suggesting that civil rights groups were drifting toward voter mobilization. Appearing ten days after the meeting between Kennedy and the Freedom Riders, the article explained that DOJ officials were predicting a shift because "Negro leaders, including young and militant newcomers, are prepared for the first time to throw their full weight behind a registration and voting drive."[62] Lewis alluded to Marshall's recent journey to Capahosic where he received feedback from SNCC activists about the DOJ's plan. Bordering on speculation, Lewis wrote, "Confidence that the Government will do its best to protect those who try to register and vote also encourages Negroes to make the attempt."[63]

The day after the *New York Times* story ran, Harry Belafonte, a popular black entertainer and longtime financial supporter of the movement, hosted a meeting for skeptical SNCC students to coax them to pursue voting rights as their main form of activism. A few days earlier, Robert Kennedy had Belafonte over to his house to ask for his help reaching out to reluctant SNCC members. Belafonte agreed that voting rights ought to be the central thrust of the southern movement. Timothy Jenkins and Charles Jones were part of the SNCC group that visited Belafonte, and both were already leaning toward voter registration as the organization's main work. The group discussed the merits of grassroots registration work, and Belafonte gave SNCC $10,000 to initiate the process. The faction within SNCC that wanted to push the organization toward voter campaigns increasingly gained power, and a series of meetings during the summer of 1961 solidified their position.[64]

Meeting in Baltimore from July 14 to 16, SNCC's executive committee discussed a range of topics, including the Belafonte meeting and shifting SNCC's emphasis to voter registration. Charles Jones gave a verbal report on the gathering between himself, Timothy Jenkins, Charles McDew, Diane Nash, Walter Williams, Lonnie King, and Harry Belafonte that took place in Washington, DC three weeks earlier. The group "felt that voter registration was the most important issue and that the real possibility to enact a successful program was at hand."[65] Led by Bob Moses, several SNCC students in Mississippi were already concentrating on registration work with the help of Amzie Moore of the state NAACP. They suggested giving greater attention to voter registration work without discontinuing direct-action protests, like

Freedom Rides and sit-ins. After more meetings, SNCC's leadership accepted the strategy to concentrate on voting rights activism. Gathering at the Highlander Folk School in August, Ella Baker mediated a compromise in which SNCC would have one wing devoted to voter registration and another to direct action. With this agreement, SNCC took the lead on grassroots voter mobilization in the South. In November 1961 at another SNCC leadership meeting, Bob Moses led a session titled "Why Voter Registration?" Marion Barry's workshop—"Why Direct Action?"—followed. By then, SNCC had accepted both strategies.[66]

As plans moved ahead for the SRC to host the joint registration project, Leslie W. Dunbar emerged as its leader. Harold Fleming later said of Dunbar, "Southern liberals of his breed are familiar with evil, for they grew up with it; discerned it among family, friends, and neighbors; learned to detect and combat it within themselves."[67] From childhood through adulthood, Dunbar, a white man, witnessed racism all around him, and as he undid its grip on him, he worked to eliminate it from society. Dunbar was born on January 27, 1921 in Lewisburg, West Virginia, but he grew up in Baltimore. He remembered Baltimore's rigid racial code that extended "from the schools to residential areas to swimming pools and everything else. We even had [segregation] in the parks, black baseball diamonds and white baseball diamonds."[68] Growing up in Baltimore's white neighborhoods, he perceived the effects of segregation, but "not in the sense that you felt it was something you needed to do something about. We just saw the order of things."[69] After graduating from the University of Maryland and briefly attending law school, Dunbar went to Cornell University and earned his doctorate in political science. He soon took a job teaching at Emory University beginning in the fall of 1948, and he moved to Atlanta to begin his academic career.[70]

Dunbar saw racism with clarity and horror during his time in Atlanta. He recalled one experience that forced him to reckon with the everyday injustices black men and women faced in the South. Soon after joining Emory's faculty, he advised the undergraduate political science club. He came up with the idea to invite an African American professor from Atlanta University to speak to their group. Dr. William Boyd earned his PhD from the University of Michigan and emerged as an expert in international relations, but when Dunbar phoned to ask him over to Emory's exclusively white campus, he asked Boyd to talk about race relations, assuming that would be his preferred topic. Boyd obliged, and he took the opportunity to detail the racist slights his family often dealt with. When they traveled to Washington, DC, Boyd told the club, his family packed their food and planned out bathroom breaks, knowing they could not pull into any store. Even more recently, he said, his daughter's school took up a collection for the segregated Atlanta Zoo to purchase a new elephant, but he had to explain that even though she had donated a dime, she could not visit the elephant. Dunbar sat stunned in the back of the room, realizing he had offended Dr. Boyd by not asking him to talk about his field of study. He apologized and Boyd accepted, but Dunbar realized that he had been blind to many everyday troubles African Americans faced in the South. Race was not Dunbar's specialty within political science, but he began to pay more attention to the subject, leading him toward a much different career path.[71]

In Atlanta, Dunbar became familiar with the SRC, befriending its executive director, George Mitchell, and Harold Fleming, and he eventually joined the staff in 1958. Mitchell gave a talk at Emory in 1949 or 1950 that Dunbar remembered as life changing: "From then on I took the [Southern Regional] Council as my guide to what was wrong about the South, and how it could be made right."[72] He became interested in the SRC's work on race relations, and Mitchell first offered him a job at the SRC in 1954, but Dunbar declined. Dunbar later joined the faculty at Mount Holyoke College, but academia bored Dunbar, and he never quite forgot the job he turned down at the SRC. Another opportunity came once Fleming became the SRC's director in 1957. Fleming offered Dunbar a summer position with the SRC during 1958, and since Dunbar did not want to return to Mount Holyoke the following fall, Fleming made the job permanent.[73] The SRC had expanded in recent years with grants from the Ford Foundation and Rockefeller Brothers Fund, and Dunbar and Fleming decided to create a permanent research department with Dunbar at the helm. The civil rights movement had taken hold across the South, and the SRC wanted to broaden its aid through research.[74]

Dunbar helped the SRC construct a national reputation as a reliable source of information on southern race relations. The revamped SRC promoted a liberal perspective on race in the South. SRC staff combed through newspapers and magazines from across the region, organizing clipping files and piling up a mass of research on various topics. They wrote news releases, pamphlets, and special reports on the state of school desegregation. As director of research, Dunbar pushed the SRC to produce information quickly. Soon after the student sit-in movement took off across the South in the winter and spring of 1960, Dunbar published a special report on the protests "while the stools at the first Woolworth's were still warm."[75] Dunbar liked to say the SRC's creed was "partisan objectivity" — clearly on the side of liberal reform but meticulous in its research to help reporters spread the word that the South was on the precipice of change.[76] "I felt in 1958, '59, and '60, that the work of the SRC was to be a leading part of a great mind changing going on in the South . . . Our role was to be something of a guide to it."[77]

With the SRC in mind, Stephen Currier met with DOJ and civil rights leaders to form an organization that would supply funds to African American voter campaigns. Currier convened meetings in his New York office on July 11 and 28, 1961 to discuss logistics. Those involved knew that interorganizational rivalries among civil rights groups endangered such a broad project, which made the SRC such an appealing choice to house the project. Behind the scenes, Fleming gauged the opinions of others about having the SRC take the lead, including Martin Luther King Jr. Fleming knew that the SRC had experience drawing together multiple organizations. More importantly, the SRC was tax-exempt, nonpartisan, and educational. Fleming approached Dunbar with the idea for the SRC to serve as a clearinghouse dispensing money to registration campaigns. Dunbar agreed, but he had conditions. Before he consented, the new venture must be guaranteed not to endanger the SRC's federal tax exemption. Dunbar also wanted Currier to oversee the fundraising, to which Currier agreed. The registration project also needed its own director, and that person must be a unanimous choice. If anyone from the NAACP, CORE, SCLC, NUL, or SNCC did not feel comfortable with the leadership, the tenuous alliance would shatter before it began. And finally, Dunbar insisted that the SRC control who received funding and that local, independent organizations be supported alongside major groups. The idea of the SRC managing the process intrigued King, but he wanted to meet Dunbar first. Dunbar heard about King's reservations, so he called King and asked to talk in person. King visited Dunbar one Saturday morning in the SRC office, and afterward, King felt comfortable with the SRC as the appropriate home for the project.[78]

Dunbar attended the July 28 meeting and forwarded his observations to the SRC executive committee, documenting the coalescence of the still-unnamed voter education program. Representatives of foundations included Stephen Currier, Jane Lee Eddy, and Lloyd K. Garrison of the Taconic Foundation; Justine Wise Polier of the Field Foundation; and Vernon Eagle of the New World Foundation. Harris Wofford and Burke Marshall represented the Kennedy administration. Civil rights leaders included King and Walker from the SCLC, Charles McDew and Marion Berry of SNCC, Roy Wilkins from the NAACP, Thurgood Marshall and Robert Carter of the NAACP Legal Defense Fund, Lester Granger and Whitney Young from the NUL, James Farmer of CORE, and Timothy Jenkins representing the National

Student Association (NSA). The group asked Marshall to discuss "the legal responsibilities of the Department of Justice in the voter registration field," which he did to their satisfaction.[79] Four hours into the meeting, King motioned that the SRC take leadership of the project, and by the end of the meeting, everyone agreed that the SRC would be "an acceptable coordinating agency."[80] Tax lawyers attended as well, and they insisted that focusing on voter registration would not imperil the SRC's tax exemption. Specific donation amounts were not discussed; nor did foundation representatives commit to join. Each organization promised to send the SRC a detailed plan of action by August 14 on how they would spend philanthropic money on voter registration. Dunbar thought the amount donated would be "substantial but not grandiose," and the attending civil rights leaders all voiced their enthusiasm for the project. The meeting appeared successful, with Dunbar noting he was "deeply impressed by the amiability and harmony of the gathering."[81]

Financial troubles had plagued the NAACP, CORE, SCLC, SNCC, and NUL, making the joint project all the more appealing. The size and bureaucracy of their operations devoured budgets, leaving little to devote to grassroots registration fieldwork. Even though the NAACP's membership grew to nearly 500,000 by the mid-1960s, the national office remained constantly in debt. The SCLC relied on church donations and labor union support, and although Walker exploited King's popularity to raise large sums of money, the SCLC spent more than it took in. Through telethons, benefit concerts, direct mail, speaking tours, and by capitalizing off the Freedom Rides, CORE raised $607,484.39 during the 1961–62 fiscal year, but its debt mushroomed to $120,000 by the next year. "Our financial cupboard is bare," James Farmer wrote in a fundraising letter.[82] While Whitney Young crafted relationships with several philanthropies, solvency likewise remained elusive for the NUL. Compared to the other four, SNCC operated in relative poverty. In 1960, SNCC took in $5,000 and in 1961 raised only $14,000 from outside sources, unable to meet its proposed budget of $15,980.[83] Leaders from these organizations felt steady pressure to raise money. The joint project offered a practical solution to take in philanthropic money for a specific purpose.[84]

Roy Wilkins composed the NAACP's response to the collective registration project. He painted the NAACP as the most competent civil rights group in the country that deserved most—if not all—of the available funds. With the exception of Alabama, which had banished the NAACP in 1956, the organization boasted 337 active branches across ten southern states. For half a century, the NAACP had promoted black registration through local drives and in court rooms. Beginning in 1957, the NAACP renewed its focus on the ballot when it created a voter registration committee with the Charlotte, North Carolina chapter president Kelly Alexander at the helm. The next year, W. C. Patton and John Brooks, two long-standing NAACP activists, took over at the NAACP's national office on matters of voter registration. Together, they coordinated a small team of field secretaries that visited branches to instigate registration campaigns. The NAACP concentrated its resources on urban areas to target the greatest number of unregistered African Americans, citing successes in cities like Memphis and Baltimore. With a precedent for registration work already in place, Wilkins stated the NAACP "has the structure and the personnel to insure that voter registration campaigns are launched and carried forward." Over the next several years, he promised, the NAACP would expand its voter registration activities in branches across the country. For these reasons, the NAACP desired to be an essential partner within the southwide registration effort, leading the way if possible.[85]

Lester B. Granger, executive director of the NUL, cited his organization's history of voter registration activism. Although its principal aim had been to promote "welfare resources, vocational guidance, and information on housing and employment," the NUL felt confident it could enhance its programs on voter registration. The NUL had chapters in thirteen southern cities, although many had been "greatly weakened in recent years by attacks from segregationist forces." But with additional funding, Granger insisted, the NUL could revitalize its work in the South and coordinate with other civil rights organizations. At the July 28 meeting, the majority had decided the project would concentrate on the South, but with the NUL's main support coming from more than fifty chapters in the North, Granger urged the group to "review its decision to limit our activity only to the South." Pointing out that over half of the country's black population resided in the urban North, Granger suggested the NUL would be in a stronger position to help if foundation resources could extend beyond the South.[86]

James Farmer penned CORE's self-evaluation and voter registration goals. With roots in communities across Florida, Louisiana, and South Carolina, CORE was ready to "carry on dynamic voter registration programs" in rural and urban areas. Drawing on years of experience, Farmer laid out how funds from the Taconic Foundation would be used to increase staff, set up offices, print materials, offer legal aid, and host citizenship workshops. Fitting with CORE's national program and ideology of nonviolence, Farmer wrote, "Our registration campaigns would be undertaken in the spirit of assuming an obligation of citizenship . . . to bring about an integrated society of friends."[87]

Martin Luther King Jr. and Wyatt Tee Walker wrote the SCLC's prospectus for the southwide voter drive. Citing evidence that only about a quarter of eligible African Americans were registered in the South, they blamed poll taxes and literacy tests, as well as outright violence and economic intimidation. Organized through the church, the SCLC's strategy would harness the power and connections of pastors and congregations to lead local movements for the ballot. King and Walker went through the list of states where the SCLC had contacts, indicating where it could be most effective. They also communicated that they were willing to work with other civil rights groups, taking careful steps to indicate their respect for the NAACP and desire for coordination. Suggesting a collaborative project of two years, the SCLC looked forward to a "dynamic Southwide Voter Registration Program."[88]

Charles McDew submitted a voter registration plan for SNCC. He pointed out SNCC's approval of the SRC as the central hub of the campaign, and he suggested creating an advisory board with members from each partner organization. For SNCC's part, it would concentrate on recruiting students to live in southern communities while organizing voting workshops and citizenship schools. In the spirit of nonviolent protest that characterized the sit-ins and Freedom Rides, SNCC envisioned stand-ins at the offices of registrars who discriminated against African Americans. SNCC also planned to host mass meetings, canvass neighborhoods, print literature, drive people to the courthouse, and embed themselves within local communities to "aid in securing the franchise for all qualified citizens."[89]

While the major civil rights organizations wrote proposals about plans for a southwide project, SRC staff drafted policy recommendations that would apply to all groups. The SRC summarized obstacles to a unified drive, including white opposition, coordination between major organizations, and "money—and regarding this no comment is necessary." Sustaining a large-scale registration campaign would be challenging as well, which "in the absence of dramatic causes, is hard, grubby, tiring, unspectacular, frequently discouraging." Yet the SRC, the Taconic Foundation, and all participating leaders believed in the idea. "Free and full participation of Negroes in southern elections," the SRC report stated, "may be the surest means of ending or at least decreasing southern preoccupation with race."[90]

On August 23, the group reconvened in New York to discuss each organization's proposal and the SRC's blueprint for a united registration drive. Stephen Currier led the meeting, along with Lloyd Garrison of the Taconic Foundation. Dunbar represented the SRC; Fleming attended as an observer;

Wofford and Marshall stood for the federal government; and James Farmer, Charles McDew, Timothy Jenkins, Whitney Young, Martin Luther King Jr., Wyatt Tee Walker, and Henry Lee Moon represented the major civil rights agencies.[91] Young raised the issue put forward in Lester Granger's NUL proposal that the group reconsider engaging with the North, but the majority insisted the project stay focused on the South where "resistance [was] the greatest."[92] At this point, Dunbar remembered, Young became upset, realizing the NUL would not get as much money as the others because of its northern base: "He wanted money. Everybody wanted money."[93] McDew wanted to know if the group could grant "immediate approval" for ten SNCC fieldworkers, but Currier expressed unwillingness to commit funds before the SRC could make sure its tax exemption would remain in place. Moon asked Currier how much the Taconic Foundation planned to donate, and Currier promised $250,000 for a two-year initiative, with the hope that he could recruit other foundations as well.[94]

Three weeks after the meeting, Dunbar wrote to everyone with a detailed plan of action coordinated through the SRC. After speaking with his executive committee, Dunbar reported that the SRC "can accept the proposed grant, for the opportunity it offers to deepen and perfect our research into voting in the South." The SRC would be the junction between major civil rights organizations while respecting each group's autonomy. It would allocate grants made possible by the Taconic Foundation and future sources, coordinate local and regional registration campaigns, offer consulting, evaluate results, and publish material based on collected data. Dunbar indicated that each group must account for all expenditures, warning that inadequate documentation would jeopardize future funds. Over objections from Wilkins and Young, the SRC stated that it would fund independent organizations as well, not only to widen the net of research but to empower grassroots agencies. Under the SRC, the voting initiative would have its own name, director, staff, and office space. Dunbar stated that publicity for the project should only be "the necessary minimum" but that others could promote it at their discretion. He noted that the voter campaign "now gives us the opportunity to study and evaluate the methods which can best change these conditions" to hasten the destruction of Jim Crow. Before moving forward, Dunbar awaited confirmation from each organization agreeing to the SRC's plan.[95]

Roy Wilkins had a conflict on August 23 and could not make the meeting, so he asked NAACP public relations director Henry Lee Moon to go. Briefing

Moon beforehand, Wilkins wrote that Currier was the "head man and has the important money . . . He is quite a 'hep' person and wants to aid in this field, but is far from being a patsy. Very nice and very sharp."[96] But Currier was upset when Wilkins did not show up. He pulled Moon aside before the meeting to ask why Wilkins did not come, stressing to Moon how important it was for each group's national leader to demonstrate his commitment. Moon apologized for Wilkins but made it clear he was more than capable of filling in for his boss, having written a book himself on the black vote in 1948. A week later, Wilkins wrote Currier to explain his absence, to which Currier expressed his relief that Wilkins did not skip the meeting out of disinterest. In order for the plan to work, he told Wilkins, the NAACP must be involved.[97]

The NAACP delayed agreeing to the coalition due to reservations from senior staff. Before committing his organization to the group, Wilkins solicited feedback from his top officers to see what they thought about the registration project. Gloster Current, the NAACP's director of branches, strongly opposed joining forces with other groups, "particularly the newer ones which have not demonstrated any degree of responsibility in such a project." Current also worried that involvement would expose the NAACP's internal administration for other organizations to see. "If the Taconic Foundation really wanted to advance registration and voting," Current wrote Wilkins, "it would give the funds directly to the NAACP," not realizing direct involvement with any single group was precisely what the Taconic Foundation wanted to avoid.[98] John Brooks, the NAACP's voter registration director, liked the idea but could "sense a big fight for organizational prestige among the groups participating" and worried that newer groups were not as committed to registration as the NAACP. "Look out for the explosion [of registration activism] when Miss Voter Registration is made real glamorous with a dress of dollar bills from the Taconic Foundation," Brooks warned.[99]

In the meantime, Louis Lomax, a well-known black journalist who had risen to fame after coproducing *The Hate That Hate Produced* in 1959 about the Nation of Islam, broke the story about the pending civil rights coalition with significant backing from a foundation. In a radio editorial on WBAI in New York on October 17, Lomax told his audience that three months earlier, "I came upon a good story, a scoop," but others asked him to stay quiet "for the good of the race because some people said if I broke the story then I'd muddy the water and the thing wouldn't come to pass." He went on to detail how back in July, a foundation that Lomax left unnamed had earmarked $250,000 for black voter registration campaigns, and after gathering together

representatives from leading African American organizations, the foundation encouraged them to form a coordinated plan of attack. They soon
settled on running the program through the SRC—"a staid and somewhat
conservative, yet very active longtime organization in the area of civil
rights"—to serve as a clearinghouse. With a plan in place, each participating group needed only to ratify the SRC's plan for action and "off to the polls
we go." But early excitement for the alliance had waned, and Lomax criticized civil rights leaders for the delay. Lomax editorialized, "I find it incred-
ible that civil rights leaders would take the better part of six months to accept
and implement such a program. Here we have a case of an interested foundation being willing to give a large sum of money to underwrite Negro voter
registration." They had the support not only of the foundation but also of
the Kennedy administration, which seemed to Lomax the perfect combina-
tion to make significant headway on racism at the ballot box. Lomax specu-
lated that the widespread problem of black disfranchisement intimidated
some leaders, for none wanted to tie themselves to a project doomed to fail
for fear of hurting their national reputation. Whatever the reason, Lomax
asked leaders not to waste the opportunity.[100]

Not coincidentally, on the same day Louis Lomax aired his commentary,
the NAACP joined, becoming the last to sign on after SNCC and CORE
pledged days earlier. But Wilkins asked Dunbar to clarify a number of points
that worried his senior staff. He expressed concern that other groups would
overshadow the NAACP and receive greater funding, even though the NAACP
had the most extensive network of chapters. Wilkins also worried that combining forces would lead to territorial disputes, and he opposed any money
directed toward grassroots campaigns unaffiliated with national groups.
Dunbar wrote back to assuage Wilkins's misgivings: "We [SRC] have made
our participation in the registration effort conditional upon yours. This is the
measure of our regard for the NAACP." Placating to Wilkins, Dunbar emphasized how crucial it was for the NAACP to participate, because if it did
not, the entire project might collapse. Dunbar explained that the joint undertaking would enhance the NAACP's voter registration efforts, not dilute
them. And while he understood the concern about working with untested
independent groups, Dunbar wrote they must "agree to disagree."[101] Dunbar's
letter arrived on Wilkins's desk on the day of a board meeting, and after
discussion, the NAACP restated its intention to join. "There is no dispute
upon the necessity of a voter education-registration project," Wilkins wrote
Dunbar. "We want to address ourselves to it, ironing out minor items as
we go along."[102]

While he awaited Wilkins's answer, Dunbar officially requested a grant of $250,000 for two years from the Taconic Foundation. Settling on the name Voter Education Project, the SRC hoped to begin operations in early 1962, but everything depended on the NAACP's acceptance and the IRS affirming the SRC's tax exemption. Classified as a 501(c)(3) tax-exempt nonprofit organization under the IRS's 1954 Internal Revenue Code, the SRC could not participate in any type of partisan political activity. After speaking with its lawyers, the SRC felt that funding nonpartisan registration drives and studying the results would not violate IRS codes. "As a matter of prudence, however," wrote Dunbar, "we have initiated discussions with the Internal Revenue Service in order to secure an advance ruling."[103]

The Taconic Foundation received the SRC's grant application in late November, but Currier and his executive board waited to hear official word from the IRS before donating the full amount. To get the project started, however, the Taconic Foundation gave $16,000 to the SRC.[104] On December 14, Adrian W. DeWind, a noted tax lawyer working at Lloyd Garrison's New York law firm, requested a ruling on the SRC's proposed voter registration project from IRS commissioner Mortimer M. Caplin. DeWind had built his reputation as an expert on tax policy, having served as chief counsel for the Treasury Department in the late 1940s and for the House Ways and Means Committee during the early 1950s. He understood how the IRS operated, and he knew how to frame the registration campaign in terms the IRS staff would approve. The SRC had first achieved tax exemption in 1947, DeWind explained, and in January 1960, the IRS reaffirmed the SRC's status as a 501(c)(3). The proposed project would not conflict with the SRC's primary mission, but it would "enable the Council to promote and to study and evaluate methods for teaching and encouraging exercise of the right to register and vote." DeWind outlined the SRC's methods for working with various civil rights organizations, none of which had their own 501(c)(3) status. The SRC would impose "stringent conditions" on all grant recipients, requiring them to submit detailed accounting for all expenditures. Grantees would not be allowed to engage in any kind of partisan activity or attempt to influence legislation. If any group violated these conditions, the SRC would terminate the relationship. As a charitable program, DeWind stated the SRC's primary purpose was to study black disfranchisement in the South by funding a massive registration drive. DeWind, along with Dunbar and Marshall, hand delivered the request to Mitchell Rogovin, Caplin's attorney adviser.[105]

Currier, Dunbar, and DeWind framed the VEP's mission as educational. Dunbar credited DeWind with formulating an "ingenious kind of theory" that the "VEP was really engaged in research, that we were researching the best ways to register voters in the South, and our method of research was [direct action]."[106] Put this way, the SRC's funding of voter registration campaigns would provide much needed data on the realities of black disfranchisement in the South. It would measure the effects of Jim Crow laws, document registrar discrimination against African Americans, and track new registration numbers across the South. The SRC positioned its registration project as educational in which black disenfranchisement would be studied and reversed. Rather than challenge the IRS's long-standing policy that foundations not engage in political advocacy, the SRC adapted its program to fit a pedagogical model. Named the Voter *Education* Project for a reason, the VEP drew attention away from its primary purpose—to blanket the South with funds for registration campaigns.

Even with a high-profile lawyer and the involvement of Burke Marshall and Harris Wofford, there was no guarantee that the IRS would extend the SRC's tax exemption to the registration program. But soon after DeWind submitted the request to the IRS, Robert Kennedy personally intervened in the matter. Kennedy had earned his law degree from the University of Virginia, and one of his professors had been Mortimer Caplin. Capitalizing on their preexisting relationship, Kennedy asked Caplin to have the IRS rule favorably for the SRC. "I was able to work out with Mort Caplin for them [SRC] to receive a tax [exemption]," Kennedy later remembered.[107] Kennedy, Marshall, Wofford, and others at the DOJ had invested too much in the idea of the VEP to see it end prematurely. The precedent for Kennedy's direct involvement had come months earlier when he strong-armed the ICC after the Freedom Rides to desegregate bus terminals, and in the same way, Kennedy used the power of his position to ensure the registration project could go forward without any federal hindrance. Kennedy kept his intervention confidential, lest the DOJ be accused of partisanship. If word leaked about the DOJ's role in the VEP, the SRC's tax exemption for the project might be questioned. Marshall, along with John Seigenthaler, believed DeWind's request was "a very fine legal document," but for a time, all they could do was wait.[108]

As 1961 ended and weeks went by in the new year without word from the IRS, Dunbar counseled the leaders of the participating groups to refrain from making public announcements about the VEP. He did not want to give the IRS any reason to be skeptical about the project, fearing that if anyone went to the press too soon, the entire operation would be off. "In the meantime," Dunbar wrote King, "we should all do what we can to keep the story from spreading."[109] By late January, the Tax Rulings Division within the IRS contacted DeWind seeking more information before making a final judgment. Accompanied by Fleming, whose Potomac Institute had just hosted a southern interagency conference to discuss VEP plans, DeWind met representatives from the Tax Rulings Division in Washington, DC on January 31. After conferring with SRC leaders, DeWind drafted a supplemental letter to the IRS going into greater detail about how the registration program fit within an educational model. At this point, DeWind and others felt confident the SRC would receive a favorable ruling. On February 22, still without notice from the IRS, the VEP went ahead and announced to cooperating agencies that its office had opened in the same building as the SRC at 5 Forsyth St. NW in downtown Atlanta, but it reminded everyone to say nothing to the press.[110]

On March 22, 1962, the IRS finally sent word to the SRC that its voter registration program qualified as tax-exempt. John W. S. Rittleton, the director of the IRS Tax Rulings Division, explained how his office reached its conclusion. Since the project would educate people "with the knowledge and will to register" without partisan bias, the SRC's tax exemption qualified. Rittleton approved of the SRC's detailed methods to oversee the program, including the immediate suspension of funds to any group violating its terms, and the SRC's plans to publish reports on the overall initiative to encourage greater black political participation. Since the project "will be useful as a source of research, knowledge and experience, it may be considered for approval."[111] With this rendered judgment, the SRC retained its 501(c)(3) designation as an institution exempt from paying federal income taxes, a precondition the Taconic Foundation and other philanthropies required.

The SRC had successfully tiptoed around the IRS's restrictions on partisan political activity. Even though it would supply funds to register black southerners, the SRC's Voter Education Project qualified for an exemption since it was "primarily a research effort designed to develop educational programs which will be most effective in providing voters with the knowledge and will to register."[112] On March 29, 1962, the VEP issued a press release citing the collaboration between the NAACP, CORE, SCLC, SNCC, and NUL. The VEP would function as "a new program to study the causes of low voter registration in the South, and to ascertain the most effective methods for increasing the southern electorate."[113] Innocuous on the surface, the VEP put itself in position to remake southern politics, empower black voters, and fight Jim Crow at the ballot box across the American South.

CHAPTER THREE

The Voter Education Project, 1962–1964

Three years before Bloody Sunday in Selma, Alabama, the VEP began invest-ing in the registration movement of Dallas County. The VEP's involvement began with a $1,500 grant to the Alabama State Coordinating Association for Registration and Voting (ASCARV). In June 1962, ASCARV helped 1,742 black Alabamians register in over thirty counties, but in Dallas County, the regis-trar refused all applicants. Selma had earned a reputation for violent oppo-sition to African American civil rights, starting with its powerful chapter of the citizens' council. The challenge of organizing Selma inspired Bernard Lafayette, a student at the American Baptist Seminary in Nashville, Ten-nessee, where he studied nonviolence under Jim Lawson and joined SNCC. Lafayette survived a beating as a Freedom Rider in 1961, and as SNCC began sending its leaders into rural communities across the South, he volunteered to lead the effort in Selma. In October 1962, a month before he married SNCC activist Colia Liddell, Lafayette researched the history of Dallas County. He documented twenty-five known lynchings between 1882 and 1913, and he found that black residents still lived in fear of the police, the citizens' council, and white vigilantes. Local leaders, including Amelia Boynton, had managed the Dallas County Voters League since the 1930s, but the group met in secret, and only 156 black residents had registered when over 15,000 met the age requirement. With the promise of VEP funding, SNCC approved Bernard and Colia Lafayette to move to Selma in early 1963. According to Lafayette, his report was "preparatory to setting up a VEP 'beach head' in Dallas County."[1]

Soon after arriving in Selma, the Lafayettes received $500 from the VEP. Along with the grant, the VEP outlined what information Lafayette needed to record and send back. Jack Minnis, the VEP's research director, instructed Bernard Lafayette to mail monthly narrative reports of registration activities and financial expenditures, writing, "It might be helpful for you to think of this narrative as an intelligence report which is designed to let us and your office know what is going on with respect to voter registration in Dallas County."[2] On March 10, Colia Lafayette drafted their first VEP field report. She chronicled how the police and local whites monitored their activities, noting, "We have been properly warned."[3] The police had visited their home, inspected their vehicle, and drove alongside the Lafayettes as they canvassed neighborhoods. Despite resistance, they held registration classes, and after a month, 21 people had tried to register, though none passed. After two months, Bernard Lafayette wrote Wiley Branton, the VEP's director, "We are financially exhausted."[4] The following month, the VEP granted the Lafayettes $1,000. Three days after the VEP sent the check, the Lafayettes helped organize a mass meeting with 350 people in attendance. A movement began to take shape, and by mid-June, the Lafayettes had helped 190 black citizens register to vote. But their activities drew unwanted attention, including a threatening advertisement in the *Selma Times Journal* from the citizens' council asking for membership dues: "Is it worth four dollars to you to prevent sit-ins, mob marches and wholesale Negro voter registration efforts in Selma?"[5] A few days later, a white man beat Bernard Lafayette outside his home, sending him to the hospital for six stitches. From his hospital bed, Lafayette promised to continue the registration campaign.[6]

The VEP continued to support the Lafayettes and the wider movement in Selma. In October 1963, the VEP approved another grant to SNCC in Dallas County to help pay for advertising, equipment, meals, office rent, supplies, postage, salaries, telephone bills, and utilities—the unglamorous but often necessary costs of a social movement. The following summer, the VEP awarded the Dallas County Voters League with a $1,000 grant. To witness firsthand how the local movement used VEP money, John Due, a VEP researcher, visited Selma in September 1964. Back in July, Due learned that the city had passed an injunction to stop all mass meetings. The registrar's office also made black registration nearly impossible. Due learned that a resident had recently applied, but the registrar "read a section of the Constitution, made her sit for five minutes in another room, and then asked her to repeat word by word what he had read to her."[7] She failed, as did most others, but the movement continued. Years later, while serving as the VEP's director, John Lewis recalled his beating on the Edmund Pettus Bridge on Bloody Sunday, March 7, 1965, telling the interviewer that the movement in Selma had already been active for years: "If there is any single event that gave birth to the Voter Rights Act, it was the Selma effort. March 7 was just sort of a combination of things. We had had a series of protests, organizing efforts in Selma in late '63 and some in '64 and '65."[8]

The events of Selma in 1965 are well known, but not the VEP's role in leading up to those dramatic moments. Not only in Selma but also in Kingstree, Atlanta, Miami, Gadsden, Asheville, Lake Charles, Lynchburg, Fort Worth, Orangeburg, Hattiesburg, Knoxville, Americus, Pine Bluff,

Gainesville, Tyler, Chattanooga, Richmond, Wilson, Anniston, and in hundreds of other towns, cities, and counties across the American South, the VEP supported grassroots movements for black poll power. By conducting research through activism, the VEP helped register nearly 700,000 African Americans between 1962 and 1964, laying the foundation for the Voting Rights Act of 1965. As the behind-the-scenes engine of the civil rights movement, the VEP brought together the major organizations and local groups for one common purpose: the right to vote.

The VEP meant to "study the effectiveness of organized effort—*political* activity in the broadest sense—in attacking the cause of low registration in the various sections of the South."[9] With single-minded purpose, the VEP stimulated communities to register and document the results. Grassroots movements utilized VEP seed money to pay for salaries, food, posters, handbills, mass meetings, bills, fuel, and other expenses. The VEP aided 129 projects, but it became especially invested in 3—the Council of Federated Organizations (COFO) in Mississippi, the Albany Movement in southwest Georgia, and Voters of Texas Enlist (VOTE). From its Atlanta office, the VEP managed the money, reviewed grant applications, conducted research, analyzed field reports, published information, coordinated between organizations, and sustained a southwide movement for the ballot. VEP staff also worked with philanthropic foundations, continuously applying for grants while keeping benefactors appraised of how their money made a difference. In two and a half years, the VEP, according to its final report, "moved Negro registration off dead center, where it had been for most of the previous decade, and reestablished momentum."[10]

ON JANUARY 2, 1962, while still waiting to hear from the IRS about tax exemption, Leslie Dunbar wrote to the leaders of the NAACP, SCLC, SNCC, CORE, and NUL that Wiley A. Branton had agreed to direct the VEP. Dunbar had previously commented, "The Project director should be Negro, a man of stature, vigor, and sagacity. He will need to have the confidence of all sponsors. These being nearly impossible qualifications, the finding of the right man will be hard."[11] Leaders of the "Big Five"—a nickname for the NAACP, SCLC, SNCC, CORE, and NUL—had suggested other candidates, but Branton's name stood out. The group unanimously approved the selection of Branton as executive director.[12]

Wiley Branton grew up in segregated Arkansas. His father owned a taxi company in Pine Bluff, and its success ensured a middle-class upbringing for him and his siblings. Influenced by Booker T. Washington, his parents encouraged him to overcome white supremacy through hard work. Branton excelled in school, but early experiences confronting racism shaped his personality as well. He once witnessed a white store clerk attack his brother Leo. Leo fought back, and then he ran out of the store when the clerk grabbed a gun. The clerk falsely accused Leo of assault with a knife. A jury found Leo guilty, but he managed to avoid jail due to a lung condition. The experience etched onto Branton's mind the injustice of white supremacy. After serving in the military during World War II, Branton returned to Arkansas. He joined the Pine Bluff NAACP, and he helped with voter registration efforts. After finishing college in 1950, he enrolled at the University of Arkansas School of Law, the fifth African American to do so. By this time, he was twenty-seven years old, an army veteran, branch president of the NAACP, married with three kids, and in charge of the family taxi business. But he wanted more, later remembering that he "decided suddenly one day that I wanted to be a lawyer, growing out of some very bitter personal civil rights experiences."[13] He excelled in law school and after graduating established his practice in Pine Bluff.[14]

On May 17, 1954, the Supreme Court ruled segregated schooling unconstitutional in *Brown v. Board of Education* and the next year vaguely instructed states to desegregate "with all deliberate speed."[15] In Little Rock, the school board adopted a desegregation plan in May 1955, but members scaled back the proposal once they realized neither the state nor the federal government would hurry integration. The NAACP and a group of parents challenged the school board's indefinite plans, and in February 1956, Branton filed a suit on their behalf in *Aaron v. Cooper*. After a year and a half of litigation, nine black students attempted to enter Central High School on September 4, 1957, but Governor Orval Faubus dispatched national guardsmen to stop them. The standoff captured national attention, and President Dwight D. Eisenhower ordered federal troops to Little Rock to escort the students into the building. The legal process continued, and Branton remained behind the scenes, working with NAACP Legal Defense Fund (LDF) leader Thurgood Marshall on behalf of the Little Rock Nine. During this long ordeal, crosses were burned on Branton's lawn, and anonymous callers threatened his family. For protection, Branton carried a gun wherever he went, and friends and family guarded his home. The case dragged on through 1962, taking up much of Branton's time until Leslie Dunbar contacted him about the Voter Education Project.[16]

While working for the Little Rock Nine, Branton became well known within the national civil rights community. He won the trust of Thurgood

Marshall and NAACP leadership. He also met members of SNCC and CORE who were part of the Freedom Rides. When Freedom Riders were arrested in Jackson, Mississippi, Marshall called Branton to ask him to go to the jail, bail them out, and provide legal aid. Branton did so, making a lasting impression on SNCC leader John Lewis, who remembered Branton as the first attorney to arrive after he and other Freedom Riders earned a sixty-six-day prison sentence.[17] From 1956 through 1961, through the legal drudgery on behalf of the Little Rock Nine, Branton developed a reputation as someone who was knowledgeable, dependable, levelheaded, and passionate about civil rights. Dunbar reached out to Branton because he had a "healthy ego," was "tough," and was "a good NAACP type" of person—the perfect blend to handle many personalities asking for money.[18] Before hearing Dunbar's offer, Branton had been close to accepting a position with the U.S. Commission on Civil Rights. At first, he told others about the VEP job, but as he later recalled, "the more I tried to sell other people on this exciting new venture, the more I became personally interested."[19]

The SRC announced the VEP on March 29, but it hoped the media would pay little attention. The *New York Times* picked up the story, identifying the roles of the five major participants and the SRC: "The actual registration drive will be carried out by these organizations. The council's role will be confined to administering financial aid through its newly organized Voter Education Project."[20] To Branton's relief, the *Times* mentioned that the chairmen of both the Democratic National Committee and the Republican National Committee endorsed the project. In the South, the *Atlanta Daily World* published a small article based on the SRC press release, and a week later, the Baltimore *Afro-American* announced the VEP.[21] The launch did not become headline news. Branton wanted the story to remain in the background, fearful that the VEP's tax exemption could be endangered if the spotlight fell on it. He suspected that more attention would come once the public realized a massive voter registration program was underway in the South, and he cautioned participants not to give away too much information. The VEP began small, with only a staff of two: Branton and his assistant, Jean Levine. Tucked away in the offices of the SRC in downtown Atlanta, the VEP guarded its semi-secrecy. Stephen Currier did not want the Taconic Foundation in the news either. Branton circulated a note instructing participants to respond to media inquiries about funding vaguely: "The foundations (plural) do not wish their grants to be publicized at this time."[22]

The VEP had just cause to worry about conservatives finding out about the campaign. On the same day that the *New York Times* printed its story,

Senator Herman E. Talmadge of Georgia, no friend to black voting rights or racial equality, wrote to IRS commissioner Mortimer Caplin about how foundations could possibly sponsor voter registration drives aimed at African Americans without losing their tax-exempt status. Caplin waited to respond until mid-May, keeping his comments brisk and outlining the legalities of 501(c)(3) organizations. He explained that the IRS had reviewed the SRC's proposal for a registration campaign, and since the program promised to remain nonpartisan and educational, the SRC had retained its tax exemption. Talmadge did not press the point any further, but his interest proved that the VEP needed to be cautious. Talmadge never forgot the VEP. Seven years later, he would lead the Senate's effort to destabilize the VEP's finances (see chapter 5).[23]

As the VEP moved ahead, DOJ officials backed away. Burke Marshall remained close for a time, along with Harris Wofford, but their involvement with the VEP waned. The DOJ believed it had done its part by helping set up the VEP. Yet SRC staff expected the DOJ to remain involved once local projects began, anticipating white backlash against registration efforts. After Marshall heard about the IRS's tax-exemption decision, he wrote Dunbar, "It is a great relief to have the waiting period over with. I have no doubt that there are going to be a lot of problems, and I urge you to feel absolutely free to call me at any time that you think that we can be of assistance in any official or unofficial fashion."[24] Marshall's promise proved shallow. The VEP and DOJ quickly grew apart after Louis Lomax published a misleading article in *Harper's* about the Kennedy administration intending the VEP to strengthen the Democratic Party's southern black electorate. "Although the public is scarcely aware of it," Lomax wrote, "the Kennedy administration is now deeply involved in an unprecedented campaign to get hundreds of thousands of Southern Negroes to vote for the first time in their lives" to "rivet the Negro's loyalty to the Democratic Party for a long time to come."[25] Branton angrily wrote to the editor to explain that the VEP operated independently of the Kennedy administration, but the exposure drove a wedge between the VEP and DOJ. By mid-1962, the VEP and DOJ no longer worked closely together, although Branton and Dunbar still counted on the DOJ to intervene should white southerners stand in the way of black registration.[26]

Although relations with the DOJ soured, the VEP strengthened bonds to philanthropic foundations. Stephen Currier helped create the VEP, and his Taconic Foundation gave the VEP its first major grant, worth $250,000 over two years.[27] With the Taconic Foundation leading the way, Currier encouraged other foundations to join, including the Field Foundation and the Stern

Family Fund. Deriving their wealth from Marshall Field's department stores, the Field family had mentored Currier in philanthropy. The family established the Field Foundation in 1940 and over two decades sponsored health programs, child advocacy groups, universities, and the American Council on Race Relations in Chicago. The Field Foundation, according to a family biographer, crafted a reputation as "a quiet sort of foundation, with no extensive fellowship program, no spectacular news releases, no multimillion-dollar grants, no museums, no showcases."[28] Beginning in the late 1950s, the Field Foundation began supporting the SRC with annual grants of $25,000.[29] Currier wrote Ruth Field to encourage her foundation to join with Taconic and support the VEP: "I think this is a dramatic opportunity. A cooperation between our two Foundations could result in massive breakthroughs in the South."[30] Once the SRC received its tax exemption for the VEP, the Field Foundation awarded the VEP with a one-year grant of $75,000.[31] Joining with Taconic and Field, the Stern Family Fund committed $124,000 over two years after Branton appeared before its board on May 5, 1962, giving what its executive director, Helen Hill Miller, described as a "persuasive presentation."[32] Founded in 1936 by the daughter of Julius Rosenwald and her husband, Edith and Edgar Stern, the Stern Family Fund continued the legacy of investing in southern African American education—this time, in the political sense.[33]

On April 17, VEP staff met with civil rights leaders in Atlanta to plan the first grants to local registration drives. The VEP decided to open with a "crash program"—a ninety-day test case taking advantage of open registration days during the summer in six states. Marvin Rich from CORE attended the meeting and informed James Farmer about the plan. The VEP would make "flat grants" to CORE and other organizations for registration campaigns, working in specific areas across the South delegated through the VEP.[34] The month before, the Big Five submitted ambitious budgets for the ninety-day crash program. In its request, the NAACP asked for $138,850 to hire eight full-time staff workers.[35] The SCLC requested $60,000.[36] Altogether, budget requests from the Big Five totaled $556,000.[37] Since the VEP only had $187,000 for the whole year, Branton could not give everyone what they asked for, but he tried to be fair. For the NUL, the VEP allocated $5,750 for voter registration programs in Winston-Salem, Richmond, and New Orleans. The VEP gave the same amount to SNCC in Mississippi and Orangeburg, South Carolina. CORE received $8,625 for its work in Baton Rouge and Jackson, along with parts of South Carolina. The SCLC and NAACP each received the largest amounts, with the SCLC taking $11,500 and the NAACP earning $17,250 for programs in Louisiana, Tennessee, Virginia, North Carolina, and South

Carolina.[38] In several cases, the VEP assigned the same locations to multiple organizations, directing them to work together and conduct coordinated registration campaigns. In Jackson, Mississippi, for example, CORE, SNCC, and the NAACP each had field organizers already on the ground. Instead of splitting them up, the VEP gave a single grant to Jackson, asking the three groups to work together. For each grant, the VEP spelled out the need to keep the money in designated bank accounts, log all expenditures, send in registration data reports, and avoid all partisan activity.[39]

With VEP money in hand, grassroots activists went to work. From SNCC in Mississippi, the VEP learned that "resistance techniques of the whites are truly amazing in their versatility."[40] SNCC reported that the authorities arrested registration volunteers on charges of vagrancy, loitering, passing out leaflets without a permit, and minor traffic violations. Intimidation and violence often followed, and SNCC recorded three arson cases against black churches hosting registration efforts, along with numerous volunteers fired from their jobs. While "quantitatively small," SNCC's work in Mississippi demonstrated "that the groundwork has been laid from which should eventually come substantial increases in Negro political participation."[41] From CORE in South Carolina and Louisiana, James Farmer informed the VEP that canvassing and handing out sample application forms resulted in over five hundred new black voters.[42] Wyatt Tee Walker sent Branton the SCLC's report describing efforts in eastern North Carolina, Virginia, Georgia, and Tennessee. While the SCLC had not kept exact figures, Walker reported "substantial increases" estimated at over seven thousand new black registrants.[43]

The VEP also received field reports from independent projects during the crash program. The VEP granted $3,600 to the All-Citizens Registration Committee (ACRC) of Atlanta, Georgia. The ACRC saturated black neighborhoods with fifty thousand handbills, purchased radio spots and newspaper advertisements, organized car pools, rented busses to ferry people to the courthouse, drove sound trucks up and down roads, and canvassed neighborhoods on foot. In a matter of weeks, Atlanta's registered black population jumped from 37,301 to 44,945. In North Carolina, the VEP gave $2,500 to the Durham Committee on Negro Affairs (DCNA) to reverse a voter purge taking place in the county. In Raleigh, the National Student Association, an organization of college student governments, registered 1,641 people between June 15 and August 3 with a grant worth $1,140. Canvassers went door to door asking people to register, and in some cases, they brought deputy registrars to register people inside their homes. In Jackson, Tennessee, the American Friends Service Committee urged over 1,500 people to register after knocking on more than 2,500 doors. Through its crash program, the VEP's experimental approach convinced activists that door-to-door canvassing and grassroots mobilization could overcome barriers to the franchise, although the work would never come easy. In its final crash program report, the VEP calculated that it helped register 21,279 black southerners in ninety days through grants worth $32,356.98 across six states, highlighting "that increased and meaningful political participation for Negroes can only be effected through arduous efforts to eliminate social, cultural, and economic disadvantages, as well as hard work on the voting front."[44]

After the success of the crash program, the VEP increased its staff and handed out numerous long-term grants. With so many field reports and quantitative data piling up at VEP headquarters, Branton hired Jack Minnis, a doctoral candidate in political science at Tulane University, as director of research. Minnis hounded grant recipients for weekly and monthly reports, insisting on thorough documentation of VEP expenditures, registration figures, and stories about what was happening in their communities. Branton later hired Randolph T. Blackwell, an economist and political scientist at Alabama A & M University, as VEP field director. Blackwell traveled the South visiting registration campaigns financed with VEP money to review the operation, offer advice, and report back to Branton.[45] As VEP staff grew, it expended more grant money. CORE received $13,800 for Louisiana, South Carolina, and Miami, Florida. The SCLC obtained $15,700 for over a dozen projects in eight southern states. For its rural organizing in Georgia, Alabama, and South Carolina, SNCC received $8,254. The NAACP received $22,000 to fund registration work in fifty-six cities and counties across nine states. The NUL received support to carry on projects in Fort Worth, Richmond, and Winston-Salem. In addition to the Big Five, the VEP funded twelve independent organizations, including the Greater Little Rock Voter Registration Movement for $1,511.60, Womanpower Unlimited in Mississippi for $1,000, the Dougherty City Voter Education League in Georgia for $4,000, and the Jefferson County Voter Registration Campaign in Alabama for $9,000. By March 1963, the VEP recorded that these seventeen organizations had registered a total of 125,007 black southerners across eleven states drawing on $111,787.60 of VEP seed money.[46]

The VEP worked closely with the Council of Federated Organizations (COFO) in Mississippi. In May 1961, Dr. Aaron Henry, a pharmacist and NAACP leader in Clarksdale, started COFO to unite civil rights activists in Mississippi who had been working through different organizations, particularly SNCC, CORE, SCLC, and the NAACP. After the VEP opened, Medgar Evers, the NAACP's field director in Mississippi, suggested to Branton that the VEP should fund all state voter registration activities through COFO. As Branton remembered it, the general feeling was "perhaps it would be better if everything was coordinated, rather than having each organization go its separate way."[47] Mississippi activists suggested that COFO operate as an "umbrella organization" that shared VEP grants.[48] Branton agreed, and he met with COFO leaders on August 22 in the basement of a Clarksdale church. Branton presided over the meeting where, long past midnight, the participants "wrote rules, drew territories, allotted future funds" and elected SNCC's Bob Moses as director of voter registration and Henry as president.[49] The VEP granted $14,000 to COFO, but over the next year, that figure mushroomed to well over $50,000, one of the largest projects the VEP ever supported.[50]

With VEP assistance, COFO projects took off across the Mississippi delta, but record keeping lagged behind. SNCC workers embedded themselves first in Bolivar, Coahoma, Leflore, Marshall, Sunflower, and Washington Counties. COFO used VEP funds to pay its fieldworkers, purchase used vehicles, bail out imprisoned volunteers, and compensate lawyers who represented them in court.[51] But COFO reports back to the VEP were inconsistent, even though Branton and Minnis emphasized to Moses and Henry the necessity. "We are not trying to hustle you unduly," Minnis wrote Moses to remind him of an upcoming deadline, "nor are we implying that you might neglect such mundane matters as reporting in favor of the more interesting problem of staying alive in Mississippi."[52] Minnis wrote Moses again in October asking COFO workers to record all registration attempts, even if no one actually tried: "After all, a VEP-2 [the form recording registration statistics] full of goose eggs tells an eloquent story in itself."[53] The VEP's patience began to run out, and Branton wrote Moses in late November, "I feel that I must impress upon you again the fact that this is primarily a research project and we simply cannot make grants to those who ignore duties."[54] A week later, Branton wrote a more conciliatory letter to Moses, "I hope that you do not feel that we have lost faith in you or COFO but we simply must get back on the right track in order for us to carry on effectively."[55]

By the end of the year, rather than strain its relationship with COFO and SNCC, the VEP changed its reporting requirements to allow for narrative accounts of registration activities rather than simple forms asking for numbers. SNCC fieldworkers seized on the change, and they began writing long, descriptive, and deeply personal stories of their work to help local people register across Mississippi. Charles McLaurin wrote about his time in Sunflower County. Along with Charlie Cobb and Landy McNair, McLaurin spent one of his first days in Ruleville walking around and meeting people: "We would ask questions about the Plantations and cotton, about the schools, parks, paved streets, stop signs at intersections and police brutality." These topics mattered to residents, and SNCC workers encouraged them to try to register as an act of resistance. Four days after an energetic mass meeting, assailants fired gunshots into the home where McLaurin lived and then shot at another house, injuring two girls getting ready for school. The shooting unnerved the community, and attendance at mass meetings plummeted as locals avoided SNCC personnel. They told McLaurin "that if we [SNCC] had not come to Ruleville all this wouldn't have happened." For the rest of the month, McLaurin, Cobb, and McNair tried to repair relationships by helping residents chop wood and pick cotton. Their efforts paid off, and the community slowly embraced the SNCC workers. McLaurin transported people to Indianola to register, helped them sign up for welfare benefits, and worked to find food and winter clothing to pass out. Around this time, Fannie Lou Hamer moved to Ruleville, who, McLaurin noted, "was a very good singer and she can do most anything . . . We feel that she will play a big part in getting people from the plantation to register."[56] Branton noted that these stories were "not exactly material for computer programming, but the stuff of which the movement was made."[57]

Not every report to the VEP was upbeat. Many, like one from Charlie Cobb from Greenville in December 1962, were downcast, reflecting the hard grind of the registration project. "This week has been really slow," Cobb opened. Only one person had attempted to register. "Voter registration wise," Cobb wrote, "we have done next to nothing this past week . . . Trying to deal with all this APATHY here in Greenville is much more frustrating than the fear one finds in the rural areas." Since few people wanted to risk their lives at the polls, Cobb started collecting statements from residents explaining their reasons. He sent these to the VEP, providing more data about disfranchisement for the project's records.[58] Combined with COFO's efforts across eleven counties in Mississippi, Cobb's work paid off. Moses informed Branton that over 1,100 black Mississippians had tried to register between May and December 1962, although only a handful succeeded.[59]

In December 1962, COFO organizers began collecting and distributing food and clothing alongside voter registration activities. Minnis visited Mississippi in January and observed the lines of people waiting for supplies while COFO workers had them fill out forms indicating their registration status. For those not registered, SNCC activists asked if they would be willing to try. Some said they would try right away, willing to march down to the courthouse "while their bundle is being prepared."[60] Branton worried that COFO used VEP funds to buy clothing and food, a violation of its tax exemption. He complained to Moses, who replied, "I know, Wiley. But what can you do when you're faced with all those people standing in line?" Branton answered, "All right, but don't document it! Don't put it in the reports."[61] Branton bent the rules for COFO in Mississippi, and to learn more about COFO's grassroots organizing, he sent his field director, Randolph Blackwell, to observe the Mississippi movement.[62]

On a cool February night in 1963, while traveling with Moses and Tougaloo College student Jimmy Travis, Blackwell's vehicle was attacked by white vigilantes. After following them for miles, the Buick pulled alongside, and three white men opened fire. They shot at least thirteen rounds, and while Moses and Blackwell escaped harm, one bullet grazed Travis's head and another lodged in his spine. In a later affidavit, Travis recalled, "I felt something burn my ear . . . They had opened fire on us . . . It sounded like a machine gun. I yelled out that I had been shot, as I let go of the wheel. Moses grabbed hold of the wheel and brought the car to a stop on the shoulder of the highway. I was scared."[63] Blackwell and Moses brought Travis to the Greenwood hospital, where doctors patched him up, but they told the group he needed to go to Jackson to have the bullet removed. The next morning, doctors at the University Hospital in Jackson removed a .45-caliber bullet from the top of Travis's spine, without using anesthesia.[64]

Branton felt a rush of emotion when he learned about the attack, but as angry as he was, he sensed an opportunity for the VEP and COFO. He contacted leaders of the NAACP, SCLC, CORE, and SNCC to explain the situation. In response to the violence, Branton suggested that each group descend on Greenwood and work through COFO to foster a larger registration movement. Everyone agreed, and Greenwood became the civil rights movement's ground zero almost overnight. Branton fired off a telegram to President Kennedy and the attorney general, writing, "This is but the latest of these vicious assaults against registration workers and applicants in Mississippi. This cannot longer be tolerated. We are accordingly today announcing a concentrated, saturation campaign to register every qualified Negro of Leflore County."[65] Branton also sent a copy to the *New York Times*, hoping to capture the attention of the national media. Branton later remembered, "It seemed to be the only way to answer this kind of violence: instead of letting up, to pour it on; instead of backing out, to move more people in . . . and that if anything was going to happen at all, there was going to be increased activity."[66]

The Greenwood movement marked a turning point for Branton and the VEP. Between March and April 1963, Branton became personally invested in COFO. As a result, the VEP embraced its role as a unique activist organization, not simply as a detached research body. Even as the VEP funded dozens of simultaneous projects across the South, Mississippi captured its attention. Branton, Minnis, and Blackwell each spent time in Leflore County. For all of COFO's work since the summer of 1962 in Leflore County, only around 250 African Americans had registered out of a total black population of 13,567.[67] The VEP had already heavily invested in Mississippi with low figures to show for it, but Branton wanted to see the result of a concentrated campaign in Greenwood. The VEP began paying ten dollars per week to over a dozen full-time organizers to canvass Leflore County's black neighborhoods. And the community responded. "For the first time in a Mississippi," Branton wrote in a press release, "there has been a breakthrough of the fear which has held Negroes back."[68]

As the movement gained traction, so too did violent responses. By the end of March, Greenwood appeared to be a "major disaster area," with the police out in full force against the black community.[69] COFO's office was burned, white mobs and police attacked African Americans on the street, and the local newspaper published the names and addresses of those attempting to register. Several marches through town provoked police officers to release dogs on the crowd resulting in several injuries, including Reverend Donald L. Tucker, an African Methodist Episcopal pastor.[70] More churches joined the movement, and attendance at mass rallies increased. At a rally packed with over 450 people inside a small church sanctuary, Branton's speech "brought the house down" after he refuted reports that outside agitators were responsible for the chaos.[71] By the end of March, the VEP noted that at least 513 residents had attempted to register, but later evidence pushed that figure higher to around 1,300.[72]

DOJ and FBI indifference toward Greenwood annoyed Branton, but he kept pushing. John Doar had been in Mississippi along with at least six FBI agents, but their duties involved litigation and observation, not direct involvement.[73] In a telegram to Robert Kennedy, Branton tried to elicit some response from the federal government: "Will you please inform me as to what steps will be taken to aid these citizens."[74] The telegram and increased media attention had an effect, and on March 30, 1963, the DOJ filed suit against Greenwood. Scheduled for a district federal court hearing on April 2, DOJ lawyers intended to order city officials to release eight registration workers from jail, cease "further interference with a registration campaign," and allow "Negroes to exercise their constitutional right to assemble . . . and protect them from whites who might object."[75] VEP staff, COFO workers, and the black community celebrated, believing this to be the first time the federal government had stepped in to protect black registration activities. At a mass meeting, Branton told his audience, "It's the greatest thing the President of the United States can do to let the world know we believe in democracy."[76]

But a week later, the DOJ cut a deal with Greenwood's white officials and abandoned the voter registration movement. Doar met Branton to break the news a few hours before the federal trial was to begin in Greenville. Branton was devastated, and he later remembered the DOJ's decision to abandon Greenwood "cause[d] us to develop some very bitter attitudes toward the role of the Justice Department. We thought that they had really sold us out."[77] Branton pleaded with Burke Marshall to do something, to no effect. The deal called for eight registration workers to be released from jail and for a promise from city officials to stop harassing people. Mississippi's two senators, James Eastland and John Stennis, had both denounced the DOJ's lawsuit against Greenwood. Wary of losing southern Democrat supporters and frightened of igniting a race war, the Kennedys decided not to pursue the lawsuit. Receiving a light punishment, white officials were emboldened. Branton tried to get the city commissioners to hold up their end of the bargain by stopping the harassment of voter applicants, but without accountability, they made no promises. Once again, just as it had during the Freedom Rides and would do so again at the 1964 Democratic National Convention, the federal government failed grassroots civil rights activists, further eroding cooperation and trust.[78]

The Greenwood movement continued on after the DOJ's decision, but it never recovered its momentum. Days later, national attention shifted to Birmingham, Alabama, where the SCLC-led mobilization campaign provoked police to spray water hoses and turn dogs loose against nonviolent demonstrators. The Greenwood movement was all but forgotten, but not by those who stayed in Mississippi. Branton crafted a new plan to build off COFO's work, one that would maintain VEP involvement but with less financial burden. Branton had previously written Aaron Henry, "Obviously, we cannot continue to maintain such a heavy financial program for one county [Leflore] for any long period."[79] A month after the DOJ's desertion, Robert Moses visited Branton in the VEP's Atlanta office to plan a new budget for COFO through September. For five months, the VEP agreed to pay COFO regular installments of $1,775, totaling $8,875. The funds supplemented the modest salaries of fieldworkers in Greenwood, Greenville, and Holly Springs, in addition to paying for office supplies, utility bills, and food.[80] The grant demonstrated the VEP's sympathy for Mississippi, but the pragmatic Branton knew that the VEP could not continue to sink money into Mississippi indefinitely without the registration results to show for it. After working out the budget with Moses, Branton wrote Henry, "I pointed out to him [Moses] the serious need for us to cut back immediately on all Mississippi expenditures."[81]

In November 1963, with the VEP grant to COFO coming to a close, Branton made the difficult choice to stop funding projects in Mississippi, except for a small NAACP project in Jackson. Branton later summarized the decision for the U.S. Commission on Civil Rights, stating that the VEP tried to be equitable with its grants for projects across the South but that "expenditures in Mississippi were heavily out of proportion, while the registration results were extremely low," totaling 3,228. He blamed the DOJ for the VEP's exit. Until the DOJ "is able to win an effective decree" to dismantle disfranchisement laws, Branton wrote, "it seemed best to the Voter Education Project staff to expend our resources in other states."[82] Many in SNCC were upset, and they suspected the VEP left because of the Freedom Vote, a mock election to demonstrate the desire for black Mississippians to register, which began a week before the VEP made the announcement. Marion Berry thought the VEP "stopped the grants because we just wouldn't do some of the things they wanted us to do . . . particularly around the political organizing, like the Freedom Vote."[83] But Branton made the decision based on numbers, sensitive to the fact that the VEP's philanthropic benefactors needed results. He later remembered, "I hoped also that our actions would spur the Justice Department to recognize that it needed to do more."[84]

While working hand in hand with COFO, the VEP also maintained a supportive relationship with the Albany Movement. Less than two hundred miles south of Atlanta, Albany served as the economic center of rural southwest Georgia, a land filled with farms, plantations, and sharecropper tenements. A few middle-class African American businessmen held some influence, but the majority of African Americans were politically powerless and isolated, spread out across hundreds of square miles. Many families worked the same land as their ancestors. In September 1961, SNCC sent fieldworkers to Albany to live in the black community and help them register. Charles Sherrod led the group, an energetic, Bible-believing Virginian who had spent a month in jail after a sit-in in Rock Hill, South Carolina. He devoted himself to nonviolence, using it as an organizing tool to encourage people to shed their fears. But the violence and intimidation that hung in the air around Albany unnerved him: "It took me time to understand how to get an old fellow who says, 'Yassuh,' 'Nawsuh,' while looking down straight at the ground, to overcome terror in southwest Georgia," remembered Sherrod.[85]

After SNCC moved into Albany and began winning the trust of the black community, they joined with local leaders and the NAACP to form the Albany Movement in November 1961. The following month, they invited King and the SCLC to join the coalition. King brought the national spotlight to Albany, where Laurie Pritchett was waiting. As chief of police, Pritchett prepared his officers to fight nonviolence with nonviolence, to calmly arrest protestors without inciting crowds. "The men were instructed that if they were spit upon, cussed, abused in any way of that nature, that they were not to take their billyclubs out," Pritchett later explained.[86] After months of protests, arrests, and constant news coverage, King withdrew from Albany in August 1962. SNCC workers believed that the SCLC's presence had disrupted the local movement in southwest Georgia, and they determined to pick up the pieces. SNCC remained in Albany after the newsmen packed their cameras and the SCLC moved on to Birmingham, but SNCC needed help to sustain the movement.

Dr. W. G. Anderson, an osteopathic doctor and president of the Albany Movement, applied to the VEP for financial assistance. An upcoming registration deadline was set for October 1, 1962, Anderson explained to Branton, and he felt the community was on the precipice of change. Branton gave the appeal "emergency consideration" and mailed a check for $2,000, the first half of a $4,000 grant. Branton explained to Anderson that Albany "offers such an interesting research problem" the VEP must study the registration results. In his proposal, Anderson floated the idea of paying fieldworkers by commission according to how many people they registered. Branton admired Anderson's ingenuity but forbid them from doing so because "such a proposal would not set well, in our opinion, with Internal Revenue nor with the foundations giving us money."[87]

VEP funds allowed SNCC to expand their operations beyond Albany. Penny Patch, a white college student who joined SNCC in southwest Georgia, submitted an early field report to the VEP about her experience. "Southwest Georgia is very, very beautiful. It just needs a little bit of fixing," she wrote.[88] With VEP assistance, more young activists like Patch joined the movement. Jack Chatfield was a white SNCC volunteer focused on voter registration. He went to the Terrell County courthouse to read the official voter rolls, but the registrar and a deputy from the sheriff's office would not allow him access. Chatfield and other SNCC workers urged people throughout the county to take citizenship classes. They pursued friendships with high school students at the all-black Carver High School, but the principle, E. E. Sykes, did not want SNCC influencing his students or passing out leaflets on campus. Some churches resisted SNCC's requests to speak to their congregations, afraid of bomb threats and the possibility that insurance companies would not pay if they learned the church hosted registration workshops. Their fears were warranted. Three churches burned during the summer of 1962 in Lee and Terrell Counties.[89] Rising concerns from the black community discouraged Chatfield, aware that he needed registration results to justify more VEP grants. In a December 1962 field report, he wrote, "One is obsessed with the feeling that nothing counts. Wiley Branton is looking over one shoulder, Sherrod over the other, and one's own self is perching on one's head."[90]

By April 1963, organizers saw an improvement in "the tone of feeling in the Negro community towards SNCC workers."[91] Many remained wary of SNCC's tenacious organizing, but they noticed a decrease in white harassment. A minister in Terrell County told one SNCC worker, Ralph Allen, "Y'all sure have done a lot 'round here. Ain't been no more killings in a long time. Used to be 'bout every week they was shooting someone."[92] In Lee County, Allen and Chatfield worked with a team of high schoolers to canvass neighborhoods. They were bold enough to visit their teachers as well, talking with them on their front porches on weeknights and Saturdays. Penny Patch paired with a black woman to canvass. "We'd go knocking on doors down these dirt roads in Albany," she reported, "recruiting people to come to mass meetings or giving them information about this and that, starting to talk to them about registering to vote."[93] During March and April 1963, fifteen people registered in Lee County and another forty in Terrell County.[94] "It [was] not easy to get people to register to vote," Janie Culbreth Rambeau recalled about her time with SNCC in southwest Georgia, "because you [had] to convince them that voting will bring about a change."[95]

Persuading people proved difficult because of the "organized economic tyranny of the whites" that kept many black adults from registering, afraid they would lose their jobs if sighted at the registrar's office.[96] Chatfield, Allen, and others heard that whites in towns across southwest Georgia swapped information, keeping each other informed about which African Americans aligned with SNCC. Mildred Beasely, an elementary-school teacher in

Terrell County, had applied to register back in 1961. Her superintendent heard, and he passed word that he would fire her if she did not rescind her application. Not wanting to lose her job, she withdrew her application before it could be processed. "I felt that if I did not get my application back, I would lose my teaching job as a result," she told Chatfield.[97] Stories like these were commonly reported, and even though SNCC's popularity rose in the region, many people felt they could not register for fear of losing their job. Even with VEP support, financial limitations persisted. In February 1963, Sherrod told Branton that money was low and he and other SNCC activists might need to resort to odd jobs to make ends meet: "Of course we don't mind that work; we have done it before, but the money from the VEP permits us to work under less tension and anxiety concerning the essential elements of life."[98] Allen included in his report, "One final thing . . . we need gas money."[99] While the numbers of registered voters in southwest Georgia remained low, SNCC's work impressed Branton and Dunbar.

As activists in southwest Georgia received VEP support, they wanted to do more than canvass and help people register. They wanted to march in the streets, sit in at restaurants, and stage nonviolent demonstrations. But they could not use VEP funds for these activities, and so "a request was made by the SNCC Southwest Georgia Project Director to break its agreement with VEP. This request was accepted."[100] Activists supplemented their voter registration work in July and August with direct-action campaigns in Albany, but by September, the protests ended, and they turned their attention back to registration. But having disassociated with the VEP, even though on friendly terms, SNCC's work in the area diminished. On March 3, 1964, Don Harris and Worth Long, two SNCC leaders, visited Branton at the VEP office with a written proposal for renewed sponsorship. They wanted to concentrate on Lee, Sumter, and Terrell Counties, convinced that locals would register in large numbers if SNCC had more resources to reach them and transport them to the registrar's office. Their ambition and strategy impressed Branton, and he awarded them $2,000 for two months. Branton was excited to renew the relationship with SNCC's southwest Georgia project, believing the data accumulated from such a long-term mission added value to the VEP's study. A week after the VEP sent the money, Randolph Blackwell, the VEP's field director, visited the SNCC project, staying long enough to watch a twenty-block registration parade, attend a mass meeting, and hear about how 345 people had registered since the new year.[101]

Registering people in southwest Georgia was no easier in 1964 than it had been in 1962. Although much of the "financial burden [had] been alleviated since VEP . . . accepted our proposal," Don Harris reported, segregationists pushed back against the renewed grassroots campaign.[102] On Saturday, March 22, black citizens arrived at the Terrell County courthouse to find three out of four doors locked and the registration testing room relocated to another part of the building. They had received official notices earlier about where to go, but the confusion wasted time and prevented many of them from taking the test.[103] Other situations turned ugly. In Americus, SNCC workers reported, "One lady had trouble filling out the application card and Sheriff Fred D. Chappell came into the registrar's office and cursed the lady and told her that she didn't know what she was voting for."[104] Less than a month later in Americus, an organizer who transported people to the courthouse went to the restroom, where the local justice of the peace, J. W. Southwell, attacked him.[105] Yet while resistance mounted, so did efforts to register. In March 1964, over 200 tried to register in Lee, Sumter, and Terrell Counties following a VEP grant. The next month, the SCLC, which had returned to Albany on a smaller scale led by Andrew Young, registered 459 people by paying for 28 canvassers with VEP funds. The VEP also provided an additional $3,000 to SNCC through September. By the end of the first VEP, Branton considered the Albany Movement as one of many success stories.[106]

Another notable VEP partnership came through Voters of Texas Enlist (VOTE)—the project that registered the highest total during the first VEP. When the VEP launched, Branton did not expect to fund many projects in Texas, where state law required annual poll taxes. But in July 1963, Blackwell attended a conference in Dallas organized by the Texas Democratic Coalition, a liberal organization founded in 1962 to bring together African Americans, Latinos, union members, and white liberals to wrest control of the Texas Democratic Party away from conservatives. Larry Goodwyn, the Coalition's executive director, led a motion to create a nonpartisan voter registration wing of the organization. Looking ahead to November 9, when Texas citizens would vote on a referendum to outlaw the poll tax, Coalition leaders wanted to register as many as possible. They had two goals in mind: conduct a massive registration campaign and strike down the poll tax. After hearing Coalition plans of voter registration across the Lone Star State, Blackwell recommended that the VEP offer support.[107]

The day after the Coalition chartered VOTE, it requested support from the VEP based on Blackwell's recommendation. Nell Goodwyn, the Coalition's finance chair, explained that VOTE "will be for voter education only, and not in behalf of any political candidate or partisan political issue."[108] Always concerned with tax exemption, Branton moved cautiously. Alone, VOTE appeared nonpartisan, but it originated from the openly political Democratic Coalition. And part of VOTE's strategy before November 9 was to help people pay their poll taxes of $1.50 or $1.75, something the VEP could not do. After thinking it over for a month, Branton agreed to help finance VOTE, as long as it accounted for its finances and used VEP money only for voter education, never poll taxes. The VEP began with a $3,500 grant to VOTE in August 1963.[109]

After receiving the grant, Goodwyn explained VOTE's strategy for voter registration. The plan hinged on motivating thousands of block workers to join together from the four legs of the Coalition—African Americans, Latinos, white liberals, and labor unions. In a 1960 registration campaign in Houston, local activists tested the model with some success, using 1,800 block workers to usher 42,000 registered African Americans to vote. By coordinating mass meetings across the state, local leaders would bring together motivated community members and have them sign pledge cards to become block workers in the upcoming election. Each block worker was responsible for 20 people. Block workers would meet their assigned people, share literature, and make sure they voted on Election Day. Using IBM computers to crunch polling data, VOTE coordinated volunteers—"generally women"—to compile lists of twenty names for block workers, usually within their neighborhood.[110] "The blockworker program is extremely complex," Goodwyn admitted to Branton, "involving the transfer of thousands of names from poll tax lists to 3×5 cards, reshuffling the cards by street address, breaking them down into groups of 20 to be given to individual blockworkers."[111] But for such a massive state in both population and geography, VOTE believed this was their best hope to beat the poll tax. Always looking for new tactics to study, the VEP wanted to see what happened in Texas.

During September and October, as VOTE worked to raise enough block workers before November 9, it went back to the VEP for more funding. VOTE planned to reach 12,000 block workers and register 240,000 people, lofty goals that required more money. The AFL-CIO and wealthy liberals donated to VOTE, but it needed a bigger financial commitment from the VEP. Demonstrating its belief in the project, the VEP committed an additional $10,500 in September and another $10,000 in October. With bills piling up, Goodwyn worried about the project collapsing before Branton called in October to let him know more dollars were on the way: "I'm afraid a bit of despair was creeping into my mind. So, your call was most timely. I feel like a vast weight has been lifted."[112] With the influx of cash, Branton warned Goodwyn again about the VEP's delicate tax exemption: "You mentioned the fact that perhaps the Texas Coalition could contribute to a campaign regarding the poll tax but since these are partisan matters we [VEP] cannot be involved."[113] VEP funds could be used for staff salaries, printing costs, stuffing envelopes, paying bills, and supplying VOTE's on-the-ground block workers. Goodwyn promised to keep funding separate, letting Branton know that political events were heating up: "The election continues to look like a cliffhanger. The other side is now openly organizing against us — elements of the Republican party, and the business community."[114]

The week before the referendum, VOTE stepped up its organizing. VOTE recruited Martin Luther King Jr. to write a letter to Texas voters urging them to the polls on November 9. "In the Delta of Mississippi, in Alabama, in Southwest Georgia, in so many places, we cannot vote," King explained. "*You can vote. And your vote on Saturday can free thousands of your brothers to vote in the future.*"[115] Goodwyn wrote block workers the week before with instructions for moving their twenty people to the polling places, adding, "*The job you will be doing this week is the most important political work you have ever done in your life.*"[116] By the time of the referendum, VOTE had not met its goal but managed to recruit around nine thousand block workers. For weeks they had canvassed neighborhoods, encouraged their twenty people, and attended mass rallies. Turnout was high but not high enough.[117]

The referendum on November 9 did not pass, and the sixty-one-year-old poll tax law remained in effect. Although 243,445 voted to repeal the poll tax, 316,008 voted to keep it in place. Goodwyn tried to find a silver lining. The block worker program was successful, having encouraged grassroots participation in an off-year election. But Goodwyn believed the repeal failed because the other three legs of the Texas Coalition did not pull equal weight to the African American contingent. Racism continued to plague the AFL-CIO, and while its leaders campaigned to end the poll tax, most local unions were indifferent to forging alliances with African Americans and Latinos. While an average of about 40 percent of registered voters turned out in black precincts across the state, only 15 to 20 percent of Latino, white liberal, and labor voters cast a ballot. Branton wrote Goodwyn four days after the referendum, "Even though we cannot support partisan politics I think it is no secret that we were all hoping that the poll tax would be outlawed in Texas."[118]

After the sting wore off, VOTE decided to renew its voter registration campaign through the end of January with a goal of registering over 300,000 African Americans and Latinos. They intended to make use once again of the block worker program after witnessing its effectiveness in the lead-up to the referendum. With a budget of $37,000, VOTE received $10,000 from the Texas AFL-CIO and more from a few private donors, "but the Lord only knows where the remaining $10,000 will come from, unless it is from the V.E.P.," pleaded Goodwyn.[119] On December 26, Branton sent Goodwyn a check for $10,000, and VOTE spent the next month prodding its block workers to register as many people as possible. They worked in twenty-two urban areas and two rural sites, eighty counties in all. During the last week of the campaign, the final state needed to ratify the Twenty-Fourth Amendment did so, outlawing the poll tax in the United States. Even though the poll tax held up on November 9, it became a moot point. Once again, VOTE extended its program, this time through March 6, coming at the end of a special thirty-day registration period initiated by the state government. The VEP supplied more money, and while VOTE did not hit its goal of registering 300,000, it oversaw the registration of a record number of African Americans and Latinos in Texas. From September 1963 through March 6, 1964, approximately 268,000 registered as a direct result of VOTE organizing. In his final report, Goodwyn thanked Branton for the VEP's crucial support: "There are so many thousands of block workers who will never know the role SRC and VEP played in the VOTE effort."[120]

While the VEP invested in VOTE, the Albany Movement, and COFO, it funded scores of other grassroots projects across the South. By supporting so much at once, the VEP nearly exhausted its finances. To reach its goal of lasting through October 1964, the VEP needed recommitments from its philanthropic benefactors. Funds from the Taconic Foundation, Field Foundation, and Stern Family Fund would last only through March 1964, but with seven months remaining until the presidential election, the VEP believed it could accomplish more. Many states held longer hours in registrar's offices during the primaries and lead-up to the general election. And quietly, after one and a half years of debate, enough states had ratified the Twenty-Fourth Amendment in January 1964, eliminating the poll tax in federal elections. To adequately study black disfranchisement during 1964, the VEP appealed to its partnering foundations. Branton wrote to the Stern Family Fund asking for $100,000. The Fund had given $124,000 over the last two years, and Branton had kept its leadership informed about how useful their grant had been. A month after Branton's request, the Fund granted $20,000 to the VEP and in February 1964 gave an additional $55,000 for the VEP's stretch run.[121] Leslie Dunbar requested additional funding from the Field Foundation and Taconic Foundation. In his letter to Maxwell Hahn of the Field Foundation, Dunbar described the VEP's ambitions and asked for $125,000.

"Voting is not a panacea," Dunbar wrote. "Yet it is unmistakably the indispensable pre-condition to all other civic advance."[122] Three months later, the Field Foundation's trustees voted to grant the VEP $75,000.[123] Dunbar's letter to Stephen Currier contained a similar message, and since the Taconic Foundation had been the VEP's principal supporter from the beginning, the VEP requested $150,000.[124] On April 22, Currier informed Dunbar that the Taconic trustees had voted to award the VEP with $80,000, and the Foundation left the door open to additional funds should the VEP require. Although the VEP did not receive its requested amounts, it entered into the final stretch with financial security.[125]

Each grant and partnership brought new data to the VEP, but Branton and his staff began to sour on working with Big Five national leadership. At the NAACP, Roy Wilkins remained skeptical of the VEP, even though its branches received dozens of grants. The NAACP often neglected its reporting to the VEP, prompting Branton to meet with Dr. John A. Morsell, Wilkins's executive secretary, to impress on him the need for branches to produce detailed reports if they wanted further VEP support.[126] Leslie Dunbar remembered that the "NAACP was a problem all the way" because it's leadership did not like being tethered to the VEP's policies.[127] Tensions between the SCLC and the VEP reached a higher pitch. In 1963, the VEP initiated a "temporary cut-off" until the SCLC could account for its finances.[128] Branton told King that the SCLC would remain "in a state of suspension" until it could account for prior funding. King "expressed great concern over this problem" and promised to intervene.[129] Minnis calculated that the SCLC had sent only three reports to the VEP, concluding that the SCLC lacked leadership at local levels and ignored VEP's policies.[130] Minnis's account passed to Andrew Young, SCLC's head of its Citizenship Education Program. He wrote Minnis, "There were several things that disturbed me about the report, but mainly it was what I'll call your 'cruel objectivity.'"[131] Young blamed poll taxes, literacy tests, workers who did not know how to research properly, and closed registration books in many counties. But by the end of his letter to Minnis, he became apologetic. "There is really no excuse for the reporting of finances the way they were reported to you," Young wrote. "This is strictly my inadequacy."[132] According to Dunbar, "In administering the voter project, we had our biggest trouble with SCLC. They weren't any good at voter registration. They wanted money for their own uses, and we had a couple of tense times with them."[133] Because of negative experiences with the national leadership of the NAACP and SCLC, the VEP shifted its emphasis onto independent agencies and local chapters of the Big Five. "We started more or less eliminating the involvement with the national organizations," Branton later recalled.[134]

One such partnership involved the Non-Partisan Voters Registration Coordinating Committee in Charlotte, North Carolina. In September 1963, the VEP granted $1,000 to the Committee and its leader, Dr. Reginald A. Hawkins, a dentist and fiery civil rights activist, for a thirty-day registration campaign. Describing the group's tactics for registering students from Johnson C. Smith University and residents in West Charlotte, Hawkins told the *Charlotte Observer*, "We're using a fan-out technique of catching people on the street and asking them to register."[135] In a field report to the VEP, Hawkins documented that between September 16 and November 9, the Committee registered 1,051 African Americans. In February 1964, the VEP answered Hawkins's application for additional money with $3,000 through May, allowing the Committee to pay bills for rent, telephone, heat, water, and electricity, as well as for supplies, an office secretary, and salaries to canvassing workers at $50 per week.[136]

The Chatham County Crusade for Voters (CCCV) in southeastern Georgia also benefitted from VEP support. On December 15, 1962, as part of a $4,000 grant for projects across the First Congressional District, the CCCV began "grass root organizing through the VEP program." Officially under the SCLC, the CCCV operated locally under the leadership of Hosea Williams, the SCLC's director of voter registration. Activists divided Chatham County into thirty-two zones and then fanned out to knock on doors, drive residents to the registrar's office, and tally the results. A telephone committee made calls to encourage community members to register, and a group of high schoolers organized film viewings and discussions about citizenship rights. The CCCV placed volunteers at the courthouse to stand guard outside of the registrar's office, to write down names of registrants, and to record stories of what happened while they tried to register. Between January and April 1963, 2,800 African Americans successfully registered. "Under the VEP in Chatham County," wrote Williams, "many advances have been made. This is the first time the white community openly expressed real concern over Negro registration." Even though many registered, resistance continued. Clerks at the registrar's office moved slowly to help African Americans in line; they spoke rudely, and they often humiliated those waiting by asking them to read a list of words and failing them if they pronounced anything to their dissatisfaction. The chief registrar, Charles Debele, complained that black registrants took too long. "I had an old colored woman about 65 or

70," Debele told Jack Minnis. "She was just nervous. I told her, come on now GIRL, take your time and don't be SCARED." In addition to the numbers of African Americans registering, Williams noted that the VEP project had "lessened the stereotype idea 'Negroes don't have intelligence enough to register in large numbers'" and that whites "began to realize Negroes are becoming politically minded and the politicians must act more and more fair toward them."[137]

In Huntsville, Alabama, the VEP granted $1,200 to the Madison County Coordinating Committee (MCCC), and after three months of organizing, the MCCC helped 752 black citizens register to vote. Huntsville had experienced a recent economic and population boom as a home for the National Aeronautic Space Administration (NASA), but the county had less than 1,400 black voters out of a total black population of 22,065. With VEP aid, local leaders spent money on advertising, carpools, mass meetings, sound trucks, and canvassing neighborhoods. Activists met little white resistance, and in a city determined to maintain its image as moderate, black registration climbed. While violence limited black registration elsewhere across the South, especially in rural areas, the VEP hoped to replicate Huntsville's success by pouring resources into urban areas where African Americans could more easily register. At the same time, the VEP continued to aid rural projects, focused on widening the scope of research as far as possible.[138]

In addition to COFO, Albany, VOTE, and local movements in Charlotte, Chatham County, and Huntsville, the VEP supported dozens of grassroots projects across the American South through October 1964, transforming southern politics. Amid the passage of the Civil Rights Act of 1964, Freedom Summer, the Mississippi Freedom Democratic Party's (MFDP) Atlantic City challenge, and the expansion of the Vietnam War, the VEP's grantees labored on. During eight days of work, 46 CORE volunteers moved throughout Iberville Parish, Louisiana, "making church appearances, staging rallies, sponsoring clinics, making speeches in halls, night clubs, etc., transporting potential registrants to the registrar's office, and filing complaints" to the DOJ.[139] William P. Mitchell, representing the Tuskegee Civic Association in Alabama, informed Branton that 703 African Americans had registered during a recent voter campaign.[140] In Chattanooga, Tennessee, the local attorney William Underwood led the NAACP chapter to register 3,800 people through "strenuous canvassing . . . radio spot announcements . . . [and] letters . . . given to the school children to take home to their parents urging them to register."[141] A registration committee formed within the Orange County, Florida NAACP chapter, and after a year of using VEP funds to mail letters, hold meetings, purchase advertisements, print handbills and post-ers, and pay babysitters to watch children while their parents canvassed Or-lando, 156 volunteers helped 3,120 African Americans register.[142] In North Carolina, the Citizens Committee of Wilson and Wilson County used $500 from the VEP to hire 20 canvassers for $1 per hour, and in a week, they reg-istered nearly 200 voters.[143] And in Birmingham, Alabama, where authori-ties unleashed dogs and water cannons on peaceful protestors, the VEP worked behind the scenes with activists to ensure that after the protests had subsided, voter registration fieldwork in the community would continue.[144]

After two and a half years, the VEP helped register an estimated 688,000 southerners. Compiled from stacks of field reports sent to the VEP by grant-ees, the total, according to Branton, was as "conservative as possible, and yet as realistic as possible."[145] For the first time in history, black southern voters topped 2,000,000, representing about 15 percent of the total southern electorate. African American registration in the South comprised 2,174,200, nearly 44 percent of those qualified to register, up from 29 percent just two and a half years earlier. Back when the VEP began, the SRC figured that black southern voters likely did not exceed 1,350,000. The VEP sparked one of the most dramatic voter increases in American history, especially considering the absence of federal legislation protecting the right to vote.[146]

The VEP's work over two and a half years influenced the 1964 elections. Lyndon B. Johnson drubbed Barry Goldwater in the presidential race, but across the South—where Goldwater expected his largest margins—African American voters pushed four states into Johnson's camp and tightened the margins in several others. After the election, VEP and SRC staff pored over the results state by state to estimate the impact of the black vote and on November 15 released a report to the press. Around 95 percent of black southerners supported Johnson. Out of the six southern states that Johnson won, "four clearly would have gone Republican had it not been for the Negro vote"—Arkansas, Florida, Tennessee, and Virginia.[147] In Virginia, for example, the SRC estimated that 166,600 African Americans had voted and that the VEP had registered around 78,700 during the previous two years. Johnson won Virginia by around 77,000 votes. According to the VEP's research, an estimated 211,800 African Americans voted in Florida, 67,600 in Arkansas, and 168,400 in North Carolina, all states that Johnson won thanks in part to black support. As the national Democratic Party inched leftward under Johnson, and as more southern African Americans registered and voted Democrat than ever before, southern white conserva-tives embraced Goldwater and the Republican Party, finding a new political base for racial demagoguery. According to SRC president John H. Wheeler, "More than any other organization, it [the VEP] deserves the credit for this amazing political revolution."[148]

Having exhausted its funding, the VEP closed after the 1964 election and looked ahead to study its data on disfranchisement. Branton remained through April 1965, using the last of the funds to pay his salary and compile the research. Rather than complete its final report internally, the VEP decided to expand the analysis and publish it as a book, intended as "a creative exploration of the new southern politics and the new people entering into political life."[149] Two journalists with connections to the SRC, Pat Watters and Reese Cleghorn, would spend the next two years combing through the information to write the book. Published by Harcourt, Brace and World in 1967, *Climbing Jacob's Ladder: The Arrival of Negroes in Southern Politics* not only served as the first VEP's final report, but it also offered an early analysis of the civil rights movement for a wider audience. In his preface, Leslie Dunbar wrote, "The voter registration campaign was not the whole of the civil rights movement, but it expressed it all."[150] Bus boycotts, sit-ins, Freedom Rides, and other nonviolent actions had spurred the movement forward, the authors argued, but what made those actions stick was voter registration. Civil rights protests highlighted the injustice of segregation, but by turning their anger toward the pursuit of democracy, African Americans won poll power. The VEP-backed surge in black voter registration demonstrated the will to vote and the need for federal protections against disfranchisement, ultimately laying the foundation for the Voting Rights Act of 1965.

Caption: Crusade for Citizenship flyer. Image WHi-135535, Box 381, Folder 3, UPWA Records, Wisconsin Historical Society.

Stephen Currier. Courtesy of the Currier Family Archive.

Audrey Currier. Courtesy of the Currier Family Archive.

THE ONLY SUCH PUBLICATION OF ITS KIND

VOTER EDUCATION PROJECT NEWSLETTER

| Volume 1 | August, 1963 | Number 1 |

INTRODUCING OUR NEWSLETTER

This is the first issue of the Voter Education Project's monthly report on voter registration work in eleven southern states, and VEP viewpoints on Negro voting. The purpose of this publication is to gather and disseminate news of the various vote drives under our auspices, for your information, and for practical political education.

We will report methods and styles developed by different local projects in persuading and helping citizens to register. We will present difficulties, successes,

Wiley Branton

and failures of these drives as pioneer experience from which other community projects may learn. The newsletter will attempt also to tabulate results of these voter efforts and pass them on in this report, to be issued the 15th of each month. The newsletter also will offer comment and interpretation on experience of groups in the field over the South.

This newsletter, as the official organ of VEP is, of course, non-political and non-partisan. It will, adhering to VEP's purpose, confine its interest to methods and results of voter registration drives, and in no way concerns itself with any political candidates, issues, or legislation. The aims of VEP

are voter registration, and acquiring information about how voters are registered, and its program is limited to these aims. So the newsletter will report and occasionally comment on the project's findings, with no political interest or policy whatever, except registering voters.

VEP was begun in the spring of 1962 and is planned to continue at least through 1964. The agency operates on funds granted to the Southern Regional Council by foundations interested in a large, free southern electorate. Project work in the main is done by the five major civil rights organizations, NAACP, CORE, SNCC, SCLC, NUL. Frequently, however, VEP makes special grants to local groups with a record of success in registering voters, where local conditions show the need for voting as-

J. Minnis

sistance and promotion. The project also functions to provide advice, materials, information and other experienced help to local groups even when it cannot give funds.

The Project has assembled a large, and perhaps unique, store of information about ways and means of register-

ing voters, and the obstacles and frustrations to be met. This information is available to any persons or groups who wish to benefit from this past and present experience in registration campaigns in their own communities.

Wiley A. Branton, civil rights lawyer from Pine Bluff, Arkansas, who was chief counsel for the plaintiffs in the school desegregation cases of Little Rock in 1957 and has practiced law for a decade in the South, is VEP director. Randolph Blackwell, law school graduate of Howard University, former political science and business law teacher in North Carolina and Alabama colleges, is director of field activities for VEP, and travels over the region to supervise, report on, and assist the local projects. Jack Minnis, a doctoral candidate in political science

R. Blackwell

at Tulane University and author of magazine articles on civil rights and political topics, is director of research and consultant to workers in the field.

Mrs. Jean Levine is office manager and administrative secretary, assisted by Mrs. Janet Shortt.

NEW TECHNIQUES IN VOTER EDUCATION

A survey of voter registration projects scattered across the eleven southern states shows a tendency of successful workers to by-pass or greatly augment the traditional house-to-house canvass means of registration. VEP found after a year's study of local projects, a great variance in results, attributable to many factors. Some success and some failure, or slight and slow progress, can be explained by the political maturity, experience and know-how of the Negro community. Memphis, where colored voters have long wielded political influence, of course is more responsive to registration projects and shows greater increases in registered voters than, say, a registration campaign in Jackson, Mississippi, where registration is attended by intimidations, and where Negroes have had very little political hope or activity in recent years. Similarly, a vote drive in Macon, Georgia, with a free and experienced Negro political organization, brought several thousand new registered voters, while a campaign in Gadsden, Alabama, had what can be considered a notable success in registering a handful of Negroes against great obstacles and threats from the white community.

It also become apparent from VEP information from the field that registration groups which invent new, untried techniques and create appealing, rousing presentation of their programs to the people, come through with excellent results in interest and the number of new registrants. In Huntsville, Alabama, for instance, the registration committee hung two signs on a mule which they paraded through the streets with the message: "This friend is not registered because he is a mule — what is your excuse?" This conspicuous appeal within a few days excited talk, laughter, and interest which started a highly successful drive. New approaches like this appear up and down the line.

Some organizations do well with

(Continued on Page 4)

VEP Newsletter, August 1963. Image WHi-135536, Box 2, Folder 10, CORE: Southern Regional Office Records, Wisconsin Historical Society.

African American lawyer Vernon E. Jordan working on a voter education project, seated at a desk with a typewriter at the Southern Regional Council, Atlanta, Georgia. Photograph by Warren K. Leffler, *U.S. News and World Report* Magazine Collection, Library of Congress, Prints and Photographs Division, LC-DIG-ds-05214.

John Lewis and Julian Bond speaking to a crowd during a voter's rights tour, August 3–5, 1971. Voter Education Project Organizational Records, Atlanta University Center Robert W. Woodruff Library.

CHAPTER FOUR

The Second Voter Education Project, 1965–1969

In February 1965, Bayard Rustin published "From Protest to Politics" in *Commentary*. Now famous for its characterization of the civil rights movement's first decade as the "classical phase," Rustin's essay called for black activists to focus on party politics. The time had come, he suggested, to stop demonstrating in the streets. Nonviolent protest had united a movement and ended public discrimination, but the remaining challenges of racial and economic inequality could only be solved through political action. Rustin wanted activists to get involved in local politics and steer the Democratic Party to the left, bringing together African Americans, union workers, and white liberals into a powerful coalition to counter the growing influence of the right. While the Civil Rights Act of 1964 protected citizenship rights, the fight continued for better education, health care, employment opportunities, housing, and voting access—none of which could be done effectively without political organization. "Here is where the cutting edge of the civil rights movement can be applied," wrote Rustin. "We must see to it that the reorganization of the 'consensus party' proceeds along lines which will make it an effective vehicle for social reconstruction."[1]

Those involved with the VEP and the SRC did not need convincing. A year before Rustin's article appeared, Leslie Dunbar argued that the only way for the American South to overcome poverty and racial affliction was "to do something that *would* matter to the world, and that is to become a rarity, a bi-racial community at peace with itself. It can do so, I think, only by integrating Negroes into its political processes."[2] From 1962 to 1964, the VEP strove to realize the political potential of southern African Americans by giving out hundreds of grants for voter registration. In the process, VEP staff worked with local activists, financed voter drives, collected data on disfranchisement, published reports, and helped register nearly 700,000 people before the presidential election. Funded by philanthropic foundations, the VEP had a vision similar to Rustin's: equip southern African Americans with the power to change their communities through grassroots political action.

But by the time Rustin's essay came out, the VEP had ceased operations, and many activists disagreed with Rustin that direct action had reached its full potential. Major events of 1965 further isolated Rustin's advice. Lyndon

Johnson's administration escalated the war in Vietnam, Malcolm X was assassinated, and Daniel Patrick Moynihan released *The Negro Family: The Case for National Action*, exasperating African Americans by blaming black poverty on weak family units caught up in a "tangle of pathology" tied to the legacy of slavery.[3] On March 7, the march from Selma to Montgomery in Alabama ended in chaos as police troopers attacked peaceful protestors on the Edmund Pettus Bridge. Bloody Sunday, as the day came to be called, provided the motivation for President Johnson and Congress to usher the Voting Rights Act into law on August 6, but less than a week later, rioting broke out in Los Angeles. To many, the United States needed direct action more than ever, not less, as Rustin advocated.

While the VEP's office sat closed for much of 1965, the SRC continued. Soon after Bloody Sunday, senior staff began exploring the possibility of restarting the VEP. Like Rustin, they believed the time had come for increased black political activism. The idea gained traction in August after the passage of the Voting Rights Act of 1965—a sweeping piece of legislation that protected the right to vote by dismantling literacy tests and promising federal intervention in counties that disenfranchised its citizens. But the Voting Rights Act did not automatically register anyone. The burden of registration still fell on individuals, and the SRC realized there would be a greater need for voter mobilization and education. With the Voting Rights Act, the possibility now existed for southern African Americans to register en masse and seize the kind of political power outlined in Rustin's essay.

From 1966 through 1969, the second VEP, under the leadership of Vernon E. Jordan Jr., answered Rustin's call and expanded its mission beyond voter registration to also include citizenship education and leadership training. The second VEP dispensed at least 403 separate grants in eleven states, spending $580,065 on grassroots projects.[4] Funding campaigns to register voters remained a priority for the VEP, but it also began aiding projects to instruct communities on the importance of local government, why voting mattered, and how black political power could be achieved. With an emphasis on leadership training, the VEP also began assisting black elected officials to solidify their new positions, to govern effectively, and to guard against racist attempts to oust them from office. Aware of how Reconstruction ended a century prior, the VEP safeguarded black political power. The Voting Rights Act enabled more African Americans to register, but the VEP helped translate easier voting access into poll power. Although Rustin's vision of a progressive Democratic Party never materialized, the VEP, once again operating as an engine converting power into motion, aided local movements moving from protest to politics across the American South.

LESLIE DUNBAR AND STEPHEN CURRIER tuned into the president's address on March 15, 1965, a week after Bloody Sunday. They listened as Johnson stated, "Many of the issues of civil rights are very complex and most difficult. But about this there can and should be no argument. Every American citizen must have an equal right to vote."[5] Five months later, the president signed the Voting Rights Act of 1965 into law. Having been involved in the VEP—Dunbar as executive director of the SRC and Currier as the VEP's primary financier—they knew that legislation alone would not be enough. For the Voting Rights Act to fulfill its promise, the VEP needed to come back. Dunbar wrote Currier the day after the president's speech, letting him know that staff at the SRC had been thinking about restarting the VEP with a new emphasis on citizenship education. Between 1962 and 1964, the VEP had focused on registration alone. The next step, with the promise of federal involvement, would be to cultivate a knowledgeable electorate. Dunbar planned to contact the Field Foundation and the Stern Family Fund for renewed financial support as well, but he first wanted to know Currier's thoughts on further Taconic Foundation sponsorship. What was clear, Dunbar wrote Currier, was that "there is a special need for resumption of VEP-type activity."[6]

The SRC remained well positioned to relaunch the VEP. Inside its Atlanta headquarters, twenty-seven black and white staff members compiled research, pored over southern newspapers, organized conferences, consulted for progressive organizations, fed information to journalists, published the monthly *New South*, and lobbied on behalf of the civil rights movement to politicians and the public. The SRC also sponsored ten separate state human relations councils across the South, whose collective membership neared ten thousand. In a program review, the Ford Foundation found the SRC to be "located to the right of the civil rights groups and to the left of the establishment, and considers itself to be a 'meeting place of men, organizations, ideas and programs' affecting the region."[7] The SRC crafted a moderate reputation with an abiding belief in the power of biracial democracy. Before rebooting the VEP, SRC leadership composed a questionnaire asking civil rights, labor, and political leaders about what the priorities of a renewed VEP should be. From responses, the SRC learned that continuing to focus solely on voter registration would not be enough. Respondents identified the main problem to be the lack of general knowledge about politics, government, policy, and voting laws. Furthermore, the Voting Rights Act of 1965 had not solved all problems. Registration slowdowns persisted, the DOJ moved slowly to send in federal registrars, and most registrar offices remained unsupervised. Drawing on history lessons from the Reconstruction era, the SRC worried that black voting gains could be reversed without vigilance. Quoting a common phrase from movement activists, the author of the SRC report summarizing responses to the questionnaire wrote, "Vote-less people are a hopeless people. This means that outlawing discrimination against qualified potential voters is not enough. Getting them registered is not enough. The primary objective should be that they use their vote and use it wisely."[8]

Dunbar initiated the VEP's renewal, but he resigned from the SRC in mid-1965 to manage the Field Foundation, moving into a role similar to Currier's as a financier of the civil rights movement. As executive director, Dunbar would oversee programs beyond the civil rights field, but his position would allow him to ensure the VEP received philanthropic support. As Dunbar later recalled, "The first assignment I gave myself when I got to New York was to get VEP re-funded."[9] During his years as SRC executive director, Dunbar had interacted with foundations and convinced them to invest in civil rights. "I believe that I have a realistic view of how much and only how much money can accomplish," as well as "how limited [money] is," Dunbar wrote a Field Foundation official soon after accepting the position.[10] Dunbar sent around the SRC's proposal for a renewed voter education program to foundations, but even though many found "virtual unanimity" on the need to restart the VEP, philanthropists were slow to promise funding.[11] Even Currier seemed hesitant about recommitting the Taconic Foundation to the VEP once again. After the success of the 1962–64 project and the promise of the Voting Rights Act, some felt that the mission had been successful. Dunbar made them see otherwise. With his new position, he first committed the Field Foundation to the new VEP. He then spoke with other philanthropists, including Currier, and convinced them to support the VEP again. Even though Dunbar had left the SRC, his move to the Field Foundation had been fortuitous, all but guaranteeing a new VEP due to his influence within the philanthropic sphere.[12]

In December 1965, the SRC applied for grants to restart the VEP. The SRC's new executive director, Paul Anthony, a thirty-seven-year-old white Virginian who had worked at the SRC since 1956 as an administrative assistant and researcher, sent the first request to Dunbar and the Field Foundation. Anthony wrote Dunbar, "Here it is. This represents the best work of a lot of people here."[13] The SRC proposed a three-year VEP "to reach those persons in the region still unregistered and bring them and others more fully into the political life of their communities."[14] According to the SRC, around 2,300,000 African Americans had registered in the South, leaving some 2,000,000 more who had yet to take advantage of the Voting Rights Act. The VEP received $100,000 from the Field Foundation, $150,000 from the Taconic Foundation, $50,000 from the Rockefeller Brothers Fund, $24,000 from the Ford Foundation, and $1,000 from the Marion Ascoli Fund. With $325,000 for its first year, the second VEP took shape.[15]

In mid-1965, after Wiley Branton accepted an offer from Vice President Hubert Humphrey to lead the President's Council on Equal Opportunity, the VEP needed a new executive director. Vernon E. Jordan Jr. became the top choice. First arriving at the SRC in 1963, Jordan worked as Dunbar's assistant, and he later served as Branton's acting assistant director for the VEP. Born on August 15, 1935, Vernon Jordan grew up in a middle-class family in Atlanta. His family lived in a neighborhood adjacent to Atlanta's community of African American universities, and Jordan grew up watching and interacting with black professors, attorneys, ministers, and community leaders. He came of age in a black metropolis, but his family's roots remained in rural Georgia, and they often took vacations to visit grandparents and cousins. On these trips, Vernon caught glimpses of the South's racial order he did not notice so readily in Atlanta, such as his aunt telling him to call his white playmate "Mr. Bobby" when they reached adolescence. Vernon stopped playing with Bobby instead.[16]

After graduating from DePauw University, Jordan attended Howard University's School of Law to train with the nation's foremost civil rights lawyers. Jordan first became interested in politics and the civil rights movement at DePauw, and during a visit home, he heard Martin Luther King Jr. speak. "King's words were so powerful, his delivery so inspired, that I knew right then and there that I was going to actively participate in the civil rights movement. There was just no doubt in my mind about that," Jordan wrote in his memoir.[17] He moved to Washington, DC in 1957 and trained with other civil rights–minded students for a life challenging segregation. He graduated in 1960 and moved back to Atlanta to begin his career.[18]

Jordan's first job out of law school was with Don Hollowell in Atlanta, a well-regarded civil rights lawyer who worked with the NAACP and Legal Defense Fund (LDF). For a year, Jordan traveled with Hollowell across Georgia to meet clients falsely accused of rape, violence, or for violating the rules of race. In 1961, Jordan helped Hollowell and the LDF defend Hamilton Holmes and Charlayne Hunter when they enrolled at the University of Georgia. Later that year, he began serving as the NAACP's field director for Georgia. For about two years, Jordan crisscrossed Georgia helping set up new NAACP chapters, leading membership drives, encouraging old branches to become more active, and promoting voter registration campaigns. Excelling at his job, he caught the attention of Leslie Dunbar in the spring of 1963, who asked Jordan to be his executive assistant at the SRC. Jordan jumped at the chance.[19]

Under Dunbar, Jordan traveled the South, researched civil rights issues, wrote reports, communicated with various activists and organizations, fundraised, and developed relationships with foundations. After the first VEP ended, Jordan took a job with the Office of Economic Opportunity (OEO), but after the Voting Rights Act passed, Jordan thought that a renewed VEP could be even more effective than the first. Years earlier when Jordan worked for the NAACP, his supervisor, Ruby Hurley, had taught him that segregationists understood two things: "the dollar and the ballot. Those interested in maintaining white supremacy worked hard to keep blacks away from both."[20] When Paul Anthony asked Jordan to return to the SRC and lead the second VEP, he had no hesitation. He planned to use the dollar to acquire the ballot.[21]

After Jordan accepted the position, news spread that the VEP would begin again. Alan Gartner, CORE's community relations director, wrote Anthony, "We are very pleased that the Southern Regional Council plans to continue voter registration work using the VEP model."[22] "Since the demise of the old voter project," Gartner later told Jordan, CORE had continued its registration work, registering about 29,000 people in 1965, but with the VEP, it could accomplish more.[23] Just before the year ended, Martin Luther King Jr. wrote Jordan, "We were very pleased with the manner in which VEP operated in the past years, and we found this quite helpful to our total movement." The Voting Rights Act, King continued, "means very little in view of the limited government action, and our situation remains essentially unchanged in the majority of southern states."[24] John A. Morsell, the NAACP's director of branches, told Jordan, "There is no question as to the immense value of SRC's previous voter registration project." The NAACP had been working to register citizens in Alabama, Mississippi, South Carolina, and Texas, "but the restriction to these four states is solely a reflection of the limited resources upon which we can draw at this time."[25]

Civil rights organizations had utilized the Voting Rights Act, but tensions grew as the DOJ sent mixed signals about how it would enforce the law. Attorney General Nicholas Katzenbach criticized civil rights groups for not doing more to register southerners, and activists accused the DOJ for hesitating to send registrars to the South and for not placing enough counties under federal supervision. As Jordan planned an early 1966 start for the resumption of VEP grants to local projects, he learned that Katzenbach wanted to help with the official kickoff. Jordan questioned Katzenbach's intentions. VEP staff feared Katzenbach wanted to soften criticism aimed at his office. But Jordan sensed an opportunity. He opposed any program that made the attorney general the center of attention at the VEP's expense, but he approved Katzenbach to speak about the federal government's support for voting rights. It would be a chance to hear directly from the attorney general in a room packed with civil rights activists demanding that the DOJ do more to enforce the Voting Rights Act.[26]

While planning for the attorney general's speech, the SRC announced the second VEP on February 18, 1966. Emphasizing that both the Republican National Committee and Democratic National Committee had once again endorsed the VEP as a nonpartisan venture, the VEP targeted the estimated 2,000,000 still unregistered African Americans in the South. The VEP would work alongside the major civil rights groups, but it also promised to heavily invest in local, grassroots organizations. So far, according to Jordan, voter registration and mobilization efforts had meant "largely middle-class enfranchisement. We need to reach down deeper into our communities and register people who have not been reached by past efforts."[27] Through registration projects, citizenship education, and leadership training, the VEP promised to empower black southerners with the franchise.

Ten days later, over 300 civil rights leaders gathered in Atlanta to hear the attorney general speak. Katzenbach heaped praise on the first VEP, which he described as "even more remarkable considering that it came entirely before the Voting Rights Act struck down so many of the barriers."[28] Since August, he stated, around 300,000 African Americans had registered, including 51,000 in Mississippi, 56,000 in Alabama, and 53,000 in Louisiana. While the Voting Right Act created safeguards, Katzenbach told his audience that the onus to help register people remained with civil rights organizations. Activists needed to move unregistered people to their local registrar's office and have them sign up—a simple act, he suggested, with most legal hurdles gone and the VEP's aid. Echoing Bayard Rustin, if only vaguely, he pleaded with leaders to "turn from protest to affirmation."[29] The audience reacted unfavorably, and Katzenbach received only minor applause when he stepped off the stage. Reporters surrounded leaders afterwards to hear their opinions. Not only were movement activists displeased that the attorney general had not promised additional federal registrars, but they expressed irritation that he blamed their organizations for not doing more. Although Katzenbach indicated his office was doing all that it could, civil rights leaders disagreed, and they disputed his claim that private groups were responsible for registration. Leaders felt that the government had distanced itself from the movement, content to let the Voting Rights Act speak for itself and do the bare minimum. "He [Katzenbach] put the burden right back on us," one SRC member told the *New York Times*.[30] Audience members were also incredulous over Katzenbach's comments that protest tactics had reached their limit. Martin Luther King Jr. told the *Atlanta Constitution*, "There has been too much caution in sending out registrars. In some cases, I think we will have to demonstrate."[31] Based on Katzenbach's comments, the path seemed clear to Jordan: the VEP and its grantees, not the government, would register southern African Americans.

The second VEP started fast. Jordan assembled a small team inside the SRC's downtown Atlanta office. He hired a high school classmate, Thaddeus Olive, as an accountant, and Marvin Wall as research director. Weldon Rougeau, a former CORE leader in Miami, later joined as field director. Together, they fielded hundreds of grant requests. An interested person or group would submit an application to the VEP for a project, often as a one- or two-page summary, along with plans for voter registration fieldwork and citizenship education, such as canvassing or workshops. The more specific the proposal, the better. Often, for shoddy proposals, Jordan sent feedback to revise before rejecting it outright. Rougeau traveled the South, meeting those asking for assistance, to get a sense of the people, the area, and the chances for registration success, offering counseling along the way to improve their grant requests. Once approved, the VEP sent checks and asked grantees to send back reports of expenditures and results. Jordan later acknowledged the power he had within the movement, whose position "made me kind of a chancellor of the exchequer. This was a heavy responsibility, and I took it very seriously."[32] Looking back, Jordan believed that the competition for money increased the efficiency of the voting rights movement by making local and national groups more accountable. "Everyone soon learned that is wasn't enough to just have a good heart and good intentions," remembered Jordan. "They had to present a viable plan to get the funds and they had to successfully execute the plan if they wanted more to undertake other projects."[33]

Over the next three years, the VEP spent $580,065 on at least 403 grants to campaigns across the Old Confederacy. The VEP kept accurate registration statistics during 1966, in which 91 projects registered 93,655 black southerners, but not in 1967 and 1968. VEP grants went to chapters of the NAACP and SCLC, but most went to independent organizations. In 1966, the VEP sent $1,925 to the Pensacola Improvement Association, which registered 590 Floridians. The Lynchburg Voters League in Virginia received $2,475 and registered 1,376 people; the Calhoun County Voters League in South Carolina used $250 to register 268; and the Fort Valley Citizens Education Commission in Georgia spent $1,000 to register 305 community members. In 1967 and 1968, VEP grants continued to fund diverse registration projects across the South, including the Screven County VEP in Georgia, the Sunflower County VEP in Mississippi, Caddo Parish VEP in Louisiana, the Lee County NAACP in Arkansas, the Lincoln County Voter Registration Project in Tennessee, and the Northampton County Voters Movement in North Carolina. The VEP coated the South.[34]

The Auburn League of Women Voters in Alabama received VEP aid in 1966. Alice Alston submitted an application to the VEP soon after funds became available. In Lee County, she wrote, many African Americans could not read, no black man or woman had ever held an elected position, and the registrar's office opened only on the first and third Monday of every month, except for special occasions. To assist black voters in her county, she wanted to rent voting machines and have people practice using them. The League would train residents on how to use the machines, taking steps to overcome the fear of embarrassment for not knowing how they operate or how to read candidate names. She only asked for $200, which the VEP approved on March 11. In June, the VEP answered a grant request from the Lee County Voters League for $1,200 for a six-week registration program, working together with the local League of Women Voters. Following the drive, the VEP gave an additional $775 to the Auburn League of Women Voters to record television programs about voting. Using the grant money to book a studio, write scripts, produce the film, and publicize, they created three shows seen by an estimated 33,000 people. Seven television and radio stations aired their programs, teaching people how to vote and why it mattered. By July, the Auburn League of Women had registered around 2,500 people.[35]

The North Carolina Voter Education Project (NCVEP) also received VEP support. The second VEP had set up state VEPs in Arkansas, Louisiana, and South Carolina—umbrella organizations uniting several independent campaigns—but the NCVEP was unique because it partnered with the North Carolina Fund (NCF) as well as the VEP. The NCF began in 1963 under Governor Terry Sanford, combining funding from the Office for Economic

Opportunity and other federal departments with philanthropic grants to support eleven antipoverty programs across the state between 1963 and 1968.[36] In 1966, black leaders in North Carolina expressed interest in forming a political training group through the NCF. George Esser, the NCF's director, asked the VEP for help. Jordan recommended keeping the NCVEP small, with one full-time staff member and a small budget, to organize voter registration campaigns, citizenship education classes, and leadership training seminars more often and in more places than the VEP could do on its own. Jordan instructed them to apply for a VEP grant as soon as possible. After receiving their application, the VEP allocated $13,000 to the NCVEP to pay for a full-time director at $7,500, a secretary for $2,600, and the rest for office supplies and travel costs. Under director John Edwards, a young NCF worker from Durham's Operation Breakthrough, the NCVEP announced its goal to go "after the potential voters who, for one reason or another, never have registered." In 1967, the NCVEP led five registration campaigns and sponsored a conference. Edwards traversed the state, helping communities orchestrate registration projects. A three-week effort in Martin County registered around 900 people. In Rocky Mount, 1,400 people registered after the NCVEP sponsored citizenship clinics. Up to 400 people registered in Goldsboro and another 600 in Kinston. In Robeson County, approximately 4,500 people registered after the county appointed deputy registrars to visit African Americans and Lumbee Native Americans to register in their homes. On July 22, the NCVEP led a Leadership Training Conference in Durham with nearly 500 participants, featuring speakers and holding workshops on local leadership, election laws, and voter mobilization.[37]

In Charleston, South Carolina, the VEP supported voting rights campaigns. In 1966, the VEP granted the ad hoc Citizens Committee of Charleston with $720, and within weeks, the project tallied 783 new black voters. At the bottom of a form documenting the results, the director hand wrote to Jordan, "We tried as hard as we could to get as many to register as possible. We are not too happy. But 783 new registered voters would never have been if it were not for the Southern Regional Council, Inc."[38] The following year, the VEP supported Charleston's NAACP branch with $2,000. Carrying into 1968, the VEP backed the Charleston County Voter Registration Project, an organization that helped black citizens register and reregister after South Carolina changed its election law to allow for reregistration by simply having the application notarized. Organizers stationed black notaries in homes, churches, and grocery stores across the county to stamp reregistration forms. In the main office on Rutledge Avenue, staff double-checked forms before sending them to the county. By February 1968, the campaign had registered or reregistered 2,543 black Charlestonians, but activists had hoped for many more. Herbert Fielding, a volunteer who worked as an undertaker, printed so many flyers advertising these notary services that his hands were stained with black ink. He told a journalist, "This is our biggest problem. Creating and generating more public interest."[39]

Along with financing grassroots campaigns, the VEP continued to support chapters of the NAACP and SCLC, but less so with CORE, the NUL, and SNCC. CORE's leadership had planned to work with the second VEP, and CORE received funding for three projects in Louisiana in 1966, but CORE had turned its attention northward. Floyd McKissick, James Farmer's successor as CORE director, asked for support in Cleveland, Ohio, but Jordan explained that the VEP would concentrate on the South.[40] The VEP awarded only two grants to the NUL worth $6,600 for citizenship education programs in Jacksonville, Florida and Hobson City, Alabama in 1967. SNCC made "one or two" grant applications to the VEP, but they "were not well conceived and therefore not funded."[41] But the NAACP capitalized on VEP resources, and between 1966 and 1969, dozens of branches received grants. Writing to thank Jordan at the end of 1966, John Morsell quipped, "There appears to have been only one fault to find: you didn't have enough money to give us."[42] The VEP also supported local affiliates of the SCLC in Alabama, Georgia, and Virginia. Martin Luther King Jr. focused on the national scene and left organizational responsibilities to his executive staff, including Hosea Williams, the director of voter registration. Williams and Jordan had an antagonistic relationship, with Williams often accusing Jordan of financial mismanagement. Jordan believed that Williams made unreasonable demands, like in 1969 when Williams requested $29,000 for a one-day registration drive. Still, the second VEP financed over a dozen SCLC projects.[43]

As the VEP financed grassroots projects, it gathered data and released reports about the impact of the Voting Rights Act of 1965. Marvin Wall compiled a list of violent acts by whites fighting back against black political action. Released a week after James Meredith was shot during his solo march from Memphis to Jackson, the VEP aimed to show journalists and the wider public that the law itself had not ended intimidation against registration workers. At least sixteen documented incidents had occurred since August 1965. In Greenwood, Mississippi, sixteen-year-old Freddie Lee Thomas died after a car struck him while he walked along the side of a road. His brother concluded that Thomas had been targeted "to discourage Negro voter registration efforts." In Barnwell, South Carolina, a gang of white men stabbed four black canvassers. In Laurel, Mississippi, someone shotgunned the house of an NAACP leader who had been collecting voting complaints for federal registrars. Vernon Dahmer, a fifty-eight-year-old leader in Hattiesburg, Mississippi, died after someone firebombed his home for leading a registration drive. Near Colerain, North Carolina, someone lit a five-foot-tall cross on the lawn of a registration activist in Bertie County. These acts demonstrated that white violence against African Americans had not stopped with the Voting Rights Act of 1965.[44]

The VEP also released a report entitled "The Effects of Federal Examiners and Organized Registration Campaigns on Negro Voter Registration" to prove that the most politically active southern counties were those with both VEP-funded projects and federal examiners. After nearly a year of the Voting Rights Act, federal registrars had gone into forty-one counties in Alabama, Mississippi, Louisiana, and South Carolina, helping register 122,905 people. Even though the Voting Rights Act had also placed Georgia, Virginia, and twenty-six North Carolina counties under watch, examiners had yet to arrive. Marvin Wall calculated that counties with both federal examiners and VEP programs had the highest percentages of black registration. The next highest numbers came from counties with only federal examiners, followed by those with just VEP projects. Counties with neither had the lowest figures. In Alabama, for example, Marengo County had both federal registrars and a VEP-financed program where 5,535 out of 7,791 African Americans had registered, about 71 percent of the total black voting-age population. Autauga County had only federal examiners, and 2,275 out of 3,651 had registered, around 62 percent. A VEP-sponsored project in Sumter County resulted in 3,369 out of 6,814 African Americans registering, only 49 percent without examiners. And a typical county without either was Clarke County, where 2,495 out of 5,833 had registered, about 43 percent. In total for Alabama, 69 percent had registered in counties with both examiners and the VEP, 64 percent with only examiners, 58 percent with only the VEP, and 45 percent without either.[45] Similar results appeared in Mississippi, Louisiana, and South Carolina. By the end of the summer of 1966, southern black registration stood at 2,620,359, compared to 14,309,704 of the white population—52 percent and 70 percent of those eligible, respectively. As black registration increased, so too did white registration. Wall logged proof of the efficacy of federal examiners and the VEP together, as well as the distance still to go.[46]

The VEP continued to amass data on disfranchisement, and in 1968, the U.S. Commission on Civil Rights borrowed heavily from VEP research in its

256-page *Political Participation*, chronicling the impact of the Voting Rights Act. Utilizing VEP studies and statistics, the Commission determined that while black registration and voting had increased, numerous barriers still existed that prevented African Americans from full political engagement. Since November 1966 when the study began, Commission attorneys and staff members visited fifty-five counties in ten states to review black political conditions. They came away with a picture of the South far from political equality. White conservatives held onto political power by diluting black votes, erecting barriers for black candidates, gerrymandering, turning elected positions into appointive ones, interfering with black poll watchers, and outright discrimination and violence. The Commission also noticed that neither the Republican nor Democratic Party had made a full effort to bring African Americans into their organizations.[47] At a time when the Republican Party was gaining strength in the white conservative South and undoing the Democratic Party's grip on the region, both parties failed to engage black southerners en masse. Jordan labeled the report "well-written, well-documented, and carefully prepared" and, along with its authors, called on the government to address these issues. For Jordan, the solution was simple: "It has been our observation that the hostility and deviousness of white officials usually decrease as Negro voting registration increases."[48]

Between 1966 and 1968, the VEP translated its research into booklets designed for citizenship education and distributed them among its grantees, such as "How to Conduct a Registration Campaign" and "Know Your Georgia Government." Patricia Collins, a sophomore at Spelman College and a summer intern with the VEP in 1967, researched and wrote the manual on registration work. At nineteen pages, the compact booklet served as a primer for groups to sponsor their own drive. "A registration campaign in full swing is exciting to watch," Collins wrote, but "doesn't happen automatically."[49] Collins advised finding an energetic director with good organizational skills, dividing areas between canvassers, documenting results, sticking to a budget, studying election laws, harnessing local issues as motivation, carpooling to the registrar's office, booking churches for mass meetings, and finding babysitters. Canvassing was the key. In "Know Your Georgia Government," the first of several state-specific civic guides, the VEP explained the structure of local and state government in twenty-three pages. The VEP found that many voted without having a clear sense of office responsibilities. Sections on city, county, and state government, the governor's office, the state legislature, the state constitution, lawmaking, courts, and juries, as well as such current issues as education, welfare, and taxes, all explained how votes mattered: "Having a vote means you have power—power to help decide who is going to run your city, your county, and your state. Whom you elect determines the sort of government, good or bad, you will have."[50]

The VEP's efforts paid off in the 1966 midterm elections. Twenty black candidates won seats in state legislatures, and many more assumed county posts. Lucius Amerson won the sheriff's race in Macon County, Georgia, believed to be the first black sheriff in the South in the twentieth century. Three African Americans were elected to the Texas State Legislature, including Barbara Jordan. In North Carolina, African American voters helped the progressive Nick Galifianakis win the Fifth Congressional District seat in the U.S. House. Demonstrating a willingness to support whichever party best served black interests, between upward of 90,000 African Americans voted in the Arkansas gubernatorial race against the segregationist Democrat candidate and for Republican Winthrop Rockefeller, giving Rockefeller the narrow victory. Black precincts in Memphis went overwhelmingly for the Democrat Ray Blanton, providing the margin to defeat Republican James Hurst in Tennessee's Seventh District. In Lowndes County, Alabama, the Lowndes County Freedom Organization ran independent candidates, although they lost every race. In Mississippi, an NAACP member in Jefferson County won a school board seat by a vote of 225 to 113, becoming the state's first black county official since Reconstruction. And significantly, in Dallas County, Alabama, African Americans voted out Sheriff Jim Clark—the face of white supremacy in Selma. During an election that witnessed the resurgence of conservatism across the United States, and while whites held on to most seats in the South, a new black political force also took shape.[51]

To foment this rising black political power, the VEP drew heavily on its philanthropic supporters, but a year into the second VEP, tragedy struck the Taconic Foundation. Since 1961, Stephen Currier had been one of the VEP's anchors of support, but in January 1967, he and his wife, Audrey, disappeared during a flight to the Virgin Islands.[52] Eulogies poured in about the Curriers' support for the civil rights movement. Although Stephen had become more comfortable in the media, the Curriers had remained largely unknown to the general public. "What Stephen and Audrey Currier have meant to the civil rights movement in this country has never been adequately described," Gertrude Wilson wrote in the *New York Amsterdam News*.[53] In the *Washington Post*, Robert Baker wrote, "He [Stephen] saw his role as a catalyst for solving problems—one of them was money—in the civil rights movement. His actions steadied the major civil rights groups at a time of despair and growing distress."[54] Although many Americans were unfamiliar with the Taconic Foundation and the Curriers, civil rights leaders had come to know them well. Whitney Young wrote, "They were white in complexion, but saw this as an accident of birth—not as a symbol of advantage, privilege or superiority over other human beings of different color."[55]

The deaths of Stephen and Audrey Currier sent the VEP into a financial panic, but, forced to expand its fundraising, the VEP emerged from the year on a stronger monetary footing. The Taconic Foundation could not carry on business as usual, leaving the VEP without its usual major sponsor. Paul Anthony asked David Hunter at the Stern Family Fund for assistance, explaining, "Their tragic death has changed things considerably and it is out of the question that Taconic could continue this support [for the VEP]."[56] In 1966, the Taconic Foundation had given $150,000 to the VEP. Now the VEP needed to make up the money elsewhere to meet its 1967 budget. The Ford Foundation gave another $24,000, and the Rockefeller Brothers Fund donated $50,000. The Field Foundation did the most to make up for Taconic's loss, with Leslie Dunbar initiating a $150,000 grant. The VEP also received $50,000 from the Mary Reynolds Babcock Foundation, $25,000 from the New World Foundation, $10,000 from the New York Foundation, and $1,645 from individual donations, totaling $310,545 for 1967. The following year in 1968, the VEP took in its highest total ever at $437,500. Another $150,000 came from the Field Foundation, as did $24,000 from the Ford Foundation, $10,000 from the New York Foundation, $4,000 from the North Carolina Fund, $15,000 from the Mary Reynolds Babcock Foundation, $2,500 from the Abelard Foundation, and $2,000 from private donors. The Taconic Foundation, still in the process of recovering, gave $5,000. In April, the tragedy of Martin Luther King Jr.'s assassination inspired the Field Foundation to give an additional $225,000 to the VEP as part of a larger donation to civil rights groups. Conscious of King's advocacy for black political power as "a lever for social and economic change," the VEP promised to put the money in the hands of voting rights activists.[57]

With financial footing, the VEP branched out from registration campaigns and citizenship education programs and began hosting leadership training conferences to empower black women and men in political office. Jordan understood what had happened the last time African Americans rose in political influence across the South. "In the years after Reconstruction came a dark period called Redemption," wrote VEP staff. "During this period, white Southerners turned back the clock and reasserted their control over the lives of black people . . . A second Redemption is unthinkable if the region—and the nation—is to survive as a multi-racial society."[58] The VEP committed to prevent a second Redemption and promised to support all of the South's newly elected black officials, whether as a state legislator, chancery clerk, school board member, county commissioner, sheriff, constable, justice of the peace, mayor, coroner, or any local position. Unlike funding individual projects, Jordan believed that leadership training necessitated bringing individuals to the VEP. During late 1966, the VEP first tried out the idea.

On December 29 and 30, 1966, the VEP hosted a seminar for state legislators in Atlanta. The VEP had no model on which to base such a conference, and it wanted to try out the idea without media scrutiny. "VEP chose not to publicize the Seminar, so that all discussions could be off-the-record and frank," summarized Paul Anthony in his year-end report.[59] Dr. Vivian Henderson, president of Clark College, spoke on "southern economics and public policy." Jack Greenberg of the LDF, with whom the VEP partnered for the seminar, lectured on how state legislators helped their constituents. State Senator Leroy Johnson from Georgia and State Representative A. W. Willis from Tennessee led a workshop on "effective law making." The next day, State Senator Barbara Jordan from Texas and State Senator Horace Ward from Georgia led an informal discussion on strategies that worked in their chambers. In total, eleven attendees came from Georgia, six from Tennessee, and three from Texas. Representatives from the Democratic National Committee, the Republican National Committee, the United Auto Workers, the AFL-CIO's Committee on Political Education, and the U.S. Commission on Civil Rights attended as well.[60] With the success of this trial meeting, Jordan pushed to host more. "The seminar was one of VEP's most successful and exciting undertakings of the year," Jordan wrote Dunbar. "The seminar sustained our belief that leadership training is important and valuable to all segments of the Negro community in the South."[61]

The next training conference took place at Clark College in July 1967. Welcoming the thirty-four elected officials who made the journey, Jordan and Dr. Anderson declared, "This is a historic occasion in the South." African Americans were registering to vote in unprecedented numbers, and black leaders held office in each of the eleven states of the Old Confederacy. "And now, for the first time, elected Negro city and county office-holders are being brought together to discuss their mutual concerns."[62] The VEP paid for their travel and lodging, and it organized several workshops, such as "Practical Problems of Negro Councilmen" and "Problem Areas of Urban Government." Bayard Rustin gave the keynote address, sending a message that "the civil rights struggle is now a matter of practical politics—not, as in the past era of demonstrations, one of ideological absolutes."[63] After the conference, attendees "returned to their constituents feeling that they knew considerably more about how to operate in their respective local governments."[64]

Six months later, the VEP held another leadership seminar for Mississippi officials. At the time, few African Americans held elected positions in the state, but as more registered, they stood poised to spike since Mississippi held the highest black population percentage in the United States. Anticipating the rise of black political power in Mississippi, the VEP invited all of the state's black elected officials. Out of twenty-two people, eighteen came from ten counties, holding such positions as county supervisor, constable, justice of the peace, chancery clerk, and coroner. They held question-and-answer sessions with VEP staff and speakers and shared ideas about how to govern with confidence. Reminding them of the past, Jordan told them, "We must avoid the perils that befell your predecessors in the Reconstruction era."[65] Bayard Rustin delivered the main address, entitled "An Overview of the Negro in the Political Process." He challenged attendees to govern for their black and white constituents alike and to entrench the ideals of the civil rights movement into legislation. Repeating familiar themes, Rustin told the eighteen officeholders, "What we need to do is to force the American society to re-evaluate its values . . . That will not be done in the streets. It will be done in the city halls, the state legislatures, in the national Congress and in the White House."[66]

In between the Clark College and Mississippi conferences in 1967, hundreds of African Americans ran for office in Louisiana, Mississippi, and Virginia. In Louisiana, 252 black men and women campaigned for positions, along with 40 in Virginia and 32 in Mississippi. On Election Day, 28 won in Louisiana, 22 in Mississippi, and 6 in Virginia. Each state also had one black candidate win a seat in the state legislature, bringing the total to six states in the South with at least one African American serving in the highest branch of state government. While the majority of candidates lost, the VEP considered these results positive, providing further evidence of a historic political shift in the making. Through his research, Marvin Wall noticed a connection between VEP projects and political races with black candidates. "As might be expected," he wrote Jordan, "there is a high correlation between counties in which the Voter Education Project has funded projects and counties in which Negroes are running for office and being elected to office."[67]

The following year, over 100 African Americans won state and local elections. Echoing the strategy of Bayard Rustin, Jordan spoke at an Associated Press convention ten days after Election Day: "We did not speak with sit-ins and demonstrations, boycotts or court action. Nor did we voice our grievances . . . through civil disobedience or violence. We spoke to America at the ballot box."[68] According to VEP research, around two-thirds of registered African Americans in the South voted. In Texas, the black vote helped secure Hubert Humphrey's lone win in the South. Elsewhere, at least 107 African Americans won their contests; 12 African Americans were elected to the Georgia State Legislature, 19 as justices of the peace in Alabama, 15 to the Election Commission in Mississippi, 5 to city councils in Arkansas, and 3 to local school boards in Louisiana. Others won races for magistrate, constable, town marshal, board of revenue, and city recorder in several states. In total, 385 black men and women now served in elected positions within the eleven southern states.[69]

With election results tallied, the VEP hosted its largest leadership training yet. The Southwide Conference for Black Elected Officials occurred in Atlanta from December 11 to 14, 1968 with 189 of the 385 black elected officials from across the South in attendance. CBS and NBC sent television crews to film highlights, and major newspapers printed stories about the historical significance of the gathering. Not since Reconstruction had so many elected African Americans been in one room. On the conference's opening night, Jordan welcomed the attendees with a warning: "The Negro officeholder is being observed closely by both races. Some of the watching eyes are friendly, but many are hostile."[70] He sympathized with them as leaders bearing the weight of unfair expectations from their constituents when they were new to government. "Black voters often feel that officeholders should produce instantly, almost magically, all those benefits and services that had been denied down through the years by callous white officials."[71]

Roaming the conference halls and peering into workshops, Reverend John Morris, the SRC's coordinator for special projects and an Episcopalian minister, found the Southwide Conference sessions "very much alive with discussion."[72] Seminars offering practical advice for school board members, law enforcement officers, state legislators, and multiple city and county officials lasted for hours and generated many new ideas. Notable speakers at the conference included Attorney General Ramsey Clark; Mayor Gordon Hatcher of Gary, Indiana; Congresswoman Shirley Chisholm from New York; Georgia State Representative Julian Bond; Reginald Hawkins and Eva Clayton from North Carolina; and Lawrence T. Guyot Jr. of the Mississippi Freedom Democratic Party. Ultimately, according to Morris, the "chief success" of the conference was simply that "for the first time, the region's black elected officials . . . assembled together."[73]

Speakers at the Southwide Conference defined their recent political success as the future of black power. The VEP encouraged those in attendance to focus on black electoral power similar to Rustin's vision. Shirley Chisholm, the first African American woman elected to Congress, told the crowd, "Black power is concerned with organizing the rage of black people" through political activism.[74] In his keynote address, Julian Bond, former SNCC communications director and Georgia state congressman, told the crowd to be proud that their constituents placed enough faith in them to give them their vote and to take it as a sign that most African Americans still believed in political solutions. Quoting the words of Reconstruction-era black politicians who were stripped of their positions a century earlier, Bond stated, "Their words are 100 years old, but their thoughts and ideas are as fresh as tomorrow. If each of us can approach his job with one half the fire and fervor that these . . . men did, then we will have vindicated the trust our constituents put in us."[75] Agreeing with the tone of the conference, the *Atlanta Constitution* editorialized, "'Black power' is a much and often misused slogan . . . But what happens when black power is achieved—when Negroes are elected to office? Then the focus of interest must shift from power to responsible use of power."[76]

After four days of speeches, networking, and workshops, the Southwide Conference ended with black elected officials more confident about their roles in government. After returning home, many wrote the VEP with sincere thanks. Sheriff Lucius D. Amerson expressed his gratitude.[77] State Representative Albert W. Thompson of Georgia wrote that the Southwide Conference was "one of the richest and most rewarding of my entire life."[78] Norfolk City Councilman Joseph A. Jordan Jr. thanked the VEP for moving "towards liberating the Southland."[79] V. A. Edwards, a board of revenue commissioner in Macon County, Alabama, wrote Jordan, thanking the VEP for "making it possible for the newly elected officials . . . to make a better adjustment than was done in the earlier days of Reconstruction."[80]

With 1968 turning out to be the VEP's busiest year, the SRC renewed the VEP for a third time through 1972. The second VEP had proven that the Voting Rights Act alone could not solve black disfranchisement. The task remained unfinished, and the VEP wanted to continue its work through voter registration, education, and leadership training. At an SRC conference, staff members discussed the possibility of disassociating the VEP from the SRC, securing its own tax exemption, so the VEP could "do more than just be a backer" and become an active civil rights group.[81] They proposed a new policy for grants to only go to counties with less than 50 percent of its black population registered and require local groups to raise matching funds. For the four-year project, Jordan created a budget worth $500,000 per year, and he sent the proposal to various foundations. Eclipsing its previous grants to the VEP, the Ford Foundation committed $250,000 for 1969. The Field Foundation pledged $125,000 for 1969 with a promise to consider three annual renewals. Leslie Dunbar, the VEP's constant supporter, wrote Jordan with news of the Field Foundation's assistance: "We are happy to have been a part, and to continue being one, of this program that has meant so much to all of us."[82]

The VEP stoked the rise of post–Voting Rights Act black political power in the South. Black registration grew from 2,689,000 in mid-1966 to 3,112,000 by the end of the summer in 1968, an increase of 423,000 people, about 14 percent.[83] The VEP ensured that scores of communities had access to resources that encouraged residents to register, vote, and get involved in local politics unlike ever before. Encapsulating the opinions of others, John Morsell wrote Vernon Jordan in March 1969 thanking him for the VEP's support to the NAACP over the last several years: "The funds which VEP has made available to us via the route of direct grants to branch campaigns have often spelled the difference between some action and no action at all."[84] Recalling his time with the VEP in his memoir, Jordan wrote, "There was never any doubt in our minds that we were doing some of the most vital work in the South. Those newly registered and voting black people would change Southern politics forever."[85] Although it intended to last another four years through 1972, the VEP's progress ruptured in 1969. According to Paul Anthony, "Through much of the year, in dramatic testimony to its effectiveness, VEP was engaged in a struggle for its life. At the end of the year, VEP's future remained clouded."[86] That struggle centered on the debate surrounding tax reform, in which congressional conservatives decimated the VEP's support from philanthropic foundations.

CHAPTER FIVE

The Tax Reform Act of 1969 and the Undermining of the Voter Education Project

Wright Patman, a populist New Dealer from Texas who had served in the House of Representatives since 1929, finally felt vindicated. On February 18, 1969, he sat as the first witness before the House Ways and Means Committee to offer his opinion on philanthropic foundations—an opinion he had been trying to share for over a decade, although few had paid attention. For years, Patman had criticized the exponential growth of philanthropic foundations and how their tax exemptions deprived the federal government of revenue. Under generous IRS guidelines, foundations had avoided paying taxes, and while philanthropists claimed these exemptions freed them to target projects for the good of society, Patman believed most harbored their money and cheated the American people. At times, Patman's evidence had bordered on the conspiratorial, but within the last two years, conservative House and Senate members started paying attention. They saw something more insidious than tax shelters, especially within the Ford Foundation, which they considered the most liberal of all. Patman saw it too and, in his opening statement, wondered aloud, "Does the Ford Foundation have a grandiose design to bring vast political, economic and social changes to the nation in the 1970s?"[1]

During the late 1960s, conservatives—both Democrats and Republicans, as the two major parties crossed ideological paths during this era—attacked philanthropic foundations as a roundabout strategy to weaken the civil rights movement. They argued that foundations had grown too large, powerful, wealthy, liberal, and supportive of black political power. The assault began in late 1967. Earlier that summer, the Ford Foundation gave $175,000 to CORE for voter registration fieldwork in Cleveland, Ohio. Months later, Carl Stokes won the city's mayoral race, becoming the first African American mayor of a major metropolis. CORE did not directly assist Stokes, but conservatives saw a connection. Without evidence, conservatives in Congress and in the press believed the Ford Foundation had meddled in politics and helped elect Stokes.[2] Over the next year and a half, more stories surfaced about alleged tax abuses by foundations. Many liberals, like Patman, were upset alongside conservatives, converging with a bipartisan national debate over taxes and whether or not philanthropy paid its fair share in society. At the same time, many Americans believed their country had descended into chaos, and major philanthropy was part of the problem. President Lyndon B. Johnson's foundation-backed War on Poverty unraveled as he sunk his political capital into expanding the Vietnam War. Riots broke out in Newark, Detroit, and other cities. The 1968 Democratic National Convention in Chicago turned violent, only months removed from the assassinations of Martin Luther King Jr. and Robert F. Kennedy. Richard Nixon and George Wallace appealed to white conservatives through their presidential campaigns, engineering a racialized populist anger across the United States. Part of this mounting national frustration took aim at liberal foundations, which conservatives claimed fomented social rebellion in cities like Cleveland.

Conservatives took advantage of popular indignation toward liberal philanthropy to undermine African American voting power. They did so through the Tax Reform Act of 1969, a long, complex law that was the product of ten months of legislative wrangling between the House, Senate, and Treasury Department. The bill eliminated loopholes for the rich while easing taxes for many Americans by updating regulations on bonds, credit, charitable deductions, and income tax. While the law addressed hundreds of separate taxation policies, Section 4945 did something else. Within this portion, Congress outlined restrictions for philanthropic foundations that supported voter registration campaigns. Southern conservatives in Congress were responsible — those once proud to identify as segregationists. To defund organizations working to register African Americans, conservatives, led by Senators Russell Long of Louisiana and Herman Talmadge of Georgia, accused tax-exempt foundations of illegally influencing politics when sponsoring voter registration activities. Most Americans agreed that tax-exempt philanthropies should not be involved in politics, but Senators Long and Talmadge and their allies enflamed the issue by exaggerating the extent to which foundations supported such projects. They also employed race-neutral and tax-oriented language to discredit black political power, pioneering strategies that would evolve during and after Nixon's presidency.[3]

Caught in this firestorm was the Voter Education Project. Scholars have chronicled how the Tax Reform Act of 1969 shifted the philanthropic landscape, but little exists about the bill's impact on the civil rights movement.[4] While the VEP remained operational in 1969 — funding ninety-eight additional projects and helping increase southern African American registration by 136,000 to a record high of 3,248,000 — the tax debate distracted executive director Vernon Jordan, frightened philanthropic supporters, and put the

VEP's future in jeopardy.[5] The VEP and its allies lobbied against the bill, help-ing forge a compromise. The Tax Reform Act of 1969 allowed for the con-tinuation of tax-exempt philanthropic support to the VEP and similar organizations but under austere rules. The new restrictions meant the VEP would have to spend an inordinate amount of time fund-raising, diversify-ing its financial support, and stretching its resources thin. Philanthropists became much more cautious when dealing with civil rights agencies, and foundations instituted tighter oversight. The SRC and VEP separated to pre-serve distinct IRS tax exemptions, cutting the VEP off from its parent organ-ization and support system. The close relationship between philanthropy and the VEP diminished, and as the money became more difficult to acquire, southern voting rights activity slowed as the movement's engine stalled. Even though the VEP functioned as a nonpartisan body, conservatives saw through the VEP's careful messaging. VEP officials never admitted so pub-licly, but they realized their actions countered white conservative politics. Conservatives sensed danger, and by disrupting the relationship between philanthropy and black voter registration projects, they won a major victory against the civil rights movement.

Although the Tax Reform Act of 1969 weakened the VEP, it survived until 1992. Amid financial uncertainty, John Lewis led the VEP from 1970 through 1976, when he decided to run for Congress. During his tenure, the VEP did what it could for local registration projects, citizenship education, and black elected officials. Along with Julian Bond, SNCC's former communications director and a state representative in Georgia, Lewis went on dozens of voter mobilization tours to encourage communities to keep registering and voting. The VEP established the Southwest Voter Registration Education Project (SVREP) in 1974 to register Latino voters across the Southwest. Following Lewis, a string of executive directors followed, but the VEP never recovered its momentum. In 1984, the Field Foundation evaluated the VEP's finances and found "very serious problems," including financial mismanagement and poor record keeping.[6] The following year, the *Atlanta Constitution* published a story about the report, ruining the VEP's reputation. The VEP never recov-ered. In February 1992, the VEP received its final grant from the Ford Foun-dation for $65,000 to transfer its records to Atlanta University Center's Robert W. Woodruff Library. Then, the VEP closed.[7]

THE ORIGINS OF THE conservative assault against foundations stretch back to the early Cold War era. In 1952, Edward E. Cox of Georgia led a House in-vestigation to determine if "tax exempt educational and philanthropic foundations are financing un-American and subversive activities."[8] Cox and his allies believed some foundations sympathized with communists. During the late 1940s and early 1950s, foundations funded social science research within the United States and abroad, projects that often pointed out problems of inequality. In particular, the Carnegie Corporation's work with the United Nations alarmed Cox. During his investigation, Cox also called executives of the Ford and Rockefeller Foundations to testify about their support for integrated schooling in the South. In an editorial for the *Chicago Defender*, NAACP executive secretary Walter White argued that the purpose of the Cox Committee was "to intimidate all foundations so that they would be afraid to contribute funds for the advancement of civil rights and equal justice for Negroes in the South."[9] Following Cox's unexpected death, B. Carroll Reece of Tennessee formed a new House committee. Calling the Cox Committee "soft," Reece promised more action to uncover how tax-exempt foundations supported propaganda "to influence public opinion for the support of certain types of ideologies that tend to the left."[10] But Reece's study began after the country had grown weary of Senator Joseph McCarthy's alleged communist conspiracies. The *Washington Post* poked fun at Reece soon after hearings started by calling him "mischievous" and arguing that another committee to inspect foundations was "wholly unnecessary, stupidly wasteful of public funds and can serve no purpose save intimidation."[11] Public opinion and House leadership moved against Reece, and he abandoned the inquiry before foundations even had the chance to respond.[12]

In 1961, as Stephen Currier pushed for greater philanthropic support for the civil rights movement, Wright Patman launched what would become an eight-year crusade against foundations. Patman's views on government stood opposite Cox and Reece, but like his conservative colleagues, he accused foundations of financial manipulation. He suspected that most foundations were nothing more than facades of altruism that horded wealth. The year before Patman began his inquiry, *Business Week* published an advice column asking its affluent readers, "Have you ever thought about setting up a 'family foundation'?" It made sense, the magazine suggested, because "if properly set up . . . it pays no federal taxes at all; yet it can be kept entirely under the control of its founder and his family."[13] This type of message alarmed Patman, and as chair of the House Select Committee on Small Business, he reviewed over five hundred foundations. Patman did uncover abuses, but errant research and a penchant for exaggeration undermined his broader call for philanthropic reform. In 1964, Patman pushed the Treasury Department to investigate foundations, but Treasury believed that most abuses were negligible. Yet Patman — "the most indefatigable of the populist gadflies on Capitol Hill" — would not relent, calling for a twenty-five-year limit on foundations, greater oversight, and an easier process to strip away tax exemption.[14]

Patman found vindication after the *New York Times* broke the story of CORE's $175,000 voter registration grant from the Ford Foundation. Calling Ford's grant "an unusual move" to a "so-called militant civil rights group," reporter Douglas Robinson noted that CORE had become "an increasingly vocal champion of the black power concept."[15] The grant raised suspicions of political activity by a major foundation, even though CORE had nothing to do with Stokes. Black newspapers did not help, with such headlines as "$175,000 Ford Grant to Help Put Stokes in Office" and "CORE's Ford Grant Could Help Get Stokes Elected."[16] Stokes won the race, becoming the first black mayor of a major American city. To many, Ford appeared to have crossed a line by getting involved in a particular city during an important race. The possibility of foul play sowed public distrust for foundations. Some feared that if foundations wanted to, they could involve themselves in more elections and manipulate outcomes through tax-exempt donations.[17]

Over the next year, more stories broke about alleged foundation abuse. McGeorge Bundy, who took over as president of the Ford Foundation in 1966 after serving in the Kennedy and Johnson administrations, pushed Ford in an increasingly ambitious direction that funded controversial projects. In particular, the Ford Foundation financed a school reform project in Brooklyn that smacked of political interference, and it awarded eight former staff members from Senator Robert F. Kennedy's presidential campaign with travel grants worth $131,000 to help them recoup after his assassination. The national press reported on these stories, deepening the Ford Foundation's growing reputation as too cozy with liberals and a provocateur of social change. At the same time, Americans grew angrier about taxes. While inflation climbed, the Johnson administration increased income taxes in 1967 to fund the Vietnam War. One of the Treasury Department's final acts under Johnson had been to release a report detailing over two hundred individuals taking advantage of tax loopholes. In February 1969, the Treasury Department received nearly two thousand letters demanding reform. With Americans irate, a new administration promised tax reform.[18]

On January 29, 1969, just over a week after Nixon's inauguration, the House Ways and Means Committee announced that hearings would begin the next month to reform the federal tax code. Chairman Wilbur D. Mills, a Democrat from Arkansas, told the press that his committee wanted nothing less than a "comprehensive reform package," including the review of tax-exempt foundations.[19] Wright Patman appeared as the first witness on February 18. According to his research, somewhere between 22,000 and 30,000 foundations existed, with around $20,500,000,000 in total assets. Philanthropy had grown too big without federal checks, Patman claimed, but he meant not "to destroy foundations, but to reform them."[20] He recommended a 20 percent tax on investment income and a twenty-five-year limit on all foundations. Alan Pifer, president of the Carnegie Corporation, likened Patman's proposals to "a remedy tantamount to using a jack hammer to crack a walnut."[21] But in Patman's mind, while some foundations gave to important causes, many more "don't do much for the nation except serve as tax evasion devices for the very rich. But they're so loaded with money that no one dares touch them — except me."[22]

The next day, Representative John J. Rooney, a Democrat from New York, fanned Patman's accusations by claiming a foundation had funded his opponent during his last campaign. "I am the first known member of Congress," Rooney declared in his testimony, "to be forced to campaign for reelection against the awesome financial resources of a tax-exempt foundation."[23] Without providing evidence, Rooney accused Frederick W. Richmond, a wealthy coffin manufacturer in Manhattan, of using his Richmond Foundation to funnel $250,000 into Jewish neighborhood groups in Brooklyn that functioned as ward clubs for his opponent. Richmond denied the allegations, but Rooney's message had its intended effect. Already distrustful of philanthropic ventures into politics, House members thought Rooney's allegations sounded plausible, even without proof.[24]

The day after Rooney's testimony, McGeorge Bundy appeared before Ways and Means representing the Ford Foundation. During four hours of questioning, Bundy acted belligerent and defensive, hardening the will of the committee to strike at foundations in the new law. Committee members from both parties brought up allegations of improper Ford Foundation grants, such as CORE's activism in Cleveland, school reform in New York City, and travel grants for Robert Kennedy's staff. Tax-exempt grants, they reminded Bundy, could not be used for anything remotely political. Bundy defended the legality and necessity of the Ford Foundation, but with too much arrogance for the committee to stomach. Responding to questions from Representative John W. Byrnes about the criteria the Ford Foundation used to determine its grantees, Bundy burst out, "We do it case by case or program by program, Mr. Byrnes."[25] Bundy claimed each grant was educational and not intended to shape public policy, but the committee remembered how

Bundy delivered the message, not the substance of what he said.[26] For weeks thereafter, committee members heard testimony from philanthropists, tax experts, and government officials before writing the bill's first draft. On April 22, two days before hearings ended, President Nixon gave a speech on tax reform promising that "exempt organizations, including private foundations, would come under much stricter surveillance."[27]

As House members wrote the law, public and congressional distrust of foundations grew. In April, the American Conservative Union circulated an inflammatory pamphlet through Congress, and in May, a scandal involving Supreme Court Justice Abe Fortas and the Wolfson Foundation further discredited philanthropy. The American Conservative Union, a lobbying firm that originated out of Barry Goldwater's 1964 presidential defeat, published "The Financiers of Revolution" by a Senate staff attorney named Allan C. Brownfeld. Without providing sufficient evidence, he outlined recent accusations against the Ford Foundation, arguing "tax-exempt foundations do, in fact, engage in partisan political activities, and on a grand scale."[28] While "The Financiers of Revolution" changed hands in Congress, William Lambert broke a story in *Life Magazine* about Abe Fortas and his ties to the Wall Street financier Louis Wolfson. Although the details remained murky, Lambert proved that Justice Fortas received a check for $20,000 from the Wolfson Foundation in 1966 for unspecified reasons. Almost a year later, Fortas returned the money, but only after Wolfson was indicted for stock manipulation, for which he was later imprisoned. Lambert implied that Wolfson had paid his friend Fortas to help his legal situation. Nixon and Chief Justice Earl Warren pressured Fortas to resign rather than face impeachment, and he turned in his letter on May 15. The situation could not have come at a worse time for the foundation community. While House members drafted legislation, speculation increased about the Ford Foundation's political intentions, and the Fortas scandal magnified public mistrust in philanthropy.[29]

As House members drafted the law behind closed doors, civil rights leaders began expressing concerns. Until then, the VEP and its allies had stayed quiet, not wanting to draw extra attention to the relationship between foundations and voter registration projects. But in April, leaders started speaking out. Whitney Young telegrammed Nixon and copied Mills with the message that restraining foundations would mean hampering voter registration efforts, thereby damaging the civil rights movement. Young raised the specter of black power and insisted that registration work kept radical tactics at bay: "By channeling black citizens' anger and frustration into voting through nonpartisan programs we have been able to make this a more constructive alternative than those methods proposed by more violent rev-olutionists."[30] Roy Wilkins wrote to Representative Emmanuel Celler to ar-gue that by limiting support for black voter fieldwork, "the registration of Negro citizens to vote would be crippled so badly that, in effect, the Admin-istration and the Congress would be the biggest biased registrars of all."[31]

On May 27, the House Ways and Means Committee released a statement about its tax reform draft, reading, in part, "No private foundation is to be permitted to directly or indirectly engage in any activities intended to influ-ence the outcome of any election (including voter registration drives)."[32] Vernon Jordan believed the statement raised more questions than it an-swered, and he felt he could no longer stand aside and watch the VEP's de-mise. He decided to break tradition and lobby on the VEP's behalf. Since the VEP's beginning in 1962, its leadership had avoided the media spotlight to safeguard its tax exemption, but with the VEP endangered, Jordan took the lead among civil rights leaders advocating against a ban on philanthropic support for registration drives. Jordan lobbied his foundation contacts to speak out against the proposed restrictions. Anne Blaine Harrison and Vernon Eagle from the New World Foundation told Mills that philanthropic support had been crucial to the civil rights movement: "We are sure you will agree that such activities do not contravene the will of the Congress, having in mind the Civil Rights Acts of 1964 and 1968 and the Voting Rights Act of 1965. On the contrary, it appears that our activities have helped to carry out the very purposes envisaged by these Acts."[33] Field Foundation staff, including Les-lie Dunbar, wrote Mills, "We find it hard to see why any voter registration, at any time, in any place, for any motive, is not in the public interest, and we would exclude foundation support from only those voter registration drives which make an overt appeal to partisan interests."[34] Jordan sent Mills information about the VEP, hoping to assuage any doubts about its neces-sity and legality, and he echoed a recent *Washington Post* editorial that stated that the VEP "has conducted voter registration drives over the past seven years, and has done so without the slightest partisanship."[35]

As Jordan concentrated on the endangerment of voter registration fund-ing, foundation executives worried about the tax bill's entirety. Before 1969, major and midsized foundations had been loosely affiliated through the Council on Foundations, an umbrella organization established in 1949, and later the Foundation Group, which compiled research on philanthropy. Foundations operated independently, but the impending tax crisis drove them together. Soon after the House Ways and Means Committee began hearings, foundation executives gathered to discuss cooperative strategy. On

July 14, fearful of a proposed tax on investment income, representatives from the Ford, Danforth, Sloan, Commonwealth, Carnegie, and other foundations met in New York. They feared Congress would enact a devastating bill on philanthropy, all because of a few foundations abusing financial loopholes and because of the Ford Foundation's sponsorship of registration activity. They also thought that the Ford Foundation inaccurately symbolized large-scale philanthropic work and that, for the time being, each foundation ought to stop making grants "that seemed to be connected with the more militant types of activity in the civil rights field and the ghettoes."[36]

Ways and Means finally finished the draft, and the House of Representatives approved H.R. 13270 on August 7 by a vote of 394–30. The bill stipulated that no more than 25 percent of a registration project's budget could come from a single tax-exempt philanthropic source and that groups undertaking such projects must operate in at least five states at once to protect against charges of partisanship in specific races. While benign on the surface, these two conditions alarmed civil rights leaders. Although the VEP had operated in eleven states, the added pressure of the five-state provision meant that it would always have to ensure that simultaneous operations were ongoing in at least five states at once. The 25 percent rule presented a greater challenge. While the VEP had applied for and won grants from many foundations, the bulk of the funding had most recently come from the Ford Foundation, well exceeding 25 percent of the total budget. The VEP had never before paid attention to balancing percentages between foundations, glad to receive as much support as possible from any source. If the House version became law, it threatened to make the VEP's job of raising money and balancing figures much more difficult. Other civil rights agencies would be affected as well. In a letter to the *New York Times*, Roy Wilkins wrote, "Regardless of the language, the proposals before the Congress in the so-called tax reform bill to bar the use of foundation funds for voter registration are principally anti-black."[37] Wilkins hoped that some members of Congress were simply unaware of the registration implications, but he believed other members were purposefully attacking black politics. He wrote, Congress "proposes to crush the rising participation of Negro voters in the election process under the guise of regulating the foundations."[38]

After the House approved H.R. 13270, it went before the Senate Finance Committee, where conservatives mounted a blatant attack on black voting rights by disputing the legality of philanthropic support for registration projects. On September 4, Senator Russell Long, chairman of the Senate Finance Committee, opened hearings by promising his committee would highlight foundations—"a special target of this tax reform bill."[39] The Finance Committee saved testimonies about foundations for last, and during the wait, Vernon Jordan and Paul Anthony drafted a statement defending the VEP's finances. Explaining the VEP's commitment to nonpartisanship, they argued that proposals in the House version were unfair because they insinuated that the VEP's work could influence targeted elections. While the VEP sponsored nonpartisan voter drives, they explained that the VEP also collected data, published reports, and provided citizenship education. Anthony and Jordan expressed concerns about capping funds from single sources at 25 percent and dictating that organizations operate in at least five states at once. There were "still relatively few foundations which are willing to support programs of social reform," they argued, but "occasionally an unusually imaginative foundation has the courage and foresight to support exclusively, or almost exclusively, a new group which has promise and a sound idea."[40] John Simon, who took over leadership of the Taconic Foundation after the deaths of Stephen and Audrey Currier, echoed Jordan and Anthony. Writing, "to bring to your attention an apparently unintended adverse effect," Simon reminded the senators that the VEP had held a special tax-exempt ruling from the IRS since 1962, and he defended its nonpartisan mission as vital to the growth of American democracy.[41] Simon contended that the 25 percent stipulation would prove devastating since it would be "almost impossible for any new voter registration programs to be undertaken."[42] Michael Harrington, the celebrated left-wing journalist, also took up his pen: "Although these provisions are phrased in dry, legislative jargon, they translate out into plain English as an attack on the democratic rights of the least powerful people in the land."[43]

Once the Senate Finance Committee turned its attention to philanthropy, civil rights advocates centered on the necessity of external funding to increase African American voter registration. But only three people had the opportunity to testify—Whitney Young, Paul Anthony, and Lucy Benson from the League of Women Voters. Benson raised concerns about the House bill being too vague about what constituted a partisan voter registration campaign. Anthony, accompanied by Vernon Jordan and SRC lawyer Joseph Haas, summarized their earlier statement on the importance of the VEP. Whitney Young gave the most powerful testimony. Part of the tax reform bill, according to Young, "had the direct result of making the black community particularly feel that it is a hostile bill, a bill that suddenly came into fruition with a purpose as much to intimidate as to legislate."[44] Foundations had already shown signs of cutting back. "There is some evidence that foundations will become again very cautious, very conservative," Young testified.[45] Young's anger continued to spill out. "You and others ask the black community to be responsible," Young testified, "but you do not give us the resources with which we can assume responsibility."[46]

Young's message failed to move Long, Talmadge, and their allies, who went even further than the House to add a "flat prohibition against foundations' financing of voter registration drives."[47] If this version passed into law, the VEP would likely end. Civil rights leaders were outraged, and Jordan redoubled his efforts lobbying against the law. Jordan sent mass mailings to political friends of the VEP, including Senator Edward M. Kennedy and Senator Daniel K. Inouye. Conservatives proposed the change, but it would not be voted on until October 31. The VEP lobbied Congress and communicated with civil rights leaders and foundation executives to expose the pending consequences. While conservatives guarded their words about motive, Jordan labeled their tactics racist and worried that others in Congress were not seeing the big picture. Under a pretense of tax reform, conservatives were undermining black political power. "Make no mistake about it," Jordan warned. "Black people in the South cannot continue to make the sort of registration gains they need to make without organized registration programs."[48]

The VEP's message resonated, and concerned citizens petitioned senators to change their minds. Nate Welch, a member of the SRC's board, wrote Talmadge that the southern African American "voter registration effort will be virtually halted if the proposed legislation is enacted."[49] Wallace L. Young Jr. of the New Orleans NAACP urged Long to drop the proposal: "Such drives increase in practice the theory of a democracy which involves all the people."[50] Conservatives on the Finance Committee remained unmoved, and they passed the resolution to ban all tax-exempt funding for voter registration projects by a 13–4 vote. While the Finance Committee spent the next several weeks amending the legislation, Jordan kept mobilizing opponents. In a mass letter that drew attention to the "little-noticed recommendation" with "an insidious racist thrust aimed at inhibiting emerging black political power," Jordan tried to help people see beyond the need for tax reform to the clandestine attempt to upend civil rights gains.[51] Roy Wilkins rallied NAACP chapters around this message, and sympathetic journalists wrote that the Finance Committee's revisions would leave the VEP "penniless and impotent."[52]

Jordan also dealt with concerns from his foundation supporters. While the VEP worried about the ban on voter campaigns, the Finance Committee also proposed to cap the lifespan of all foundations at forty years. Foundation executives panicked that their entire world might crash and thereafter paid less attention to registration concerns. The Council on Foundations reconvened following the Finance Committee's recommendations, and executives dreaded what might happen. Not only were executives worried about their foundations; they were also scared personally, for the tax legislation carried with it strict penalties for executives who used tax-exempt funds to sponsor political activities. Foundations could be penalized up to 100 percent of the offending grant if misappropriated funds were not returned within ninety days, and executives could be additionally liable for up to 50 percent of the grant value. Philanthropists felt overwhelmed by the complexity of the law and the threat of personal accountability, and they did not want to provoke Congress any further. As the Council on Foundations worked on a statement, Jordan pressed them to include language denouncing the proposed ban on registration support. Jordan kept pushing, and Eli Evans of the Carnegie Corporation informed him that the Council on Foundation's response would dispute the registration prohibition. "Please note it includes voter education and mentions Southern Regional Council," Evans wrote Jordan. "It wasn't easy."[53] Evans's message implied that many executives wanted to leave the issue of voter registration out in hopes of placating Congress. Their response to Congress stated that the VEP "represents a major contribution to the maintenance and improvement of the American system of democratic government."[54]

After the Senate's harsh version, the House's earlier bill began to look much sweeter. The Council on Foundations recommended that the Senate turn back to the House's provisions rather than institute an outright ban against registration drives. Jordan also came to see the House's version as the lesser of evils, and he began promoting its readoption. Senators Ralph Yarborough, a Democrat from Texas, and Hugh Scott, a Republican from Pennsylvania, drafted an amendment to accomplish that goal—to nullify the Finance Committee's proposal and return the tax legislation closer to the original House version. On December 1, they introduced what became known as the Yarborough-Scott Amendment to H.R. 13270. It included a more lenient application of the House's original ideas, including requirements that organizations receiving tax-exempt funds conduct voter campaigns in more than one state at a time, have at least three philanthropic supporters, and receive no more than 40 percent from a single source. The Senate Finance Committee's actions, Yarborough and Scott stated, "harms all Americans, [and] would destroy such universally approved organizations as the League of Women Voters Education Fund and the Voter Education Project."[55]

On December 4, the Senate adopted the Yarborough-Scott Amendment by a vote of 52–36. Calling the vote "a very significant victory," Jordan praised those senators who saw the value of nonpartisan voter registration field-work.[56] But Talmadge complained that the amendment lacked clarity concerning the meaning of nonpartisanship. In his mind, the Ku Klux Klan, John Birch Society, and Black Panther Party could all claim nonpartisanship and receive tax-exempt funds for registration projects. Talmadge also objected to the more-than-one-state requirement, citing it as much too easy to overcome. Three days after the amendment passed, Senator Paul Fannin hastily put together a counteramendment to forbid all tax-exempt registration field-work, but it failed. It appeared as though conservatives would not be able to bankrupt foundation-backed voter registration fieldwork, and the VEP's supporters celebrated a successful lobbying effort. The chairwoman of the League of Women Voters thanked Jordan: "It seems a little presumptuous for me to thank you for all you did for us—since obviously the Voter Education program of the Southern Regional Council was the really significant and critical matter at stake—but we're pleased to have benefitted, too."[57]

But Talmadge, Long, and their conservative allies had one more play. Capitalizing on their deep knowledge of congressional rules, they waited until after the Senate approved the tax bill. The legislation next went to conference committee to resolve disagreements between both chambers before going to Nixon's desk. Between December 15 and 19, Senate and House members negotiated terms and straightened out the language of H.R. 13270, and they did so behind closed doors. Before the committee met, David E. Rosenbaum of the New York Times explained the shadowy proceedings: "Their negotiations will be in private session, with neither the press, the public nor even other members of Congress allowed in the conference room, and the proceedings of the meetings will never be published."[58] During these private sessions, conservatives pushed the Yarborough-Scott Amendment terms back to the original House version—five or more states at once and no more than 25 percent from one foundation for voter campaigns. Conference committee members reversed the more generous terms of one state and 40 percent without any explanation. In his account of the conference committee, Rosenbaum wrote, "In theory the conferees argue for the provisions of the bill passed by their chamber. In practice, they have considerable latitude."[59] What took place within the conference committee will never be known, but somehow Long, Talmadge, and their allies took one last shot at foundations and voter registration projects. The day the conference committee began meetings, Talmadge wrote Jordan, signaling his resolve: "I am sorry that you and I cannot agree on this issue . . . I have always felt that voter registration drives are the very essence of politics and I do not believe that Foundation money should be used to promote a candidate or a party."[60] David F. Rock, a VEP lawyer, later wrote that the law "served as a vehicle for angry elements in Congress who regarded their interests as somehow jeopardized by Voter Registration drives."[61]

After the conference committee finalized the legislation, the House approved the Tax Reform Act of 1969 by a vote of 381–2, and the Senate did so by 71–6. Nixon signed it into law on December 30, immediately sending the VEP and foundations into chaos.[62] McGeorge Bundy circulated a memorandum among Ford Foundation trustees that the law's constraints required "reexamination of our relations to the Southern Regional Council and the League of Women Voters."[63] In Atlanta, the SRC suspended all VEP activities while staff met with lawyers to determine what to do next. On January 22, 1970, Paul Anthony and SRC lawyers met with IRS representatives seeking advice. After this meeting, the SRC decided to cut the VEP loose. Lawyers counseled that if the VEP continued to spend tax-exempt philanthropic dollars on voter registration, the entire SRC could be subject to the 25 percent rule. "The Council is not limited to the amount of income it may receive from another private foundation," wrote Anthony, "so long as that income is expended on tax-exempt activity within one year of receipt. If, however, the Council engages in voter registration campaigns . . . it is the opinion of counsel that the entire income of SRC is subject to the [25 percent] limitation."[64] Anthony and SRC leadership feared entanglement with the VEP— that if they remained conjoined, the SRC's finances would be dragged down along with the VEP. On January 31, 1970, SRC lawyers filed paperwork with the IRS to establish the Voter Education Project, Inc., a wholly separate 501(c)(3) nonprofit, tax-exempt organization.[65]

Years later, Leslie Dunbar recalled the split between the SRC and VEP as something that "did not have to be done." He blamed it on panic and the ignorance of SRC lawyers, as well as on Paul Anthony's self-interest. In the immediate aftermath of the Tax Reform Act, lawyers had not yet mastered the legislation's complexities, and the SRC's counsel advised to err on the side of caution by disassociating from voter registration activities. Dunbar also believed foundations and the IRS pressured Anthony to disconnect from the VEP to maintain their associations. "I think, at that time," remembered Dunbar, "they [SRC] may have felt that this was not legally necessary, but maybe politically necessary." Plus, Anthony and Jordan did not get along, and Dunbar believed that Anthony did not want to have to work with the VEP's next leader. "Paul had had the problem of Vernon. He could not control Vernon. Vernon was a better-known person than he, and becoming more so."[66] On February 24, 1970, VEP, Inc., filed for its own corporate charter. Three months later, the IRS approved VEP, Inc. as a 501(c)(3). Although they continued to share office space on Forsyth Street in downtown Atlanta for another year, the VEP and SRC became independent of one another, a move that ultimately weakened both.[67]

As the VEP and SRC separated, Vernon Jordan announced his resignation to lead the United Negro College Fund, and the new VEP board of directors hired John Lewis as executive director in February 1970.[68] Born on February 21, 1940, Lewis grew up on a rural farm in Pike County, Alabama. His parents had been sharecroppers, but in 1944, they purchased 110 acres for $300. Lewis spent his adolescence working on the farm alongside his nine siblings. They lived in a world of strict segregation. When he was eleven, he went with his uncle Otis on a trip to Buffalo, New York, and when he returned to Alabama, he saw racial inequality in his home county clearer than ever. He enjoyed some aspects of farm life, but he loved school and books. By reading everything he could, he learned about the world outside Pike County. He studied the *Brown v. Board of Education* decision, which inspired him to imagine Alabama as a place without segregation. In 1955, he listened to Martin Luther King Jr. preach on the radio, hearing for the first time about the social gospel. Later that year, Emmett Till was murdered. Till's death shocked Lewis, imagining that someone near his age could be killed without consequence. The next year, two days after he preached his first sermon at the age of sixteen, his great uncle Thomas Brewer, an NAACP leader in Columbus, Georgia, died after sustaining seven gunshot wounds. Black community members believed the store owner who murdered Brewer—who was never indicted—had ties to the Ku Klux Klan. These violent events, plus the bus boycott in Montgomery and Alabama's attorney general banning the NAACP, inspired Lewis to apply for a library card. He was denied, but he had his first taste of nonviolent protest. Soon after, he won acceptance to the American Baptist Theological Seminary, and he moved to Nashville, Tennessee in 1957.[69]

In Nashville, Lewis learned how to protest and fight for civil rights—skills that served him during the sit-in movement, as a Freedom Rider, as a founding member of SNCC, as chairman of SNCC for three years, and as the VEP's third executive director. As a freshman, Lewis tried to start an NAACP chapter on campus, but the president discouraged him due to the seminary's ties to the Southern Baptist Convention. The following year, he met James Lawson, a student at Vanderbilt Divinity School who led community workshops in nonviolence based on Mahatma Gandhi's philosophy that challenged British colonialism. In November 1959, he and other Nashville students began

sit-ins in downtown department stores, and after four students in Greens-
boro captured national headlines in February 1960, the Nashville movement gained momentum. Later that year, Lewis helped organize SNCC, and
the following year, he went on several Freedom Rides, endured physical attacks, and served prison time in Mississippi. As SNCC's chairman, Lewis
oversaw the expansion of the student-led organization into rural communities urging locals to register. He helped coordinate Freedom Summer in
Mississippi in 1964, and police cracked his skull on the Edmund Pettus
Bridge in Selma, Alabama on March 7, 1965. In May 1966, Stokely Carmi-
chael won a plurality of votes to become SNCC's chairman. Two months
later, Lewis left SNCC after it became clear to him that the organization's embrace of black nationalism and the ouster of its white members signaled a
turn away from its founding principles. Lewis went to work for Leslie Dunbar and the Field Foundation in New York for about a year, after which he
aided Robert F. Kennedy's presidential campaign during part of 1968. Lewis
then returned to Atlanta to head the SRC's Community Organization Project until February 1970, when he accepted the job to lead the new VEP, Inc.[70]

The VEP moved ahead with Lewis in charge, foundations surveyed the
altered landscape after the Tax Reform Act of 1969 and considered the future
of voter registration grants. The Ford Foundation, the Field Foundation, and
other philanthropies told Lewis that they remained committed to funding
the VEP, but the 25 percent provision complicated their ties. "The Foundation's commitment to you and the VEP is, if anything, stronger than ever,"
Basil Whiting, a Ford program officer, assured Lewis. But the Ford Foundation
needed to decide on new policies because of the Tax Reform Act, and Whiting wrote, "We are not sure what that will be yet but will inform you."[71] Ford
wanted to closely monitor the VEP and review its policies for funding registration campaigns. After he heard that the SRC had stopped all VEP activities in the wake of the tax legislation, Dunbar wrote Anthony that he was
"disturbed to learn that voter registration activity ceased the first of January,"
especially since 1970 was a midterm election year.[72] But Dunbar also feared
the law's implications for the Field Foundation, and he asked lawyers for clarity on tax-exempt funds used for registering voters. They recommended to
Dunbar that "as a matter of protecting itself [Field Foundation] against a possible claim of the Internal Revenue Service for liability to the tax imposed by
section 4945," it should be cautious and specific that its donations only be
used for nonpartisan activities.[73]

The 25 percent requirement compromised the VEP's finances. After the
VEP and SRC separated, both organizations worked with foundations to

move money that had originally gone to the SRC into the new VEP, Inc. This process highlighted the difficulty of raising money and balancing figures between foundations to meet the 25 percent rule. In 1968, the Ford Foundation had committed $590,000 to the VEP over three years, but "in accordance with the 'twenty-five percent rule,'" wrote Assistant Secretary William H. Nims to McGeorge Bundy, "it is recommended that the Foundation contribute only $120,000 of the amount originally allocated."[74] Dunbar alerted Lewis, "I think it is premature to specify just how we should proceed in the future."[75] The Rockefeller Brothers Fund had not donated to the VEP during 1969 "due to pending tax reform legislation," but gave $50,000 for 1970 and another $50,000 for 1971 — smaller amounts that they hoped would prompt the VEP to reach out to other potential backers.[76] By August 1970, the VEP had received nearly $131,000, but it could only speculate about how much the Carnegie Corporation, New World Foundation, Irwin-Sweeney-Miller Foundation, Aaron E. Norman Fund, and other past supporters would give. Lewis feared the VEP might have to forfeit money if the 25 percent balance could not be met. "If these arrangements . . . are not carried out," Lewis wrote Anthony, "the result will be a serious crippling of the VEP."[77]

John Lewis still believed in politics as the primary battlefield of the civil rights movement. "When I took over as the executive director of the Voter Education Project," remembered Lewis, "we felt and truly believed that we had to create a real movement to dramatize the need for people to get registered and have an opportunity to cast a vote."[78] In a VEP fund-raising letter, he wrote, "The goal of a truly representative government is still distant. If we fail to realize how incomplete this movement is now and do not attend to the remaining needs, the accomplishment thus far may turn out to be empty achievements."[79] By July 1970, the VEP had received over two hundred applications from local groups wanting support to conduct voter registration drives. VEP staff and board members met for three days in Capahosic, Virginia to discuss the future. During the retreat, they discussed strategy, programs, and how to comply with the Tax Reform Act. Along with Lewis, the new VEP staff was comprised of Thaddeus Olive as administrative assistant, Marvin Wall as research director, and Janet Shortt as administrative secretary—all holdovers from the previous VEP. Charles Rooks, Marilyn Adamson, and Patricia Madsen joined in support roles. The VEP also retained a lawyer. With enough funds to begin, the VEP tried to salvage the election year and began financing dozens of grassroots campaigns.[80]

By the end of 1970, the VEP had spent $210,513 on one hundred projects in eleven states. The Citizens Coordinating Committee of Daytona Beach,

Florida, received $1,200. The Southwest Georgia Voter Education Project in Albany earned $1,800. The San Patricio and Bee County Voter Registration Council in Texas received $1,500. These projects helped push black registration in the South to 3,357,000—an increase of 212,000 since November 1968. By the end of the year, an estimated 644 African Americans held elected positions.[81] The VEP did all of this on a tighter budget. Lewis pulled in a total of $292,017, but he had hoped for much more. By the end of 1970, seven foundations had donated to the VEP, supplemented by five religious and civic organizations giving small amounts. The Ford Foundation had promised $125,000, but based on all other giving under the new tax law's requirements, it had to reduce its contribution to $73,000—exactly 24.9985 percent of the VEP's budget to meet the new 25 percent rule.[82]

Between 1970 and 1976, the VEP sponsored at least 449 local registration campaigns across the American South.[83] The movement in Thomas County, Georgia was one. Through a VEP grant worth $700, the local NAACP launched a six-week registration campaign in May 1972. The VEP had supported a similar project in Thomas County in 1966, resulting in 1,600 new black registrants. Curtis Thomas, the director of the registration effort, wanted to recreate the enthusiasm of the 1966 drive. Recently, according to Thomas, the black community had grown indifferent toward voting, made worse by complaints that the county had taken many people off the rolls without explanation. Thomas organized volunteers to canvass the county and drive elderly people to the courthouse. He even convinced the county to appoint temporary black and white deputy registrars with the power to register people in their homes. VEP funds allowed him to print flyers, organize car pools, and feed his volunteers. He described one ninety-year-old woman who lived twenty miles from the courthouse: "She might come into town on Saturday to shop, but the courthouse was closed and nobody had encouraged her to go register. So she was happy that she could register. We found a lot of 65 and 70-year-olds who were just waiting for us to come along."[84] The NAACP also boycotted local businesses during the campaign to push for more African Americans to be hired. Members printed bumper stickers that read, "Save Your Bucks, Use Your Ballot—Register and Vote."[85] John Lewis, Hosea Williams, and Shirley Chisholm visited and spoke at mass rallies. After six weeks, 1,300 had registered. Lenzie Adams, a resident of Pavo, described how black voting power had pushed elected officials to pave roads, put in sewers, and improve the lives of Thomas County's African American citizens: "We got these streets, street lights, and paved roads by voting—it was our vote. This is what you have to look at—how all these things came about."[86]

To keep assisting places like Thomas County, Lewis believed he needed to expand the VEP's ability to raise its own capital. But by devoting more time and energy to fund-raising, the VEP became less efficient. The VEP had always relied on philanthropic support alone, enabling it to concentrate on moving money quickly into the hands of activists. To meet the demand, Lewis hired more staff and created a fund-raising division within the VEP. Between 1970 and early 1977 when Lewis resigned, the VEP developed several fund-raising programs, but each one siphoned away employee energy and resources that could have gone directly to grassroots organizers if philanthropic support had been higher.

During the 1970s, the VEP coordinated direct mail campaigns, and unlike such conservatives as Jesse Helms, who mastered the strategy, the VEP spent more than it earned. In October 1970, Lewis hired Shirley Cooks to coordinate the VEP's direct mail. In April 1971, she sent out around fifteen thousand letters costing $2,250, and by June, the VEP had taken in $11,000 from about one thousand people donating in small sums. Within each envelope, Cooks included a letter and brochure about the VEP. In the fall, Lewis decided to professionalize fund-raising and hired Grizzard Advertising to handle direct mail. Grizzard upped the VEP's mailing capacity into the hundreds of thousands, and over the next year, the VEP sent color brochures and letters to people across the United States. A fund-raising letter signed by a diverse cast of supporters, including Julian Bond, Fannie Lou Hamer, Senators Edward Kennedy and Jacob Javits, Governors Winthrop Rockefeller and John West, the president of Duke University and former governor Terry Sanford, and Sheriff John Hulett of Lowndes County, Alabama informed readers that "foundation support for VEP has been restricted by the 1969 Tax Reform Act" and that the VEP had been unable to fund over fifty applications in 1971.[87] By June 1972, Grizzard's strategy had netted the VEP over $44,000, but it had cost the VEP $58,460.64 to hire the firm. To make matters worse, another agency that Lewis hired to expand its mailing list had computer problems, and for over a year, the VEP's contact list sat inaccessible. In late 1973, Lewis contracted another advertising firm in New York to handle direct mail, but by the following summer, less than 1 percent of people had responded, giving less than $16,000 after the VEP had paid nearly $12,000 to the firm. The year 1977 was worst of all—$87,000 spent while netting $31,000. In seven years, the VEP lost more than it made on direct mail.[88]

To make up for the philanthropic deficit after the Tax Reform Act of 1969, the VEP courted potential donors through benefit dinners and by appealing to corporations, but neither initiative proved lucrative. The VEP hosted a benefit dinner in 1974 with Senator Edward Kennedy as the featured speaker. Over eight hundred people attended and spent $50 per plate, hearing Kennedy praise black political participation with "the Voting Rights Act [acting] as their protector and the Voter Education Project as their shepherd."[89] The VEP invited union officials and corporate executives to the dinner, including representatives from the United Auto Workers, the AFL-CIO, Coca-Cola, and Delta Airlines. Lewis remained hopeful that some of these unions and businesses would fund the VEP, but long-term support remained negligible. The VEP hosted two more benefit dinners in 1975 and 1976 with speakers Senator Jacob Javits and Governor Jimmy Carter. While the events generated some immediate funds, including around $50,000 from the Carter dinner, they did not produce long-term solutions.[90]

Although financially volatile, the VEP spent high-dollar amounts on print, radio, and television advertisements. Under Vernon Jordan, the VEP pushed citizenship education as a prerequisite for greater African American political power, and Lewis believed that in addition to grassroots investment, popular media could reach millions more about the power of the ballot. The idea gained a stronger foothold within the VEP after ratification of the Twenty-Sixth Amendment on July 1, 1971, lowering the voting age to eighteen nationwide.[91] With millions of young people now eligible to vote, Lewis wanted to make sure African American youth knew what to do. Lewis suspended the newsletter *VEP News*, except for the occasional update, and instead concentrated on mass appeals to the public. Lewis hired the Atlanta artist Herman "Kofi" Bailey to create an attention-grabbing poster. Bailey came up with "Hands That Pick Cotton Now Can Pick Our Elected Officials," illustrating one black hand picking cotton and another dropping a ballot into a box. Lewis recalled, "10,000 copies were made and distributed all through the South, where they wound up on the walls of beauty parlors and barber shops, schools and churches."[92] In 1972, the VEP hired characters from such television series as *All in the Family*, *Maude*, and *Chico and the Man* for commercials and radio spots encouraging people to register and vote. Over 150 television stations aired the commercials. The VEP spent another $54,000 on a single flyer: an image of Muhammad Ali ready to strike, reading, "It's your fight. Vote. It's the greatest equalizer."[93] The VEP recognized that voter registration "sometimes seems mundane and non-glamorous," and it drew on popular culture to resonate with the public.[94]

To energize southern communities, Lewis went on dozens of voter mobilization tours with his friend Julian Bond. Their first tour came in June 1971 to Mississippi, where they made thirty-nine stops in twenty-five counties in a little over a week. Lewis and Bond spoke at mass rallies in churches, schools, colleges, and out in the open, and for every community visited, their message included "that they were not alone in their struggle. We did not tell them who to vote for or what political party to join, but simply that they could begin to control their own destiny by registering to vote."[95] VEP staff visited all eleven southern states in 1971 and 1972, and they continued making trips throughout Lewis's tenure to stimulate black voting power. Lewis intended these tours to inspire and link African Americans together across counties and states—to impart confidence that their vote had the potential to change the political and racial order of their hometowns. Whites no longer carried out mass violence against African Americans trying to register, but after another tour of Mississippi in 1975, Lewis concluded that intimidation was still a reality in the South: "At several of the meetings and rallies in Mississippi we heard people saying the boss man told them they didn't need to vote, they didn't need to register. People on the farms, the plantations are afraid to come in to register."[96]

Alongside registration projects, the VEP spent money to support black elected officials, whose number across the South had risen to 873 in 1972.[97] As an extension of the Southwide Conference in December 1968, the VEP established five service centers for local officials on historically black college campuses—Tougaloo College, Clark College, Southern University, Talladega College, and Miles College. The VEP designed these centers to be in-state resource hubs "on the procedures, duties, and responsibilities of their positions" and "libraries of knowledge for helping officials take advantage of federal programs."[98] These centers hosted their own conferences, worked with state leaders, and brought political scientists in academia together with grassroots politicians. The Carnegie Corporation donated $200,000 in 1969 for the service centers—before the new tax law went into effect—and the Ford and Aaron E. Norman Foundations later contributed. For a brief time, these service centers provided crucial assistance for African American elected leaders in state politics where their presence unsettled and angered long-serving white Democrats.[99]

At the Tougaloo College service center, Taunya Banks became a force within Mississippi politics. A recent law school graduate of Howard University, Banks served as the director of the center, where she counseled black politicians, hosted workshops, wrote political manuals, and contacted the DOJ when whites discriminated against black candidates and officials. She learned that often, after black candidates won elections over white incumbents, officials "literally walked out of the office with all of their staff and

[took] all of the records, and there wasn't the orderly transition that you normally have when offices change."[100] The center provided a home base while Banks organized over the phone and traveled the state to advise black elected officials. Banks worked with officials in Bolton, Mound Bayou, and Edwards to make sure aldermen were seated without resistance. She counseled Geneva Collins from Claiborne County, who served as the state's only African American chancery clerk. Banks stayed informed about changes to election laws, and she contacted African Americans when new legislation affected their offices. Although Banks effectively led the Tougaloo College center until she resigned in mid-1970, the others struggled, and the VEP terminated the program in mid-1972 amid financial challenges.[101]

Since its beginning in 1962, the VEP had tried forging relationships with Latino voters to expand minority voting power, but this strategy gained new momentum under John Lewis. During Vernon Jordan's tenure, the VEP began reaching out to Chicano activists about potential registration projects in the Southwest. Several visited the VEP's Atlanta headquarters to glean ideas about starting a Latino-focused VEP, including Willie Velásquez. A Mexican-American political activist, Velásquez cofounded *La Raza Unida* in Texas but left after he became convinced that an independent, ethnically singular party would win few electoral contests. Soon after taking over the new VEP, Lewis began working with Velásquez, and in May 1974, the Southwest Voter Registration Education Project (SVREP) received its charter and set up headquarters in San Antonio. Velásquez built up the Latino vote in Texas, New Mexico, Arizona, Colorado, Utah, Nevada, and California. The SVREP received funding from several donors with ties to the VEP, including the Field Foundation, Rockefeller Brothers Fund, and the United Auto Workers. In 1976 alone, the group sponsored almost fifty projects aimed at registering Latinos. "While many Americans are celebrating the Bicentennial Anniversary of their participation in American government," Velásquez said in a joint statement with the VEP, "we are still working so that Blacks, Spanish-Speaking, and Native Americans can have a voice and full participation in the social, political, and economic arenas."[102] That year, the SVREP helped register 161,500 Latinos across the Southwest. Over the next decade, the SVREP organized hundreds of registration campaigns, conducted research, published reports, and filed dozens of lawsuits challenging racial redistricting. "It's similar to what happened in the South with blacks," Velásquez told the *Washington Post* in 1977. "The same thing is happening with Latinos except we're a couple of years behind."[103]

As the VEP evolved under Lewis, its finances remained precarious. The reality after the Tax Reform Act of 1969 was most evident through the VEP's partnership with the Ford Foundation. At a May 1971 meeting with VEP staff, Bryant George of the Ford Foundation said, "The IRS watches the Foundation very closely and therefore VEP in turn will have to be monitored to assure the Foundation that it is adhering to the law."[104] Ford promised a new hands-on approach if the VEP wanted to continue receiving major grants, including Ford staff visits to local projects, observing VEP staff in the office, reviewing printed materials to ensure nonpartisanship, and monitoring the VEP's overall effectiveness. One event threatened to rupture the relationship. In April 1974, Lewis went on a voter mobilization tour in Alabama with Julian Bond and Hosea Williams during the gubernatorial race, where the incumbent, George Wallace, had drawn unprecedented support—even from segments of the black community. A *New York Times* reporter covered the story, writing that Lewis, Bond, and Williams "told black Alabamians in half a dozen cities and towns that a vote for George Wallace was a traitorous step backward."[105] The story reached Ford Foundation executives, and they launched a full-scale investigation of the tour to see if the VEP had violated its grant conditions by engaging in partisan politics. Ford representatives brought VEP staff into the foundation's New York headquarters to review grant policies. Lewis maintained that he had done nothing wrong and that the journalist has misinterpreted several details. He stood up for his actions, saying that many African Americans were confused about the election after several black mayors, including Tuskegee's Johnnie Ford, endorsed the former segregationist when he appealed to black communities as a changed man. Ford's lead investigator determined "certain liberties may have been taken which, in light of the highly sensitive status of VEP, were both unfortunate and, possibly, inappropriate," but recommended no further action beyond a stern reproach.[106]

The VEP continued to receive funding from a handful of other foundations, but balancing figures for the 25 percent rule proved difficult, compounded by the economic recession that weighed on the United States during the 1970s. Between 1971 and 1973, the VEP kept increasing its budget, but it stretched resources thin as it expanded programs. By 1974, the money started drying up. "The VEP's entire range of financial supporters, from individual donors to foundations, is suffering from the recession," Lewis wrote Dunbar.[107] Stock values dropped, and since foundations tied their wealth to markets, they scaled back grants. The Ford Foundation alone lost around one billion dollars in total assets in 1974. The VEP felt these reverberations.

Lewis laid off five staff members in 1974 after a year plagued by money shortages. Speaking at the Butler Street YMCA in Atlanta, Lewis told the crowd, "the current economic recession threatens to wipe out the social and political gains" of the civil rights revolution.[108] Paul West, a reporter with the *Atlanta Constitution*, followed up on the story and interviewed foundation executives who sounded the alarm about how much they would be able to give to civil rights groups. "Hard times may do more damage to the civil rights movement in one year than resistance by white supremacists did in twenty," West concluded.[109]

Amid financial trouble, Lewis testified before Congress in the spring of 1975 to advocate for congressional renewal of the Voting Rights Act. He listed the benefits of the legislation, but he also took the opportunity to blast the Tax Reform Act of 1969 for impeding the work of the VEP. "The Congress," Lewis explained to House members, "with one hand, removed some of the barriers to the ballot; four years later, it turned around and, with its other hand, placed a serious restriction on private financial support to achieve the franchise."[110] Lewis could not separate the two pieces of legislation, for one curtailed the other and few seemed to know or care. He blamed the Tax Reform Act for limiting the VEP, forcing him to lay off staff members and reduce assistance to communities trying to organize registration campaigns.[111] Meanwhile, conservatives found ways around the Voting Rights Act. "Every conceivable tactic has been used by the southern states to violate, oppose, circumvent, and ignore both the letter and spirit of the Voting Rights Act," Lewis told the Senate Judiciary Committee.[112] For example, Mississippi created a voter application form that required registrants to write down license plate numbers, list crimes, record all properties, and indicate where they worked and went to church. If the federal government would not do anything about these disfranchisement tactics, Lewis explained, the VEP would try, but the tax law impeded its reach. In August, Congress extended the Voting Rights Act to 1982 but did not address Lewis's concerns about the Tax Reform Act of 1969.[113]

John Lewis resigned in January 1977 to run for Congress, and the VEP never regained its footing. The next year, Lewis's successor, Vivian Malone Jones, the first African American graduate from the University of Alabama, mailed a fund-raising letter stating that "our cash flow has been depleted."[114] By 1979, the VEP went in debt by $55,000 and ceased operations. In 1982, Geraldine Thompson, a former staff member in Atlanta's mayoral office and NAACP leader, took over the VEP, and while she led a brief renaissance of VEP activities, a Field Foundation study uncovered numerous operational and financial discrepancies. The report discovered no actual budget, no work plans for employees, no concrete goals, no research protocols, and almost nothing in the VEP's bank account. The following year, the *Atlanta Constitution* obtained a copy and published a story about the VEP's financial problems, wrecking its reputation. Peter Scott, the journalist who broke the story, wrote, "VEP does not appear to have any systematic strategies or programs to increase voter registration/education among minorities."[115] Thompson and the entire VEP staff soon left. A Ford Foundation report blamed poor leadership, along with unrealistic budget aims and unfulfilled promises to local groups that had requested funds. The VEP also "suffered severe cash flow problems," the Ford report's author, Tonya Lewis, wrote. "Because of matching requirements and the uncertainty in arrival of funds, VEP could not accurately predict the amount of money it would have at any given moment."[116]

VEP barely held on through the early 1990s. Clarence D. Coleman, a retired educator and former staff member of the SRC, took over as the VEP's executive director and only employee. "I was determined that this organization not be allowed to just wither away and die," he told a reporter at the VEP's twenty-five-year anniversary celebration in 1987.[117] But by then, the VEP held debts over $160,000. The Ford Foundation provided some relief, and Coleman worked without a salary for most of his tenure. He moved the VEP to Atlanta University in 1987, where faculty members in political science provided some assistance. In 1990, Ed Brown became the VEP's final executive director. He obtained the VEP's last philanthropic grant: $65,000 from the Ford Foundation for the "orderly closing down of the organization and disposition of its records" to Atlanta University's archive.[118]

Conservatives used the Tax Reform Act of 1969 as a cover to undermine the growing strength of the black southern vote. Careful to avoid incriminatory statements about their intentions, conservatives went after the money supply. Senators tried to sink the VEP but, in the face of the VEP's lobbying campaign, settled for the 25 percent rule and five-state provision. The VEP breathed a sigh of relief at the time, but challenges multiplied. The VEP and the SRC separated, foundations became cautious, and the VEP stretched its resources thin as it fund-raised on its own. These changes distracted the VEP from what it had done best between 1962 and 1964 and again from 1966 to 1969—empower communities with resources to register, vote, and compete for political power. Although the VEP carried on for another two decades, the tax overhaul destabilized this vital, behind-the-scenes civil rights agency. Without a robust VEP, black communities across the American South lost a key ally in the fight for black poll power.

Epilogue

The VEP accomplished so much during its brief life-span. Although they have received little fanfare, Wiley Branton, Vernon Jordan, Leslie Dunbar, Stephen Currier, Alice Alston, John Lewis, Taunya Banks, and many others spurred on a political revolution—the empowering of the southern African American vote at the end of the Jim Crow era. They did so outside the spotlight and with the unglamorous tools of grant applications, monetary checks, and research reports. The VEP linked together not only the five major civil rights groups but scores of local grassroots organizations—all around the central goals of registering, voting, and increasing black political power. Although far from perfect, the VEP helped fulfill the promise of the Fifteenth Amendment. Without the VEP, the southern civil rights movement would have lacked more than just money—it would have been without its primary support.

The VEP bound the civil rights struggle together by uniting scores of separate movements together around the united goal of voting rights. Their opponent, however, was not the absence of federal voter protections but white supremacy itself, a value system that considers people of color to be lesser beings, undeserving of human rights, and appropriate targets of violence. The VEP believed in a simple yet difficult-to-achieve strategy to fight back—registration and voting, which the SRC correctly labeled "hard, grubby, tiring, unspectacular, frequently discouraging" in 1961.[1] Registration campaigns never came easy, but the VEP helped lift the burden, kept them going, and chipped away at black disfranchisement. The VEP converted grassroots power into southwide motion.

The VEP provided what the historian J. Morgan Kousser called "institutional stability," serving as "a prerequisite for minority success." White southerners, who had larger numbers and deeper roots of political power, could "accept fluctuations in political outcomes and rules. [But] smaller, more isolated minorities . . . need protective institutions, which cannot rapidly be rebuilt if they are destroyed."[2] In weakening the VEP through the Tax Reform Act of 1969, conservatives sabotaged the civil rights movement, and by veiling their intentions through the guise of tax reform, conservatives shielded themselves from charges of partisanship. Conservatives use similar tactics today, and the deck remains stacked against African Americans. Through racial gerrymandering, voter identification cards, purges, reduced polling places, scaled-back early voting, the disfranchisement of ex-convicts and the incarcerated, the dissemination of conspiracy theories, violence, intimidation, the right wing's hollow outrage over voter fraud, and the Supreme Court's shredding of the Voting Rights Act in 2013, conservatives have continued the assault on black political power in the South and across the United States. During an oral history interview in 2013, Vernon Jordan lamented the VEP's absence and what remains at stake: "The VEP should be alive and well right now. It never should have gone the way it did. It faded, and it never should have. And it faded in part on the theory that our work was done. It is very clear now that our work is not done."[3]

Acknowledgments

I want to start by thanking my family. My parents, Terry and Phyllis Faulkenbury, encouraged my interest in history from a young age, and they have always been there for me. The same goes for my grandparents, Pat and Lester Shelton. My in-laws, Tony and Loretta Lippold, and my sisters-in-law, Laken, Shelby, and Sydney, welcomed me into the family. I'm most grateful to my wife, Alex, and daughter, Clara. For some reason I still haven't figured out, Alex signed up for a life with me. Clara came along at the worst possible time for any graduate student, right in the middle of preparing for comprehensive exams. But looking back, I wouldn't have it any other way. I love those two more than words can express.

I learned how to be a historian as an MA student in the History Department at the University of North Carolina at Charlotte. Even though I had no idea what I was doing half the time, professors mentored me. Thanks especially to David Goldfield, John David Smith, Sonya Ramsey, Gregory Mixon, Christopher Cameron, Karen Cox, Jürgen Buchenau, Christine Haynes, and Mark Wilson. Thanks also to the staff of the J. Murrey Atkins Special Collections Unit, especially Katie McCormick, who gave me my first academic job and introduced me to studying the civil rights movement inside an archive.

One of the happiest moments of my professional career came when I received an email telling me that I had moved off the waiting list and had been accepted into the PhD program in history at the University of North Carolina at Chapel Hill. Jim Leloudis, my adviser, took a chance on me, and I owe him much for guiding my ideas, research, and writing. I'm also grateful to the rest of my committee who challenged me to do justice to the VEP's story: Bob Korstad, Benjamin Waterhouse, William Sturkey, Jerma Jackson, and Fitz Brundage. I also received ideas and support from Jacquelyn Dowd Hall, Kathryn Burns, Claude Clegg, Kathleen DuVal, Bill Ferris, Malinda Maynor Lowery, John Sweet, Katherine Turk, Harry Watson, Zaragosa Vargas, Patrick Horn, Kenneth Janken, and Joy Mann Jones. In Chapel Hill, I found a home inside the Southern Oral History Program and the Center for the Study of the American South. Working for the SOHP gave me a love of oral history and public history, and I especially thank Rachel Seidman for letting me in to the club. Thanks to fellow writing group members Jessica Auer, Robert Richard, Samuel Finesurry, Joshua Tait, Jeanine Navarrete, and Benjamin Waterhouse for not ending our friendship after I once circulated a particularly long dissertation chapter. I stayed sensible thanks to fellow graduate students and friends, especially Robert Colby, Robert Shapard, Ansev Demirhan, and Neil Floetke.

Another happy moment came when I took a phone call from Randi Storch offering me a position at SUNY Cortland. Since starting in fall 2016, I've felt welcomed and part of an innovative history department in central New York. Thanks to Randi Storch, Brett

Troyan, Girish Bhat, Scott Moranda, Laura Gathagan, Kevin Sheets, Amy Schutt, Judy Van Buskirk, Gigi Peterson, Luo Xu, Benjamin de Lee, Bekeh Ukelina, Celeste Mc-Namara, and Gilda Votra for making Old Main such an enjoyable place to be. I'm also thankful to my students, who constantly require me to explain why understanding history matters.

As I researched, I received assistance from those who also believe the VEP's story matters. Soon after moving to Chapel Hill, I met Steven Lawson, a historian whose work has been instrumental to my own. We shook hands, and he handed me a brief-case full of photocopied sources related to the VEP from his own research decades earlier. His generosity set me on my way. I benefitted from the kindness of Andrea Currier, daughter of Stephen and Audrey Currier, who allowed me access into her private family archive. Thanks also to Jamie Duffy, who curated the Currier's collection and assisted me. I was fortunate to meet Leslie W. Dunbar before he passed away, and I'll always remember his pleasure discussing part of his life's work. Thanks to his son, Tony Dunbar, for arranging our meeting. I'm indebted to John Lewis, Vernon E. Jordan Jr., Hodding Carter III, Taunya Banks, and the late Julian Bond for allowing me to interview them about the VEP. At conferences and through informal conversations, I received feedback and encouragement from Eric Abrahamson, Katherine Mellen Charron, Brandon Winford, Hasan Kwame Jeffries, Gavin Wright, Herbert Haines, Emilye Crosby, Lawrence Glickman, Charles McKinney, Robert Greene II, Wesley Hogan, and Louis Ray.

I received financial support from the Archives Research Center of the Robert W. Woodruff Library at Atlanta University Center, the John F. Kennedy Presidential Library, the Dolph Briscoe Center for American History of the University of Texas at Austin, the Rockefeller Archive Center, the History Department at UNC Chapel Hill, the Center for the Study of the American South, the Southern Oral History Program, and the Institute for African American Research, as well as from the Haines Fund, President Erik Bitterbaum, and the History Department at SUNY Cortland. Without their assistance, I could not have completed this project. In addition to those at institutions that provided funding, I want to thank the librarians and archivists at the Stuart A. Rose Manuscript, Archives, and Rare Book Library at Emory University, the Martin Luther King Jr. Center for Nonviolent Social Change, the Boston University Howard Gotlieb Archival Research Center, the Harvard Law School Historical and Special Collections, the Wisconsin Historical Society, and the Moorland-Spingarn Research Center at Howard University, as well as those at the Southern Historical Collection and Davis Library at UNC Chapel Hill. And thanks to the *Southern Historian* journal for granting permission to reuse parts of my 2015 article in chapter 4.

It has been a privilege to work with everyone at UNC Press. Thanks especially to my editor, Brandon Proia, who first saw my project's potential when I was still years away from defending my dissertation. His work and attention to detail motivated me to keep pace. And thanks to the series editors of Justice, Power, and Politics, Heather Ann Thompson and Rhonda Y. Williams, and to two anonymous reviewers whose insights strengthened this book.

In a single book, there was no way I could write about every one of the hundreds of voter registration campaigns that the VEP backed. But I didn't want to leave them out, either. Thanks to R. J. Ramey and AUUT Studio, whose creativity and technical expertise made this project possible: anyone with an internet connection can explore each VEP-backed campaign between 1962 and 1970 through our digital map project. This map tells a story that I couldn't with words alone — namely, about the scale of the VEP and its impact on so many local communities across the Old Confederacy. My hope is that students and teachers alike will find this public history project valuable and that many more historians and community members will research these individual movements in greater detail. My deepest thanks to R. J. Ramey for all the help.

Lastly, I want to acknowledge the women and men who worked for the VEP or whose local movement received a VEP grant. I had the comparatively easy role of writing about their history, while they risked their lives to make democracy real. Never miss an opportunity to cast a ballot. Vote!

Notes

Introduction

1. Randolph T. Blackwell to Wiley A. Branton, February 4, 1964, Reel 176, Microfilm Collection of the Southern Regional Council Papers, 1944–1968 (Ann Arbor, MI: University Microfilms International, 1983) (hereinafter SRC Papers).

2. Notice, Orangeburg Office on Voter Registration, n.d., Reel 181, SRC Papers (emphasis in original).

3. James W. McPherson, Report from Orangeburg Area, VEP Registration Program for the Second Congressional District of South Carolina, n.d., Reel 181, SRC Papers. On the civil rights movement in Orangeburg and across South Carolina, see Peter F. Lau, *Democracy Rising: South Carolina and the Fight for Black Equality since 1865* (Lexington: University Press of Kentucky, 2006); and Winfred B. Moore Jr. and Orville Vernon Burton, eds., *Toward the Meeting of the Waters: Currents in the Civil Rights Movement of South Carolina during the Twentieth Century* (Columbia: University of South Carolina Press, 2008).

4. VEP Policy and Procedure Manual, Reel 176, SRC Papers.

5. Dr. C. H. Thomas Jr. to the Voter Education Project, Attn. Wiley Branton, July 17, 1963, Reel 181, SRC Papers; and Wiley Branton to Dr. C. H. Thomas Jr., August 19, 1963, Reel 181, SRC Papers.

6. McPherson, Report from Orangeburg Area (emphasis in original).

7. VEP Orangeburg Report, October 18, 1963, Reel 181, SRC Papers.

8. VEP Orangeburg Report, November 14, 1963, Reel 181, SRC Papers.

9. Jean Levine to Wiley Branton, Re: "Final Accounting on VEP 3-20," November 24, 1964, Reel 181, SRC Papers.

10. Randolph Blackwell to Wiley Branton, October 16, 1963, Reel 176, SRC Papers.

11. John Due and Joe Tucker to Wiley Branton, August 10–12, 1964, Reel 176, SRC Papers.

12. McPherson, Report from Orangeburg Area; and "Negro Voter Group Opens Office; Hundreds Register," *The State* (Columbia, SC), August 16, 1964, Reel 181, SRC Papers.

13. McPherson, Report from Orangeburg Area.

14. VEP Financial Statement, January 1962–May 1, 1965, Reel 173, SRC Papers; Annual Report of the Executive Director of the Southern Regional Council, A Review of Program Activities during 1964, April 1965, Box 12, Folder 15, Leslie W. Dunbar Papers, Stuart A. Rose Manuscript, Archives, and Rare Book Library, Emory University (hereinafter Dunbar Papers); and Pat Watters and Reese Cleghorn, *Climbing Jacob's Ladder: The Arrival of Negroes in Southern Politics* (New York: Harcourt, Brace and World, 1967), 26–27.

15. Interview with Wiley Austin Branton by Steven Lawson, October 21, 1970, Columbia Center for Oral History.

16. Maurice Waite, ed., *Pocket Oxford English Dictionary*, 11th ed. (Oxford: Oxford University Press, 2013), 296.

17. Watters and Cleghorn, *Climbing Jacob's Ladder*, 44–50; Steven F. Lawson, *Black Ballots: Voting Rights in the South, 1944–1969* (New York: Columbia University Press, 1976), 260–66; William Jefferson Hinson Jr., "A History of the Voter Education Project, 1962–1975" (senior thesis, Emory University, 1977); "The Voter Education Project: A Concise History, 1962–1979," Box 34, Folder 14, Printed and Published Materials, VEP Organizational Papers, Archives Research Center, Robert W. Woodruff Library, Atlanta University Center (hereinafter VEP Papers); and Judith Kilpatrick, *There When We Needed Him: Wiley Austin Branton, Civil Rights Warrior* (Fayetteville: University of Arkansas Press, 2007), 97–108. Vernon Jordan and John Lewis wrote memoirs detailing accounts of the VEP. See John Lewis with Michael D'Orso, *Walking with the Wind: A Memoir of the Movement* (New York: Simon and Schuster, 1998), 413–20; and Vernon E. Jordan Jr. with Annette Gordon-Reed, *Vernon Can Read! A Memoir* (New York: PublicAffairs, 2001), 166–204.

18. Arthur M. Schlesinger Jr., *A Thousand Days: John F. Kennedy in the White House* (Boston: Houghton Mifflin, 1965), 935; Carl M. Brauer, *John F. Kennedy and the Second Reconstruction* (New York: Columbia University Press, 1977), 112–16; David J. Garrow, *Bearing the Cross: Martin Luther King Jr. and the Southern Christian Leadership Conference* (New York: William Morrow, 1986), 161–62; Taylor Branch, *Parting the Waters: America in the King Years, 1954–1963* (New York: Simon and Schuster, 1988), 477–82; Mark Stern, *Calculating Visions: Kennedy, Johnson, and Civil Rights* (New Brunswick, NJ: Rutgers University Press, 1992), 63–66; Nick Bryant, *The Bystander: John F. Kennedy and the Struggle for Black Equality* (New York: Basic Books, 2006), 283–86; David C. Carter, *The Music Has Gone Out of the Movement: Civil Rights and the Johnson Administration, 1965–1968* (Chapel Hill: University of North Carolina Press, 2009), 46; and Françoise N. Hamlin, *Crossroads at Clarksdale: The Black Freedom Struggle in the Mississippi Delta after World War II* (Chapel Hill: University of North Carolina Press, 2012), 104.

19. For a selection of local studies that credit the VEP, see John Dittmer, *Local People: The Struggle for Rights in Mississippi* (Urbana: University of Illinois Press, 1994), 119–20, 147–48; Charles M. Payne, *I've Got the Light of Freedom: The Organizing Tradition and the Mississippi Freedom Struggle* (Berkeley: University of California Press, 1995, 2007), 108–9, 141–72; Adam Fairclough, *Race and Democracy: The Civil Rights Struggle in Louisiana, 1915–1972* (Athens: University of Georgia Press, 1995); 294–95, 302–17; and J. Todd Moye, *Let the People Decide: Black Freedom and White Resistance Movements in Sunflower County, Mississippi, 1945–1986* (Chapel Hill: University of North Carolina Press, 2004), 103–14. For a selection of southern and national perspectives that take the VEP into account, see August Meier and Elliot Rudwick, *CORE: A Study in the Civil Rights Movement, 1942–1968* (New York: Oxford University Press, 1973), 172–81; Harvard Sitkoff, *The Struggle for Black Equality* (New York: Hill and Wang, 1981, 1993, 2008), 106–11; Garrow, *Bearing the Cross*, 161–63; Branch, *Parting the Waters*, 573–79; Clayborne Carson, *In Struggle: SNCC and the Black Awakening of the 1960s* (Cambridge, MA: Harvard University Press, 1981, 1995), 70, 78, 97; Adam Fairclough, *To Redeem the Soul of America:*

The Southern Christian Leadership Conference and Martin Luther King Jr. (Athens: University of Georgia Press, 1987), 76–77, 82–83, 95–96; Timothy J. Minchin and John A. Salmond, *After the Dream: Black and White Southerners since 1965* (Lexington: University Press of Kentucky, 2011), 10, 70–71; and Ari Berman, *Give Us the Ballot: The Modern Struggle for Voting Rights in America* (New York: Picador, 2015), 100–105.

20. On the debate between the top-down and bottom-up perspectives, or the "View from the Nation" versus the "View from the Trenches," see Steven F. Lawson and Charles Payne, *Debating the Civil Rights Movement, 1945–1968* (Lanham, MD: Rowman and Littlefield, 1998, 2006); and Emilye Crosby, "Introduction: The Politics of Writing and Teaching Movement History," in *Civil Rights History from the Ground Up: Local Struggles, a National Movement*, ed. Emilye Crosby, 1–39 (Athens: University of Georgia Press, 2011). On nonviolence and self-defense, see Timothy B. Tyson, *Radio Free Dixie: Robert F. Williams and the Roots of Black Power* (Chapel Hill: University of North Carolina Press, 1999); Lance Hill, *The Deacons for Defense: Armed Resistance and the Civil Rights Movement* (Chapel Hill: University of North Carolina Press, 2004); Akinyele Omowale Umoja, *We Will Shoot Back: Armed Resistance in the Mississippi Freedom Movement* (New York: New York University Press, 2013); and Charles E. Cobb Jr., *This Nonviolent Stuff'll Get You Killed: How Guns Made the Civil Rights Movement Possible* (New York: Basic Books, 2014). On black power periodization debates, see Sundiata Keita Cha-Jua and Clarence Lang, "The 'Long Movement' as Vampire: Temporal and Spatial Fallacies in Recent Black Freedom Studies," *Journal of African American History* 92, no. 2 (Spring 2007), 266–68; and Peniel E. Joseph, "The Black Power Movement: A State of the Field," *Journal of American History* 96, no. 3 (December 2009): 751–76. On the long civil rights movement, see Jacquelyn Dowd Hall, "The Long Civil Rights Movement and the Political Uses of the Past," *Journal of American History* 91, no. 4 (March 2005): 1233–63.

21. Charles W. Eagles, "Toward New Histories of the Civil Rights Era," *Journal of Southern History* 66, no. 4 (November 2000), 833.

22. On philanthropy and the civil rights movement, see David J. Garrow, "Philanthropy and the Civil Rights Movement," working paper for the Center for the Study of Philanthropy, The Graduate Center at the City University of New York, October 1987; Claude A. Clegg III, "Philanthropy, the Civil Rights Movement, and the Politics of Racial Reform," in *Charity, Philanthropy, and Civility in American History*, ed. Lawrence J. Friedman and Mark D. McGarvie, 341–62 (New York: Cambridge University Press, 2003); Olivier Zunz, *Philanthropy in America: A History* (Princeton, NJ: Princeton University Press, 2012), 201–31; and Sean Dobson, "Freedom Funders: Philanthropy and the Civil Rights Movement, 1955–1965," commissioned by the National Committee for Responsive Philanthropy, June 2014. On the role of philanthropy, particularly the Ford Foundation, on the black power movement, see Alice O'Connor, "The Ford Foundation and Philanthropic Activism in the 1960s," in *Philanthropic Foundations: New Scholarship, New Possibilities*, ed. Ellen Condliffe Lagemann, 169–94 (Bloomington: Indiana University Press, 1999); and Karen Ferguson, *Top Down: The Ford Foundation, Black Power, and the Reinvention of Racial Liberalism* (Philadelphia: University of Pennsylvania Press, 2013). On the economics of segregation and the civil rights movement, see Gavin Wright, *Sharing the Prize: The Economics of the Civil Rights Revolution in the American South* (Cambridge, MA: Belknap Press of Harvard University Press, 2013).

23. On conservative resistance to the civil rights movement before and after 1965, see Dan T. Carter, *The Politics of Rage: George Wallace, the Origins of the New Conservatism, and the Transformation of American Politics* (New York: Simon and Schuster, 1995); J. Morgan Kousser, *Colorblind Injustice: Minority Voting Rights and the Undoing of the Second Reconstruction* (Chapel Hill: University of North Carolina Press, 1999); Kevin Kruse, *White Flight: Atlanta and the Making of Modern Conservatism* (Princeton, NJ: Princeton University Press, 2005); Matthew D. Lassiter, *The Silent Majority: Suburban Politics in the Sunbelt South* (Princeton, NJ: Princeton University Press, 2006); Jason Sokol, *There Goes My Everything: White Southerners in the Age of Civil Rights, 1945-1975* (New York: Alfred A. Knopf, 2006); Joseph Crespino, *In Search of Another Country: Mississippi and the Conservative Counterrevolution* (Princeton, NJ: Princeton University Press, 2007); Keith M. Finley, *Delaying the Dream: Southern Senators and the Fight against Civil Rights, 1938-1965* (Baton Rouge: Louisiana State University Press, 2008); and Jason Morgan Ward, *Defending White Democracy: The Making of a Segregationist Movement and the Remaking of Racial Politics, 1936-1965* (Chapel Hill: University of North Carolina Press, 2011). See also Kim Phillips-Fein, "Conservatism: A State of the Field," *Journal of American History* 98, no. 3 (December 2011): 723–43.

24. Quoted in Stanley Nelson, *Devils Walking: Klan Murders along the Mississippi in the 1960s* (Baton Rouge: Louisiana State University Press, 2016), 18.

25. Henry Lee Moon, *Balance of Power: The Negro Vote* (New York: Doubleday, 1948), 9.

26. Sociologists have long been interested in how social movements function. For a selection of sociological scholarship on the civil rights movement, see Aldon D. Morris, *The Origins of the Civil Rights Movement: Black Communities Organizing for Change* (New York: The Free Press, 1984); Doug McAdam, *Political Process and the Development of Black Insurgency, 1930-1970* (Chicago: University of Chicago Press, 1982, 1999); and Kenneth T. Andrews, *Freedom Is a Constant Struggle: The Mississippi Civil Rights Movement and Its Legacy* (Chicago: University of Chicago Press, 2004). Sociologists have also tracked the finances of major civil rights organizations. See Herbert H. Haines, "Black Radicalization and the Funding of Civil Rights, 1957-1970," *Social Problems* 32, no. 1 (October 1984): 31–43; and J. Craig Jenkins and Craig M. Eckert, "Channeling Black Insurgency: Elite Patronage and Professional Social Movement Organizations in the Development of the Black Movement," *American Sociological Review* 51, no. 6 (December 1986): 812–29.

27. McPherson, Report from Orangeburg Area.

28. Nancy Wilstach, "She Can't Vote, but She Signs Up New S.C. Voters," *Rock Hill Evening Herald*, June 18, 1969, reprinted in *VEP News* 3, no. 7 (July 1969).

Chapter One

1. On the pursuit of black political power from Reconstruction through the Jim Crow era, see Leon Litwack, *Been in the Storm So Long: The Aftermath of Slavery* (New York: Alfred A. Knopf, 1979); Eric Foner, *Reconstruction: America's Unfinished Revolution, 1863-1877* (New York: Harper and Row, 1988); Paul Ortiz, *Emancipation Betrayed: The Hidden History of Black Organizing and White Violence in Florida from Reconstruction to the Bloody Election of 1920* (Berkeley: University of California Press, 2005); Volney R. Riser,

Defying Disfranchisement: Black Voting Rights Activism in the Jim Crow South, 1890–1908 (Baton Rouge: Louisiana State University Press, 2010); Carole Emberton, *Beyond Redemption: Race, Violence, and the American South after the Civil War* (Chicago: University of Chicago Press, 2014); and Justin Behrend, *Reconstructing Democracy: Grassroots Black Politics in the Deep South after the Civil War* (Athens: University of Georgia Press, 2015).

2. On the left-labor coalitions and the post–World War II Red Scare in the South, see Patricia Sullivan, *Days of Hope: Race and Democracy during the New Deal Era* (Chapel Hill: University of North Carolina Press, 1996); Mary L. Dudziak, *Cold War Civil Rights: Race and the Image of American Democracy* (Princeton, NJ: Princeton University Press, 2000); Robert R. Korstad, *Civil Rights Unionism: Tobacco Workers and the Struggle for Democracy in the Mid-Twentieth Century South* (Chapel Hill: University of North Carolina Press, 2003); George Lewis, *The White South and the Red Menace: Segregationists, Anticommunism, and Massive Resistance, 1945–1965* (Gainesville: University Press of Florida, 2004); Jeff Woods, *Black Struggle, Red Scare: Segregation and Anti-Communism in the South, 1948–1968* (Baton Rouge: Louisiana State University Press, 2004); Landon R. Y. Storrs, *The Second Red Scare and the Unmaking of the New Deal Left* (Princeton, NJ: Princeton University Press, 2013); and Yasuhiro Katagiri, *Black Freedom, White Resistance, and Red Menace: Civil Rights and Anticommunism in the Jim Crow South* (Baton Rouge: Louisiana State University Press, 2014).

3. Margaret Price, "The Negro Voter in the South," SRC Special Report, July 1957, Reel 220, SRC Papers. The number of incidents at 530 comes from a report by the American Friends Service Committee, quoted in Margaret Price, "The Negro and the Ballot in the South," SRC Special Report, August 1959, Reel 218, SRC Papers. See also Margaret Price, Draft of "Joint Interagency Fact-Finding Project on Violence and Intimidation," n.d., Reel 218, SRC Papers; and Reverend Ben F. Wyland, "Voting Restrictions in Florida," Southern Conference Educational Fund's (SCEF) Conference on Voting Restrictions in Southern States in Washington, DC, April 27, 1958, Reel 208, SRC Papers.

4. "The Move to Disenfranchise the Negro Voter," SRC Report, April 17, 1958, Reel 208, SRC Papers. See also "Civil Rights in the South," Remarks by Guy B. Johnson before the President's Committee on Civil Rights, May 14, 1947, Folder 001541-004-0594, Harry S. Truman Presidential Library, accessed via ProQuest History Vault; Price, "The Negro Voter in the South," 1957; Cleghorn and Watters, *Climbing Jacob's Ladder*, 123; and Lawson, *Black Ballots*, 55–85.

5. Ella Lee White, Complaint Card, July 28, 1964, Box 5, Folder 9, Congress of Racial Equality, Monroe Chapter (LA) Records, Wisconsin Historical Society. See also Price, "The Negro Voter in the South," 1957; Lawson, *Black Ballots*, 87–88; Alexander Keyssar, *The Right to Vote: The Contested History of Democracy in the United States* (New York: Basic Books, 2000), 89, 207, 258; and Evan Faulkenbury, "'Monroe is Hell': Voter Purges, Registration Drives, and the Civil Rights Movement in Ouachita Parish, Louisiana," *Louisiana History* (Winter 2018): 40–66.

6. Grover S. McLeod, "A Study of Voter Registration in Jefferson County, Alabama," Jefferson County Citizens Council, 1958, Reel 208, SRC Papers. See also Price, "The Negro Voter in the South," 1957; B. R. Brazeal to Harold Fleming, Re: "Summary of Laurens County Interviews and Findings About Negro Political Participation in Politics,"

August 31, 1956, Reel 218, SRC Papers; and "The Negro Voter in the South," SRC preliminary findings report, November 2, 1958, Reel 220, SRC Papers.

7. Riser, *Defying Disfranchisement*.

8. "'Break' Party Lines Says NAACP Head," *Afro-American*, June 26, 1926.

9. Edgar T. Rouzeau, "'Black America Wars on Double Front for High Stakes'— Rouzeau," *Pittsburgh Courier*, February 7, 1942; and "The *Courier's* 'Double V' for a Double Victory Campaign Gets Country-Wide Support," *Pittsburgh Courier*, February 14, 1942. On the "Double V" campaign, see Kimberly L. Phillips, *War! What Is It Good For?: Black Freedom Struggles and the U.S. Military from World War II to Iraq* (Chapel Hill: University of North Carolina Press, 2012), 20–63. On *Smith v. Allwright*, see Darlene Clark Hine, *Black Victory: The Rise and Fall of the White Primary in Texas* (Columbia: University of Missouri Press, 1979, 2003); and Charles L. Zelden, *The Battle for the Black Ballot: Smith v. Allwright and the Defeat of the Texas All-White Primary* (Lawrence: University Press of Kansas, 2004).

10. Moon, *Balance of Power*, 156–65; Lawson, *Black Ballots*, 116–39; and Sullivan, *Days of Hope*, 193–220.

11. A Brief Statement on the History and Aims of the Southern Regional Council, from "The Attack on the Southern Regional Council and the Georgia Committee on Interracial Cooperation," October 1955, Box 2S440, Folder "Southern Regional Council 1955–1957," Field Foundation Archives, 1940–1990, Dolph Briscoe Center for American History, the University of Texas at Austin (hereinafter Field Foundation Archives).

12. See A Brief Statement on the History and Aims of the Southern Regional Council, October 1955; SRC Report No. L-1, "The Southern Regional Council—Its Origin and Aims," April 27, 1959, Box 2S440, Folder "Southern Regional Council 1955–1957," Field Foundation Archives; Morton Sosna, *In Search of the Silent South: Southern Liberals and the Race Issue* (New York: Columbia University Press, 1977), 20–41, 115–20; Julia Anne McDonough, "Men and Women of Good Will: A History of the Commission on Interracial Cooperation and the Southern Regional Council, 1919–1954" (PhD diss., University of Virginia, 1993), 20–251; Jacquelyn Dowd Hall, *Revolt against Chivalry: Jesse Daniel Ames and the Women's Campaign against Lynching* (New York: Columbia University Press, 1993), 256–60; David L. Chappell, *Inside Agitators: White Southerners in the Civil Rights Movement* (Baltimore: The John Hopkins University Press, 1994), 34–41; John Egerton, *Speak Now against the Day: The Generation before the Civil Rights Movement in the South* (Chapel Hill: University of North Carolina Press, 1995), 47–51; 301–15; and Sullivan, *Days of Hope*, 163–66.

13. "Civil Rights in the South," remarks by Guy B. Johnson before the President's Committee on Civil Rights, May 14, 1947.

14. SRC Report No. L-1, "The Southern Regional Council—Its Origin and Aims," April 27, 1959.

15. A Brief Statement on the History and Aims of the Southern Regional Council, October 1955. See also Sosna, *In Search of the Silent South*, 142–54; McDonough, "Men and Women of Good Will," 375–580; and Chappell, *Inside Agitators*, 46–48.

16. Benjamin Mays, "Why an Atlanta School Suit?" *New South* 5 (September–October 1950), 3. See also McDonough, "Men and Women of Good Will," 548–49.

17. "'Outsiders' Hit by Talmadge," *Atlanta Daily World*, August 21, 1951.

18. "Southern Regional Council Financed by Ford as Haven for Commies," *Augusta Courier*, June 28, 1954.

19. "Do-Gooders Stirring Bloodshed," *News and Courier*, October 28, 1955.

20. Eugene Cook, "The Ugly Truth about the NAACP," speech to the 55th Annual Convention of the Peace Officers Association of Georgia, October 19, 1956, Reel 19, SRC Papers. See also A Brief Statement on the History and Aims of the Southern Regional Council, October 1955; and McDonough, "Men and Women of Good Will," 548–70.

21. Leon Racht and Jeffrey Roche, "Name 21 Pro-Reds on Board Dixie Race Study Council," *New York Journal-American*, November 7, 1955. See also "Fund for Republic—'A Good Investment'—For What?," paid advertisement in the *Virginian-Pilot*, November 12, 1955, Reel 19, SRC Papers.

22. Price, Draft of "Joint Interagency Fact Finding Project on Violence and Intimidation."

23. "Pro-Segregation Groups in the South," SRC Special Report, November 19, 1956, Reel 220, SRC Papers; "The South and the Supreme Court's School Decisions: A Chronology, May 17, 1954–December 31, 1956," SRC Special Report, Reel 220, SRC Papers; and McDonough, "Men and Women of Good Will," 548.

24. John N. Popham, "Lag in Negro Vote Reported in South," *New York Times*, February 8, 1953.

25. Price, "The Negro Voter in the South," 1957 (all quotes).

26. Dr. Brailsford R. Brazeal to Harold Fleming, Re: "Summary of Laurens County Interviews and Findings about Negro Political Participation in Politics," August 31, 1956, Reel 218, SRC Papers (all quotes).

27. For an explanation of the SRC's tax exemption, see Adrian W. DeWind to Mortimer M. Caplin, December 14, 1961, Folder "Southern Regional Council: Voter Education Project, 1961–1962," Taconic Foundation Records, Rockefeller Archive Center (hereinafter Taconic Foundation Records). Thanks to Mary Ann Quinn and the staff at the Rockefeller Archive Center, I was able to research the Taconic Foundation Records before final processing. See bibliography for details.

28. Martin Luther King Jr., *Stride toward Freedom: The Montgomery Story* (New York: Harper and Brothers, 1958; Beacon Press reprint, 2010), 58.

29. King, *Stride toward Freedom*, 18–20, 58; and foreword by Harold C. Fleming to Price, "The Negro Voter in the South," 1957.

30. "The Next Step for Mass Action in the Struggle for Equality," working paper #2, Southern Negro Leaders Conference on Transportation and Non-Violent Integration, January 10–11, 1957, Folder 001565-001-0074, Part 2: Records of the Executive Director and Treasurer, Records of the Southern Christian Leadership Conference, 1954–1970, ProQuest History Vault (all quotes).

31. Constitution and Bylaws of the Southern Christian Leadership Conference, Folder 001565-001-0052, Part 2: Records of the Executive Director and Treasurer, Records of the Southern Christian Leadership Conference, 1954–1970, ProQuest History Vault.

32. Lawson, *Black Ballots*, 152–65.

33. "'We'll March': Prayer Pilgrimage to Capital Planned," *Afro-American*, February 23, 1957.

34. Prayer Pilgrimage for Freedom, New York Organizational Meeting, April 18, 1957, Folder 001608-024-0613, A. Philip Randolph Papers, ProQuest History Vault. See also "Behind the Scenes," *Chicago Defender*, March 9, 1957; "Rev. Martin King, Billy Graham on Baptist Program," *Atlanta Daily World*, March 17, 1957; and "Negroes to Mass in Capital May 17," *New York Times*, April 6, 1957. On King's impressions of Ghana, see Martin Luther King Jr., "The Birth of a New Nation," sermon delivered at Dexter Avenue Baptist Church, April 7, 1957, in *The Papers of Martin Luther King Jr.*, vol. 4, January 1957–December 1958 (Berkeley: University of California Press, 2000), 155–67.

35. On the March on Washington Movement, see William P. Jones, *The March on Washington: Jobs, Freedom, and the Forgotten History of Civil Rights* (New York: W. W. Norton, 2013), 1–78; and David Lucander, *Winning the War for Democracy: The March on Washington Movement, 1941–1946* (Urbana: University of Illinois Press, 2014). On the Prayer Pilgrimage, see Garrow, *Bearing the Cross*, 90–94; Branch, *Parting the Waters*, 216–17; and Fairclough, *To Redeem the Soul of America*, 39–40.

36. Roy Wilkins Statement, May 10, 1957, in response to UPI Query, Folder 001608-024-0696, A. Philip Randolph Papers.

37. "'Subversive' Groups Barred from the Prayer Pilgrimage," *Philadelphia Tribune*, May 14, 1957.

38. Edward Peeks, "'We Will March on DC'—Abernathy," *Afro-American*, March 9, 1957.

39. Bayard Rustin to Rosa Parks, n.d., Rosa Parks Papers: Subject File, 1937–2005, Box 16, Folder 3, Manuscript/Mixed Material, Library of Congress, https://www.loc.gov/item/mss859430197/

40. Bayard Rustin to Martin Luther King Jr., May 10, 1957, Folder 001581-004-1005, Bayard Rustin Papers, accessed via ProQuest History Vault. See also Martin Luther King Jr., A. Philip Randolph, and Roy Wilkins, "Call to a Prayer Pilgrimage for Freedom," Folder 001608-024-0696, A. Philip Randolph Papers; "King Outlines Aims, Plans for Pilgrimage," *Atlanta Daily World*, April 27, 1957; and "Use of Lincoln Memorial Is Granted Prayer Pilgrimage," *Afro-American*, May 4, 1957.

41. Septima Clark to A. Philip Randolph, May 21, 1957, Folder 001608-024-0631, A. Philip Randolph Papers. On Septima Clark, see Katherine Mellen Charron, *Freedom's Teacher: The Life of Septima Clark* (Chapel Hill: University of North Carolina Press, 2009).

42. A. Philip Randolph Address at the Prayer Pilgrimage, Folder 001608-024-0631, A. Philip Randolph Papers; Program, Prayer Pilgrimage for Freedom, May 17, 1957, Folder 001581-004-1005, Bayard Rustin Papers; and Jay Walz, "Negroes Hold Rally on Rights in Capital," *New York Times*, May 18, 1957.

43. Text of Martin Luther King Jr. Address at the Prayer Pilgrimage for Freedom, May 17, 1957, Folder 001581-004-1005, Bayard Rustin Papers.

44. Alice A. Dunnigan, "Prayer Pilgrimage for Freedom Hailed as Nation's Most Impressive Demonstration," Associated Negro Press, May 20, 1957, Folder 001585-062-0698, Claude A. Barnett Papers: The Associated Negro Press, 1918–1967, Part 1: Associated Negro Press News Releases, 1928–1964, Series C: 1956–1964, ProQuest History Vault.

45. Dunnigan, "Prayer Pilgrimage for Freedom Hailed"; and "Prayer Pilgrimage: Its Meaning," *Chicago Defender*, May 20, 1957.

46. Hugh Morris, "Over 15,000 in Washington in Protest for Civil Rights," *Atlanta Daily World*, May 18, 1957; and "Crowd Chants for the Ballot at Pilgrimage," *Washington Post*, May 18, 1957.

47. Reverend Hamilton T. Boswell, "Washington Prayer Pilgrimage a Great Success," *Associated Negro Press*, May 20, 1957, Folder 001585-062-0698, Claude A. Barnett Papers.

48. Earl Brown, "Not Prayer Alone," *New York Amsterdam News*, June 1, 1957.

49. "Prayer Pilgrimage: Its Meaning," *Chicago Defender*, May 20, 1957.

50. "Vice President Nixon Assures Top Leaders Support," *Atlanta Daily World*, June 14, 1957.

51. C. P. Trussell, "Civil Rights Foes Set Back in House," *New York Times*, June 14, 1957; "Prayer Pilgrimage: Its Meaning," *Chicago Defender*, May 20, 1957; and Lawson, *Black Ballots*, 176.

52. Civil Rights Act of 1957, 85th Congress, H.R. 6127, Public Law 85-315, September 9, 1957 (all quotes). See also Lawson, *Black Ballots*, 140–202.

53. Dr. Martin Luther King Jr. to Vice President Richard M. Nixon, August 30, 1957, in *The Papers of Martin Luther King Jr.*, vol. 4, 263–64 (all quotes).

54. Harold L. Keith, "Randolph Calls for Vote 'Crusade,'" *Pittsburgh Courier*, June 1, 1957.

55. Dr. Martin Luther King Jr., Invocation Delivered at Billy Graham Evangelistic Association Crusade, New York, New York, July 18, 1957, in *The Papers of Martin Luther King Jr.*, vol. 4, 238; Martin Luther King Jr. to Billy Graham, August 31, 1957, in *The Papers of Martin Luther King Jr.*, vol. 4, 264–66; and Steven P. Miller, *Billy Graham and the Rise of the Republican South* (Philadelphia: University of Pennsylvania Press, 2009), 43.

56. Press Release, SCLC Announcement of the Crusade for Citizenship, November 5, 1957, in *The Papers of Martin Luther King Jr.*, vol. 4, 307–8; Emory O. Jackson, "Dr. King Calls for Massive Voter-Registration in South," *Atlanta Daily World*, August 9, 1957; and "$200,000 Drive Opens to Register Negroes," *Washington Post*, August 10, 1957; Thaddeus T. Stokes, "Southern Christian Leaders Plan Southwide Voter-Drive," *Atlanta Daily World*, November 8, 1957; and Branch, *Parting the Waters*, 229.

57. Interview with Ella Baker by John Britton, June 19, 1968, RJB-203, Ralph J. Bunch Collection, Moorland-Spingarn Research Center, Howard University; Barbara Ransby, *Ella Baker and the Black Freedom Movement: A Radical Democratic Vision* (Chapel Hill: University of North Carolina Press, 2003), 172–83; Branch, *Parting the Waters*, 231–32; and Garrow, *Bearing the Cross*, 100–104. See also Interview with Ella Baker by Eugene P. Walker, September 4, 1974, G-0007, in the Southern Oral History Program Collection #4007, Southern Historical Collection, Wilson Library, University of North Carolina at Chapel Hill.

58. Ella Baker interview, June 19, 1968.

59. Ransby, *Ella Baker*, 180.

60. "Southern Christian Leadership Conference Pushes Registration," *Atlanta Daily World*, January 19, 1958.

61. Ella Baker interview, June 19, 1968. See also Ella Baker to Reverend Edward T. Graham, January 21, 1958, Folder 001565-001-0344, Records of the Southern Christian

Leadership Conference, 1954–1970, Part 1: Records of the President's Office; Ella Baker to Reverend E. T. Brown, January 25, 1958, Box 32, Folder 7, SCLC Papers, the Martin Luther King, Jr. Center for Nonviolent Social Change, Inc. (hereinafter King Center); W. H. Hall to Ella Baker, February 4, 1958, Folder 7, Box 32, Folder 7, SCLC Papers, King Center; and "Southern Leadership Group Maps Final Plans for Voter Crusade," *Atlanta Daily World*, January 31, 1958.

62. Stokes, "Southern Christian Leaders Plan Southwide Voter-Drive."

63. Memorandum from Dr. Martin Luther King Jr. to Speakers, Local Contacts, Participants in SCLC, Re: "Crusade for Citizenship Mass Meeting, February 12, 1958," February 4, 1958, in *The Papers of Martin Luther King Jr.*, vol. 4, 358–60 (all quotes, emphasis in original).

64. Dr. Martin Luther King Jr. to Congressman Adam Clayton Powell, February 7, 1958, Box 32, Folder 7, SCLC Papers, King Center. See also "Congressman Powell Joins Southern 'Crusade' Group," *Atlanta Daily World*, February 8, 1958.

65. SCLC Press Release, Re: "Crusade for Citizenship," n.d., Box 381, Folder 3, United Packinghouse, Food, and Allied Workers Records, 1937–1968, Wisconsin Historical Society (hereinafter UPWA Records).

66. Reverend King's Statement on the Crusade, n.d., Box 381, Folder 4, UPWA Records.

67. Dr. Martin Luther King Jr., Address at Greater Bethel AME Church in Miami, Florida, February 12, 1958, in *The Papers of Martin Luther King Jr.*, vol. 4, 367–71. See also "Scheduled Meetings," January 20, 1958, Folder 001581-005-0619, Bayard Rustin Papers; "Launch Crusade for Citizenship," *Chicago Defender*, February 13, 1958; Dr. C. O. Simpkins to Ella Baker, February 14, 1958, Folder 001563-002-0493, SCLC Papers, King Center, ProQuest; "King, Powell Address 'Crusade' Meetings," *Chicago Defender*, February 22, 1958; and Inez J. Baskin, "Why Hope Remains; Topic of Speaker at Crusade Meet," *Atlanta Daily World*, March 4, 1958.

68. Ella J. Baker to Reverend J. E. Lowry, March 28, 1958, Folder 001563-002-0493, SCLC Papers, King Center, ProQuest. See also Ella Baker to Reverend Edward T. Graham, April 16, 1958 and Reverend Edward T. Graham to Ella J. Baker, May 7, 1958, Folder 001565-001-0344, SCLC Papers, King Center, ProQuest.

69. Reverend Ralph D. Abernathy to Reverend E. T. Graham, March 10, 1958, Box 1, Folder 1, SCLC Papers, King Center.

70. Congressman Charles C. Diggs to Martin Luther King Jr., March 13, 1958, in *The Papers of Martin Luther King Jr.*, vol. 4, 389.

71. "Southern Survey Shows Negroes Stay Home, Vote Crusade Fails," *U.S. News and World Report*, May 2, 1958, 52–54.

72. Ella Baker interview, June 19, 1968.

73. Ella Baker to Martin Luther King Jr., October 10, 1959, Box 3, Folder 8, SCLC Papers, King Center. See also "Two Named to Atlanta Office of 'Crusade for Citizenship,'" *Atlanta Daily World*, June 19, 1958; John Tilley to Reverend Henry C. Bunton, September 25, 1958, Box 1, Folder 1, SCLC Papers, King Center; and Fairclough, *To Redeem the Soul of America*, 48.

74. Interview with Maxwell Hahn by Kathy Schwarzschild, November 12, 1979, Box 4X98, Folder "Max Hahn Interview, 1979," Field Foundation Archives; Leslie Dunbar

to Maxwell Hahn, May 17, 1962, Box 4X97, Folder "SRC FA 1962," Field Foundation Archives; and "Maxwell Hahn Dies; Charity Director, 94," *New York Times*, August 28, 1994.

75. Margaret Price, "The Negro and the Ballot in the South," August 1959, Reel 218, SRC Papers. See also Margaret Price to Florence Irving, September 11, 1958, Reel 208, SRC Papers.

76. SRC Press Release, August 30, 1959, Reel 208, SRC Papers.

77. Price, "The Negro and the Ballot in the South."

78. Price, "The Negro and the Ballot in the South."

79. James M. Nabrit Jr., "Summary of Reports on Voting Restrictions in Southern States," SCEF conference, April 27, 1958, Reel 208, SRC Papers.

80. Nabrit, "Summary of Reports on Voting Restrictions."

Chapter Two

1. Diane J. Nash to President John F. Kennedy, June 7, 1961, Box 5, Folder "Nash, Diane J., June 21–October 16, 1961," Harris Wofford Papers, John F. Kennedy Presidential Library (hereafter Wofford Papers).

2. Interview with Charles Jones by Taylor Branch, November 24, 1986, Taylor Branch Papers #5047, Southern Historical Collection, Wilson Library, University of North Carolina at Chapel Hill (hereafter Branch Papers); and Branch, *Parting the Waters*, 480.

3. Interview with Charles Sherrod by Taylor Branch, October 7, 1985, Branch Papers.

4. Branch, *Parting the Waters*, 480–81.

5. Quoted in Burton Hersh, *The Mellon Family: A Fortune in History* (New York: William Morrow, 1978), 417.

6. Eric Pace, "Edward Warburg, Philanthropist and Patron of the Arts, Dies at 84," *New York Times*, September 22, 1992; Margalit Fox, "Mary Warburg, a Noted Philanthropist, Dies at 100," *New York Times*, March 11, 2009; and Ron Chernow, *The Warburgs: The Twentieth-Century Odyssey of a Remarkable Jewish Family* (New York: Vintage, 1994), 456–57. See also "Stephen Currier Missing on Flight," *New York Times*, January 19, 1967; "Gifts by Curriers $3-Million in 1966," *New York Times*, January 26, 1967; "800 Attend Rites for the Curriers," *New York Times*, February 16, 1967; and John Egerton, introduction to Harold C. Fleming with Virginia Fleming, *The Potomac Chronicle: Public Policy and Civil Rights from Kennedy to Reagan* (Athens: University of Georgia Press, 1996), xxv.

7. Hersh, *The Mellon Family*, 414–15; David E. Koskoff, *The Mellons: The Chronicle of America's Richest Family* (New York: Thomas Y. Crowell, 1978), 534; and David Cannadine, *Mellon: An American Life* (New York: Alfred A. Knopf, 2006), 610–12.

8. Mary V. R. Thayer, "There's a Wedding in the Mellon Clan," *Washington Post*, April 7, 1956; "Mellon Heiress Weds," *Chicago Daily Tribune*, April 24, 1956; Hersh, *The Mellon Family*, 415; and Nelson D. Lankford, *The Last American Diplomat: The Biography of David K. E. Bruce, 1898–1977* (Boston: Little, Brown and Company, 1996), 273.

9. Unpublished Memoir by Lloyd K. Garrison, 42, Box 1, Folder 3, Lloyd K. Garrison Papers, 1893–1990, Harvard Law School Library, Harvard University; and Egerton, introduction in Fleming, *The Potomac Chronicle*, xxv. On the Rosenwald Fund, see

Stephanie Deutsch, *You Need a Schoolhouse: Booker T. Washington, Julius Rosenwald, and the Building of Schools for the Segregated South* (Evanston, IL: Northwestern University Press, 2011).

10. Garrison unpublished memoir, 41.

11. Garrison unpublished memoir, 41.

12. Garrison unpublished memoir, 41–42; "Man of Many Posts: Lloyd Kirkham Garrison," *New York Times*, May 4, 1967; Hersh, *The Mellon Family*, 417–18; and Dennis C. Dickerson, *Militant Mediator: Whitney M. Young, Jr.* (Lexington: University Press of Kentucky, 1998), 177.

13. "Introduction," *Taconic Foundation: Report 1959–1984*, in *Taconic Foundation: Twenty-Five Years* (June 1985), 9.

14. John G. Simon, "The Better Angels of Our Nature: A Preface," *Taconic Foundation: Twenty-Five Years* (June 1985).

15. Egerton, introduction in Fleming, *The Potomac Chronicle*, xxvi, emphasis in original. See also "He gives a $Million for Rights but Shuns Publicity Limelight," *Afro-American*, August 24, 1963.

16. "Gifts by Curriers $3-Million in 1966," *New York Times*, January 26, 1967. See also Taconic Foundation: Grants 1958/1959–1969, *Taconic Foundation: Report 1959–1984*, 29–35.

17. Cannadine, *Mellon: An American Life*, 616.

18. Quoted in Hersh, *The Mellon Family*, 417.

19. "800 Attend Rites for the Curriers," *New York Times*, February 16, 1967; Koskoff, *The Mellons*, 511, 535–36; and Lankford, *The Last American Diplomat*, 348.

20. Egerton, introduction to *The Potomac Chronicle*, xvi.

21. Minutes, Consultative Conference on Desegregation, Southern Interagency Meeting, November 5–6, 1957, Box 116, Folder 3, Dr. Martin Luther King, Jr. Archive, Boston University Howard Gotlieb Archival Research Center (hereinafter MLK Archive, Boston University).

22. Harold C. Fleming, "Some Observations on Foundation Giving in the Field of Race Relations," October 19, 1959, Reel 28, SRC Papers.

23. Memorandum, Harold C. Fleming to Stephen Currier, "Summary Report on Projects Assisted by December 1958 Contributions," October 19, 1959, Folder "Southern Regional Council: General Program, 1958–1964," Taconic Foundation Records. For a list of other foundations that supported the SRC during the late 1950s, see Report No. L-1, "The Southern Regional Council: Its Origin and Aims," April 17, 1959, Box 2S440, Folder "Southern Regional Council, 1955–1957," Field Foundation Archives.

24. Quoted in Hersh, *The Mellon Family*, 419.

25. Garrison unpublished memoir, 43–44.

26. Garrison unpublished memoir, 43.

27. Fleming, *The Potomac Chronicle*, 8.

28. Harold C. Fleming, *The Potomac Institute Incorporated, 1961–1971*, report published by the Potomac Institute, 1972, 2.

29. Fleming, *The Potomac Chronicle*, vii (also 2–3, 7–8); and Fleming, *The Potomac Institute Incorporated, 1961–1971*.

30. Zunz, *Philanthropy in America*, 89 (also 85–89).

31. Section 511, Article 13, Regulations 79 Relating to Gift Tax under the Revenue Act of 1932, as Amended and Supplemented by the Revenue Acts of 1934 and 1935, U.S. Treasury Department, Bureau of Internal Revenue (Washington, DC: Government Printing Office, 1936).

32. Zunz, *Philanthropy in America*, 89–103. On early interpretations of the Revenue Act of 1934, see Roy G. Blakey and Gladys C. Blakey, "The Revenue Act of 1934," *American Economic Review* 24, no. 3 (September 1934): 450–61.

33. C. Lowell Harriss, "Philanthropy and Federal Tax Exemption," *Journal of Political Economy* 47, no. 4 (August 1939): 528.

34. B. W. Patch, "Tax-Exempt Foundations," *Editorial Research Reports*, January 5, 1949, 10.

35. Anthony Lewis, "Kennedy Salutes Negroes' Sit-Ins," *New York Times*, June 25, 1960. See also Interview with John Seigenthaler by William A. Geoghegan, July 22, 1964, John F. Kennedy Library Oral History Program.

36. Interview with Leslie W. Dunbar by Jacquelyn Hall, Helen Bresler, and Bob Hall, December 18, 1978, G-0075, in the Southern Oral History Program Collection #4007, Southern Historical Collection, Wilson Library, University of North Carolina at Chapel Hill.

37. Daniel H. Pollitt to Mima Riddiford Pollitt, October 23, 1960, Series 4, Box 37, Folder 348, Daniel H. Pollitt Papers #5498, Southern Historical Collection, Wilson Library, University of North Carolina at Chapel Hill.

38. Fleming, *The Potomac Chronicle*, 14; and Leslie Dunbar interview, December 18, 1978.

39. Southern Regional Council, "The Federal Executive and Civil Rights," January 1961, Section 8, Civil Rights during the Kennedy Administration, 1961–1963, Part 1: The White House Central Files and Staff Files and The President's Office Files. For a shortened summary of "The Federal Executive and Civil Rights," see *New South* 16, no. 3 (March 1961): 11–14.

40. Confidential Report on the Southern Regional Council, Public Affairs Program of the Ford Foundation, May 7, 1965, 3, Series 010437, Unpublished Reports, Office of the President, Office Files of Harry T. Heald, Ford Foundation Records, Rockefeller Archive Center (hereinafter Ford Foundation Records).

41. Harris Wofford, *Of Kennedys and Kings: Making Sense of the Sixties* (New York: Farrar, Straus, and Giroux, 1980), 159.

42. For more on Harris Wofford's nonviolent philosophy, see Harris and Clare Wofford, *India Afire* (New York: J. Day, 1951).

43. Schlesinger, *A Thousand Days*, 935.

44. Interview with John Doar by Taylor Branch, May 12, 1986, C-5047/8-9, Taylor Branch Papers; Interview with John Doar, conducted by Blackside, Inc., November 15, 1985, for *Eyes on the Prize: America's Civil Rights Years (1954–1965)*, Washington University Libraries, Film and Media Archive, Henry Hampton Collection. See also Branch, *Parting the Waters*, 382; and Brauer, *John F. Kennedy and the Second Reconstruction*, 72, 120. For personal memories of African Americans forced off land in Fayette County, see James Forman, *The Making of Black Revolutionaries* (Seattle: University of Washington Press, 1972, 1997), 116–30.

45. Memorandum from Harris Wofford to President-Elect Kennedy on Civil Rights—1961, 7, Box 68, Folder "Civil Rights [Reports] (2 of 4)," Burke Marshall Personal Papers, John F. Kennedy Library (hereinafter Marshall Papers) (emphasis in original).

46. Memorandum from Harris Wofford to President-Elect Kennedy on Civil Rights—1961, 16.

47. Memorandum from Harris Wofford to President-Elect Kennedy on Civil Rights—1961, 16.

48. Memorandum from Harris Wofford to President-Elect Kennedy on Civil Rights—1961, 17.

49. John Doar interview, May 12, 1986. See also Interview with Burke Marshall by Taylor Branch, September 26, 1984, C-5047/18, Branch Papers; Interview with Louis Martin by Taylor Branch, June 10, 1985, C-5047/19, Branch Papers; and Branch, *Parting the Waters*, 382–83.

50. Robert F. Kennedy address at the Law Day Exercises at the University of Georgia, May 6, 1961, 6, Box 253, Folder "University of Georgia Law School, May 6, 1961," Robert F. Kennedy Attorney General Papers, John F. Kennedy Library.

51. Harold Fleming to Stephen Currier, February 8, 1961, Reel 28, SRC Papers. See also Robert Wallace, "Non-Whiz Kid with the Quiet Gun," *Life*, August 9, 1963, 75–80; and Wofford, *Of Kennedys and Kings*, 90–92.

52. Martin Luther King Jr., "Equality Now," *The Nation*, February 4, 1961; and Martin Luther King Jr. to Harold Fleming, February 15, 1961, Box 116, Folder 1, MLK Archive, Boston University.

53. Interview with John Seigenthaler by Ronald J. Grele, February 22, 1966, 425, John F. Kennedy Library Oral History Program.

54. John Seigenthaler to the Attorney General, "Luncheon Meeting March 6, 1961, Background Information on Those Attending," March 6, 1961, Box 68, Folder "Seigenthaler, John: 1961–1962," Robert F. Kennedy Attorney General Papers, John F. Kennedy Library; Wofford, *Of Kennedys and Kings*, 216; and Branch, *Parting the Waters*, 403–7. Since this meeting was secret, Branch corroborated the evidence and believes it to have taken place in the spring of 1961 between the Bay of Pigs invasion on April 17 and the initial Freedom Rides on May 4. See Branch, *Parting the Waters*, 962n405.

55. Leslie W. Dunbar, "The Freedom Ride," Special Report from the Southern Regional Council, May 30, 1961, Box 2, Folder 14, Dunbar Papers.

56. On the Freedom Rides, see David Niven, *The Politics of Injustice: The Kennedys, the Freedom Rides, and the Electoral Consequences of a Moral Compromise* (Knoxville: University of Tennessee Press, 2003); Raymond Arsenault, *Freedom Riders: 1961 and the Struggle for Racial Justice* (New York: Oxford University Press, 2006); and Derek Catsam, *Freedom's Main Line: The Journey of Reconciliation and the Freedom Rides* (Lexington: University Press of Kentucky, 2009).

57. Interview with Burke Marshall by Louis F. Oberdorfer, May 29, 1964, 39, John F. Kennedy Library Oral History Program.

58. Branch, *Parting the Waters*, 478.

59. Branch, *Parting the Waters*, 381–82. See also Interview with Wyatt Tee Walker by Evan Faulkenbury, March 15, 2013, U-1035, in the Southern Oral History Program

Collection #4007, Southern Historical Collection, Wilson Library, University of North Carolina at Chapel Hill; Dunbar interview, December 18, 1978; Interview with Leslie W. Dunbar by Robert Korstad, February 5, 1992, Southern Rural Poverty Collection, DeWitt Wallace Center for Media and Democracy, Sanford School of Public Policy, Duke University; and Charron, *Freedom's Teacher*, 293–303.

60. Fleming, *The Potomac Institute*, 33 (also 15–16, 18, 32–34).

61. Interview with Timothy Jenkins by Taylor Branch, March 11, 1986, C-5047-48-49, Branch Papers; and Branch, *Parting the Waters*, 479–80.

62. Anthony Lewis, "Negro Vote Surge Expected in South," *New York Times*, June 26, 1961.

63. Lewis, "Negro Vote Surge"; and Branch, *Parting the Waters*, 481.

64. Interview with Harry Belafonte by Taylor Branch, March 6–7, 1985, C-5047-34-40, Branch Papers; Carson, *In Struggle*, 39–43; and Branch, *Parting the Waters*, 481.

65. Minutes, Student Nonviolent Coordinating Committee Meeting, July 14–16, 1961, Baltimore, Maryland, Box 62, Folder 3, Carl and Ann Braden Papers, Wisconsin Historical Society.

66. Program, SNCC Leadership Training Institute, November 23–24, 1961, Box 2, Folder 9, Constance Curry Papers, Stuart A. Rose Manuscript, Archives, and Rare Book Library, Emory University (hereinafter Curry Papers). See also Minutes, Student Nonviolent Coordinating Committee Meeting, July 14–16, 1961; "Report of Harry Belafonte Committee to SNCC," August 11, 1961, Box 62, Folder 3, Carl and Ann Braden Papers, Wisconsin Historical Society; Carson, *In Struggle*, 39–43; Branch, *Parting the Waters*, 481; and Ransby, *Ella Baker and the Black Freedom Movement*, 268–71.

67. Harold C. Fleming, "Introduction of Leslie W. Dunbar," Southern Regional Council Annual Meeting, November 5, 1969, Box 4X98, Folder "Introduction of Les Dunbar with Correspondence, 1967–1988," Field Foundation Archives.

68. Dunbar interview, February 5, 1992.

69. Dunbar interview, February 5, 1992.

70. Cullen B. Gosnell to Leslie Dunbar, May 11, 1948, Box 7, Folder "Correspondence 1948," Dunbar Papers.

71. Dunbar interview, February 5, 1992; and Dunbar interview, December 18, 1978.

72. Speech by Leslie Dunbar, SRC Annual Dinner, November 9, 1991, Box 2, Folder 17, Dunbar Papers.

73. Harold C. Fleming to Leslie Dunbar, April 23, 1958, Box 8, Folder "Correspondence 1958," Dunbar Papers.

74. Dunbar interview, February 5, 1992; and Interview with Leslie Dunbar by Susan Glisson, May 10, 2002, Southern Regional Council Oral History Collection, UF Digital Collections, George A. Smathers Libraries, University of Florida.

75. Fleming, "Introduction of Leslie W. Dunbar," November 5, 1969; Dunbar interview, May 10, 2002; and "The Student Protest Movement, Winter 1960," Southern Regional Council Special Report 13, April 1, 1960. See also Harold C. Fleming to Leslie Dunbar, October 31, 1958, Box 8, Folder "Correspondence 1958," Dunbar Papers.

76. Dunbar interview, May 10, 2002.

77. Dunbar interview, December 18, 1978.

78. Dunbar interview, December 18, 1978; and Fleming, *The Potomac Chronicle*, 32–34.

79. Memorandum, Burke Marshall to Voter Registration File, "July 28, 1961 meeting of Taconic Foundation," July 31, 1961, Box 34, Folder "Voter Registration 1961–1963," Marshall Papers.

80. Southern Regional Council Memorandum, Leslie W. Dunbar to members of the executive committee, July 31, 1961, Reel 173, SRC Papers.

81. Southern Regional Council Memorandum, Leslie W. Dunbar to members of the executive committee, July 31, 1961.

82. Quoted in Meier and Rudwick, *CORE*, 149.

83. Minutes, SNCC Meeting, February 3–5, 1961, Box 2, Folder 4, Curry Papers; and Haines, "Black Radicalization and the Funding of Civil Rights: 1957–1970," 36.

84. On the NAACP's budget, see Yvonne Ryan, *Roy Wilkins: The Quiet Revolutionary and the NAACP* (Lexington: University Press of Kentucky, 2014), 159–60. On the SCLC's finances, see Rhonda D. Jones, "Tithe, Time and Talent: An Analysis of Fundraising Activity for the Southern Christian Leadership Conference (SCLC), 1957–1964" (PhD diss., Howard University, 2003); Walker interview, March 15, 2013; Glenn T. Eskew, *But for Birmingham: The Local and National Movements in the Civil Rights Struggle* (Chapel Hill: University of North Carolina Press, 1997), 37–40; and Nikhil Pal Singh, "'Learn Your Horn': Jack O'Dell and the Long Civil Rights Movement," in *Climbin' Jacob's Ladder: The Black Freedom Movement Writings of Jack O'Dell*, ed. Nikhil Pal Singh, 28 (Berkeley: University of California Press, 2010). On CORE's finances, see Statement of Income and Expense, Year Ended May 31, 1962, Reel 17, Series 5, Papers of the Congress of Racial Equality, 1941–1967; A. D. Moore to CORE Groups and Friends, Re: Freedom Ride Costs, December 29, 1961, Reel 17, Series 5, Papers of the Congress of Racial Equality, 1941–1967; and Meier and Rudwick, *CORE*, 42, 78, 81–83, 148–49. On NUL budgets, see Guichard Parris and Lester Brooks, *Blacks in the City: A History of the National Urban League* (Boston: Little, Brown and Company, 1971), 394; Dickerson, *Militant Mediator*, 2; and Nancy J. Weiss, *The National Urban League, 1910–1940* (New York: Oxford University Press, 1974), 80–83, 155–59. For a chart of contributions to organizations, see Haines, "Black Radicalization and the Funding of Civil Rights: 1957–1970," 36.

85. Roy Wilkins, "Memorandum on Structure and Activities of NAACP in Voter Registration," Box 34, Folder "Voter Registration Miscellaneous and Undated," Marshall Papers. See also Lawson, *Black Ballots*, 263–64; and Ryan, *Roy Wilkins*, 101–3.

86. Lester B. Granger to Stephen Currier, August 14, 1961, Box 34, Folder "Voter Registration Miscellaneous and Undated," Marshall Papers.

87. Memorandum, James Farmer to Stephen Currier, "CORE Voter Registration Program," n.d., Box 34, Folder "Voter Registration Miscellaneous and Undated," Marshall Papers.

88. Martin Luther King Jr. and Wyatt Tee Walker, "Southwide Voter Registration Prospectus," Southern Christian Leadership Conference, n.d., Box 34, Folder "Voter Registration Miscellaneous and Undated," Marshall Papers.

89. Memorandum, Charles McDew, "Proposed (student) project in voter registration," August 14, 1961, Box 34, Folder "Voter Registration Miscellaneous and Undated," Marshall Papers.

90. Memorandum from the Southern Regional Council, for discussion August 23, 1961, Box 34, Folder "Voter Registration Miscellaneous and Undated," Marshall Papers.

91. Jenkins, while also a SNCC member, represented the National Student Association (NSA), which did not join in the VEP as a full member, although at least one local NSA chapter later won a grant from the VEP. Fortunately, the NSA did not join, since it was later revealed to be a front for the Central Intelligence Agency. See Karen M. Paget, *Patriotic Betrayal: The Inside Story of the CIA's Secret Campaign to Enroll American Students in the Crusade against Communism* (New Haven, CT: Yale University Press, 2015).

92. Memorandum, Henry Lee Moon to Roy Wilkins, "Conference of Taconic Foundation, August 23, 1961," August 28, 1961, Folder 001519-006-0525, Group III, Series A, General Office File, Subject File—Register and Vote, Papers of the NAACP, Part 4, Library of Congress, accessed via ProQuest History Vault (hereinafter NAACP Papers).

93. Dunbar interview, December 18, 1978.

94. Moon to Wilkins, August 28, 1961.

95. Leslie Dunbar to James Farmer, Roy Wilkins, Whitney Young, Wyatt Tee Walker, Charles McDew, and Timothy Jenkins, September 13, 1961, Folder "Southern Regional Council: Voter Education Project, 1961–1962," Taconic Foundation Records.

96. Roy Wilkins to Henry Lee Moon, August 21, 1961, Folder 001519-006-0525, Group III, Series A, General Office File, Subject File—Register and Vote, Part 4, NAACP Papers.

97. Memorandum, Henry Lee Moon to Roy Wilkins, "Conference of Taconic Foundation, August 23, 1961," August 28, 1961; and Stephen Currier to Roy Wilkins, September 8, 1961, Folder 001519-006-0525, Group III, Series A, General Office File, Subject File—Register and Vote, Part 4, NAACP Papers.

98. Memorandum, Gloster Current to Roy Wilkins, "The Special Project," n.d., Folder 001519-006-0525, Group III, Series A, General Office File, Subject File—Register and Vote, Part 4, NAACP Papers.

99. Memorandum, John M. Brooks to Roy Wilkins, "Taconic Foundation," September 22, 1961, Folder 001519-006- 0525, Group III, Series A, General Office File, Subject File—Register and Vote, Part 4, NAACP Papers.

100. Louis Lomax, Transcript of Radio Broadcast on WBAI, October 17, 1961, Box 34, Folder "Voter Registration, 1961–1963," Marshall Papers (all quotes).

101. Leslie Dunbar to Roy Wilkins, November 10, 1961, Folder 001519-006-0525, Group III, Series A, General Office File, Subject File—Register and Vote, Part 4, NAACP Papers.

102. Roy Wilkins to Leslie Dunbar, November 22, 1961, Folder 001519-006-0525, Group III, Series A, General Office File, Subject File—Register and Vote, Part 4, NAACP Papers.

103. Leslie Dunbar to Stephen R. Currier, November 10, 1961, Folder 001519-006-0525, Group III, Series A, General Office File, Subject File—Register and Vote, Part 4, NAACP Papers.

104. Memorandum, Henry Lee Moon to Roy Wilkins, November 27, 1961, Folder 001519-006-0525, Group III, Series A, General Office File, Subject File—Register and Vote, Part 4, NAACP Papers.

105. Adrian W. DeWind to the Honorable Mortimer M. Caplin, December 14, 1961, Folder "Southern Regional Council: Voter Education Project, 1961–1962," Taconic

Foundation Records. See also Adrian W. DeWind to Burke Marshall, December 14, 1961, Box 34, Folder "Voter Registration, 1961–1963," Marshall Papers; and Dennis Hevesi, "Adrian DeWind, Tax Expert and Human Rights Watch Founder, Dies at 95," *New York Times*, August 19, 2009.

106. Dunbar interview, May 10, 2002.

107. Fifth Oral History Interview with Robert F. Kennedy and Burke Marshall by Anthony Lewis, December 4, 1964, John F. Kennedy Library.

108. Burke Marshall to John Seigenthaler, December 18, 1961, Box 34, Folder "Voter Registration, 1961–1963," Marshall Papers. For more on Robert Kennedy's role in influencing the IRS to extend the SRC's tax exemption to the voter registration campaign, see Wofford, *Of Kings and Kennedys*, 159; Stern, *Calculating Visions*, 65; and Branch, *Parting the Waters*, 479. Harold Fleming's account differs. He remembers Burke Marshall telling him that Kennedy thought it would be wrong to intervene directly with the IRS but admitted it was possible Kennedy pressured the IRS without his knowledge. See Fleming, *The Potomac Chronicle*, 35.

109. Leslie Dunbar to Martin Luther King Jr., January 2, 1962, Box 22, Folder 32, Martin Luther King Jr. Papers, King Center.

110. Wiley Branton to Roy Wilkins, Whitney Young, Martin Luther King, James Forman, and James Farmer, February 22, 1962, Series 1: Director's Files, Box 9, Folder 8, CORE Records, Wisconsin Historical Society (hereinafter CORE Records); Proposed Agenda, Southern Interagency Conference, Potomac Institute, January 11–12, 1962, Box 69, Folder 12, Program Department, CORE Records; and John W. S. Rittleton to Southern Regional Council, March 22, 1962, Folder "Southern Regional Council: Voter Education Project, 1961–1962," Taconic Foundation Records.

111. John W. S. Rittleton to Southern Regional Council, March 22, 1962, Folder "Southern Regional Council: Voter Education Project, 1961–1962," Taconic Foundation Records.

112. Leslie Dunbar and Wiley Branton, "First Annual Report of the Voter Education Project of the Southern Regional Council, Inc. for the Fiscal Year April 1, 1962 through March 31, 1963," Box 1, Folder 1, Financial Records, VEP Papers.

113. SRC Press Release, March 29, 1962, Box 22, Folder 33, MLK Papers, King Center.

Chapter Three

1. Bernard Lafayette, Report on Dallas County, Alabama, October 1962, Box 1, Folder 2, Project Files, VEP Papers. See also "Bernard Lafayette" and "Colia Liddell (Lafayette)," *SNCC Digital Gateway*, SNCC Legacy Project and Duke University, https://snccdigital.org/people/bernard-lafayette/ & https://snccdigital.org/people/colia-liddell-lafayette/ (accessed July 27, 2017); Gary May, *Bending toward Justice: The Voting Rights Act and the Transformation of American Democracy* (New York: Basic Books, 2013), 1–24; and Bernard Lafayette Jr. and Kathryn Lee Johnson, *In Peace and Freedom: My Journey in Selma* (Lexington: University Press of Kentucky, 2013).

2. Jack Minnis to Bernard Lafayette, February 15, 1963, Box 1, Folder 2, Project Files, VEP Papers.

3. Colia Lafayette, VEP Field Report, Dallas County, Alabama, March 10, 1963, Box 1, Folder 2, Project Files, VEP Papers.

4. Wiley Branton to Bernard Lafayette, April 4, 1963, Box 1, Folder 2, Project Files, VEP Papers.

5. Advertisement, Dallas County Citizens' Council, *Selma Times Journal*, June 9, 1963, Reel 173, SRC Papers.

6. Wiley Branton to Jim Forman, February 5, 1963, Box 1, Folder 2, Project Files, VEP Papers; Wiley Branton to Jim Forman, May 10, 1963, Box 1, Folder 2, Project Files, VEP Papers; SNCC News Release, "SNCC Worker Beaten in Selma, Alabama," June 12, 1963, Box 2, Folder 12, Curry Papers; and "Bernard and Colia Lafayette Begin Selma Project," *SNCC Digital Gateway*, SNCC Legacy Project and Duke University, https://snccdigital.org/events/bernard-colia-lafayette-begin-selma-project/ (accessed July 27, 2017).

7. John Due to Wiley Branton, Field Trip to South Alabama, September 21, 1964, Reel 176, SRC Papers.

8. Interview with John Lewis by Jack Bass and Walter Devries, November 20, 1973, A-0073, in the Southern Oral History Collection #4007, Southern Historical Collection, Wilson Library, University of North Carolina at Chapel Hill. See also Jean Levine, VEP Grant Approval, October 17, 1963, Box 1, Folder 2, Project Files, VEP Papers; and Randolph Blackwell to Wiley Branton, Field Trip to Selma, Alabama, June 5, 1964, Box 1, Folder 3, Project Files, VEP Papers.

9. VEP First Annual Report (emphasis in original).

10. Watters and Cleghorn, *Climbing Jacob's Ladder*, 47.

11. SRC Memorandum for discussion August 23, 1961, Box 34, Folder "Voter Registration Miscellaneous and Undated," Marshall Papers.

12. Leslie W. Dunbar to Martin Luther King Jr., January 2, 1962, Box 22, Folder 32, MLK Papers, King Center.

13. Branton interview, October 21, 1970.

14. Branton interview, October 21, 1970; and Kilpatrick, *There When We Needed Him*, 1–51.

15. Brown v. Board of Education, 349 U.S. 294 (1955).

16. Interview with Wiley A. Branton by Robert Penn Warren, March 17, 1964, Louie B. Nunn Center for Oral History, University of Kentucky; Branton interview, October 21, 1970; and Kilpatrick, *There When We Needed Him*, 63–96. On the Little Rock Nine case, see Elizabeth Jacoway, *Turn Away Thy Son: Little Rock, the Crisis That Shocked the Nation* (New York: The Free Press, 2007); and Karen Anderson, *Little Rock: Race and Resistance at Central High School* (Princeton, NJ: Princeton University Press, 2010).

17. John Lewis, "Wiley Branton Was There for Us," *Legal Times*, January 2, 1989, 16.

18. Dunbar interview, December 18, 1978. See also Branton interview, October 21, 1970; and Kilpatrick, *There When We Needed Him*, 93–94.

19. Branton interview, October 21, 1970.

20. "Negro Vote Drive Opened in South by Rights Groups," *New York Times*, March 29, 1962. See also SRC Press Release, March 29, 1962, Box 22, Folder 33, MLK Papers, King Center.

21. "Voter Education Project Announced," *Atlanta Daily World*, March 29, 1962; and "2-Year Project Set to Spur Dixie Voter," *Afro-American*, April 7, 1962.

22. "Guides for Answering of Inquiries from the Press or Others," Box 22, Folder 43, MLK Papers, King Center.

23. Commissioner Mortimer Caplin to Senator Herman E. Talmadge, May 15, 1962, Box 34, Folder "Voter Registration 1961–1963," Marshall Papers.

24. Burke Marshall to Leslie Dunbar, March 30, 1962, Box 2, Folder "D 1961–1962," Marshall Papers.

25. Louis E. Lomax, "The Kennedys Move In On Dixie," *Harper's Magazine*, May 1, 1962, 27.

26. Wiley A. Branton to Russell Lynes, May 31, 1962, Steven Lawson Research Papers (in author's possession, hereinafter Lawson Papers). In 2013, Steven Lawson gave me a briefcase of VEP and SRC primary sources from his research on *Black Ballots*. See also Branton interview, October 21, 1970.

27. Stephen Currier to Leslie Dunbar, March 30, 1962, Folder "Southern Regional Council: Voter Education Project 1961–1962," Taconic Foundation Records.

28. Stephen Becker, *Marshall Field III* (New York: Simon and Schuster, 1964), 189.

29. Leslie Dunbar to Maxwell Hahn, May 17, 1962, Box 4X97, Folder "SRC Fall 1962," Field Foundation Archives.

30. Stephen Currier to Mrs. Marshall Field, November 16, 1961, Folder "Southern Regional Council: Voter Education Project 1961–1962," Taconic Foundation Records.

31. Leslie Dunbar to Maxwell Hahn, January 8, 1964, Box 2S438, Folder "SRC, Voter Registration, 1962–1965," Field Foundation Archives.

32. Helen Hill Miller to Wiley Branton, May 7, 1962, Box 17, Folder 19, Stern Fund Records, Wisconsin Historical Society (hereinafter Stern Fund Records).

33. *The Stern Fund: The Story of a Progressive Family Foundation* (New York: Institute for Media Analysis, 1992), 1–39.

34. Marvin Rich to James Farmer, April 20, 1962, Series 5: Community Relations Department, Box 23, Folder 9, CORE Records.

35. Roy Wilkins to Wiley Branton, April 4, 1962, Reel 172, SRC Papers.

36. Martin Luther King Jr. and Wyatt Tee Walker to Wiley Branton, April 6, 1962, Reel 173, SRC Papers.

37. Minutes, VEP Conference, May 1–2, 1962, Reel 174, SRC Papers.

38. Wiley Branton to Whitney Young, Re: VEP 2-7, May 4, 1962, Reel 173, SRC Papers; Wiley Branton to James Forman, Re: VEP 2-5, May 4, 1962, Reel 173, SRC Papers; Wiley Branton to James Farmer, Re: VEP 2-3, May 4, 1962, Series 1: Director's File, Box 9, Folder 8, CORE Records; Wiley Branton to Wyatt Tee Walker, Re: VEP 2-4, May 4, 1962, Box 138, Folder 1, SCLC Papers, King Center; and Wiley Branton to Roy Wilkins, Re: VEP 2-6, May 4, 1962, Reel 173, SRC Papers.

39. Wiley Branton, "Conditions Governing Grants," Voter Education Project, May 1962, Box 138, Folder 1, SCLC Papers, King Center.

40. VEP Summary Report, SNCC Program in Mississippi, May 11, 1962–July 31, 1962, Reel 176, SRC Papers.

41. VEP Summary Report, SNCC Program in Mississippi, May 11, 1962–July 31, 1962.

42. James Farmer to Wiley Branton, June 8, 1962, Series 1: Director's File, Box 9, Folder 8, CORE Records.

43. Wyatt Tee Walker to Wiley Branton, June 22, 1962, Reel 173, SRC Papers; and VEP Summary Report, SCLC Crash Program Grant, n.d., Reel 176, SRC Papers.

44. VEP First Status Report, September 20, 1962. See also Field Report, All-Citizens Registration Committee of Atlanta, n.d., Reel 176, SRC Papers; Interoffice Request for Payment Form, Voter Education Project, VEP 2-2, April 27, 1962, Reel 173, SRC Papers; VEP Summary Report, NSA Project, Raleigh, North Carolina, June 15–August 3, 1962, Reel 176, SRC Papers; and VEP Summary Report, AFSC Project—Jackson, Tennessee, June 15–August 10, 1962, Reel 176, SRC Papers.

45. Wiley Branton to All Interested Parties, July 12, 1962, Box 138, Folder 1, SCLC Papers, King Center; "Introducing Our Newsletter," *Voter Education Project Newsletter* 1, no. 1 (August 1963), Box 2, Folder 10, Congress of Racial Equality Southern Regional Office Records, Wisconsin Historical Society; Annual Report of the Executive Director of the Southern Regional Council for 1963, Box 12, Folder 15, Dunbar Papers; and Alec Fazackerley Hickmott, "Randolph Blackwell and the Economics of Civil Rights" (MPhil thesis, University of Sussex, 2010).

46. See Table II VEP First Annual Report; and Table III in VEP Second Annual Report. In some cases, the VEP ended up paying more than originally agreed upon. For example, Wiley Branton first told James Farmer that CORE would receive $12,800, but the final figure recorded at the end of the fiscal year was $13,800. On Womanpower Unlimited, see Tiyi Makeda Morris, *Womanpower Unlimited and the Black Freedom Struggle in Mississippi* (Athens: University of Georgia Press, 2015).

47. Testimony of Wiley Branton before the United States Commission on Civil Rights, February 16–20, 1965, in Jackson, Mississippi, Volume I: Voting, 182.

48. Testimony of Wiley Branton before the United States Commission on Civil Rights, February 16–20, 1965.

49. Branch, *Parting the Waters*, 635.

50. Wiley Branton to Aaron Henry, September 5, 1962, Reel 177, SRC Papers. On COFO, see also Watters and Cleghorn, *Climbing Jacob's Ladder*, 59–64; Carson, *In Struggle*, 77–81; Dittmer, *Local People*, 143–57; Payne, *I've Got the Light of Freedom*, 132–79; and Laura Visser-Maessen, *Robert Parris Moses: A Life in Civil Rights and Leadership at the Grassroots* (Chapel Hill: University of North Carolina Press, 2016), 95–97. I use "COFO" and "SNCC" interchangeably. Most people in COFO were originally from SNCC, but operations often fell under the banner of COFO.

51. COFO Financial Report, October 1962, Reel 177, SRC Papers; and COFO Comprehensive Report, August–November 9, 1962, Reel 177, SRC Papers.

52. Jack Minnis to Bob Moses, October 3, 1962, Reel 177, SRC Papers.

53. Jack Minnis to Bob Moses, October 16, 1962, Reel 177, SRC Papers.

54. Wiley Branton to Bob Moses, November 29, 1962, Reel 177, SRC Papers.

55. Wiley Branton to Bob Moses, December 6, 1962, Reel 177, SRC Papers.

56. VEP Field Report, Charles McLaurin, "Report on Activity in Ruleville and Sunflower County from August 19th to December 28th," n.d., Reel 177, SRC Papers (all quotes). On the longer movement in Sunflower County, see Moye, *Let the People Decide*. On Fannie Lou Hamer, see Chana Kai Lee, *For Freedom's Sake: The Life of Fannie*

Lou Hamer (Urbana: University of Illinois Press, 1999); Kay Mills, *This Little Light of Mine: The Life of Fannie Lou Hamer* (Lexington: University Press of Kentucky, 2007); and Christopher Myers Asch, *The Senator and the Sharecropper: The Freedom Struggles of James O. Eastland and Fannie Lou Hamer* (New York: The New Press, 2008). See also Cobb, *This Nonviolent Stuff'll Get You Killed.*

57. VEP First Annual Report; and Watters and Cleghorn, *Climbing Jacob's Ladder,* 50.

58. Report from Charlie Cobb on Voter Registration Project in Greenville, Mississippi, received at VEP office on December 19, 1962, Reel 177, SRC Papers (emphasis in original).

59. Field Report, Bob Moses, December 1962, Reel 177, SRC Papers.

60. Jack Minnis, "Mississippi Field Trip," January 9–11, 1963, Reel 177, SRC Papers.

61. Quoted in Branch, *Parting the Waters,* 714–15. See also Bob Moses to Wiley Branton, February 22, 1963, Reel 177, SRC Papers.

62. Wiley Branton to Bob Moses, February 27, 1963, Reel 177, SRC Papers.

63. Quoted in Forman, *The Making of Black Revolutionaries,* 295.

64. "Two Shots Hit Voter Worker," *Delta Democrat-Times,* March 1, 1963, clipping in Box 2, Folder 12, Curry Papers; and First VEP Annual Report, 29–30.

65. Wiley Branton to President John F. Kennedy, March 1, 1963, Part 1, Reel 8, Civil Rights During the Kennedy Administration, 1961–1963.

66. Quoted in Payne, *I've Got the Light of Freedom,* 163. See also Claude Sitton, "Negro's Shooting Spurs Vote Drive," *New York Times,* March 2, 1963.

67. Watters and Cleghorn, *Climbing Jacob's Ladder,* 59.

68. VEP News Release, March 31, 1963, Box 2S438, Folder "SRC, Voter Registration, 1962–1965," Field Foundation Archives. See also VEP First Annual Report, 30–32; and Branton interview, October 21, 1970.

69. Wiley Branton, "Description of Problems Encountered by the Voter Education Project in the State of Mississippi between April 1, 1962 and November 1, 1963," 8, Prepared for the United States Commission on Civil Rights, n.d., Reel 177, SRC Papers.

70. Wiley Branton, "Description of Problems Encountered by the Voter Education Project in the State of Mississippi between April 1, 1962 and November 1, 1963," 8–9; and Field Report, Joe McCastor, "Report on Voter Registration Activities in Greenwood, Mississippi," n.d., Reel 177, SRC Papers.

71. Field Report, Bobby Talbert, March 25, 1963, Reel 177, SRC Papers; Dittmer, *Local People,* 151; and Payne, *I've Got the Light of Freedom,* 170.

72. VEP First Annual Report, 32.

73. Dittmer, *Local People,* 153.

74. Wiley Branton to Robert F. Kennedy, March 29, 1963, Reel 175, SRC Papers.

75. Claude Sitton, "U.S. Court Hears Race Plea Today," *New York Times,* April 1, 1963.

76. Quoted in Dittmer, *Local People,* 154.

77. Branton interview, October 21, 1970.

78. Dittmer, *Local People,* 152–57; and Payne, *I've Got the Light of Freedom,* 173–74.

79. Wiley Branton to Aaron Henry, March 28, 1963, Reel 177, SRC Papers.

80. Wiley Branton and Robert Moses, "Proposed Budget for Mississippi Registration Program," May 1–September 30, 1963, May 3, 1963, Reel 177, SRC Papers.

81. Wiley Branton to Aaron Henry, May 7, 1963, Reel 177, SRC Papers.

82. Branton, "Description of Problems Encountered by the Voter Education Project," 10–11.

83. Quoted in Dittmer, *Local People*, 212.

84. Branton interview, October 21, 1970.

85. Interview with Charles Sherrod by Joseph Mosnier, June 4, 2011, Civil Rights History Project, Smithsonian Institution's National Museum of African American History and Culture and the Library of Congress. On the Albany Movement, see especially Carson, *In Struggle*, 56–65; Wesley C. Hogan, *Many Minds, One Heart: SNCC's Dream for a New America* (Chapel Hill: University of North Carolina Press, 2007), 66–77; and Thomas F. Jackson, *From Civil Rights to Human Rights: Martin Luther King Jr. and the Struggle for Economic Justice* (Philadelphia: University of Pennsylvania Press, 2007), 148–54.

86. Interview with Laurie Pritchett by James Reston, April 23, 1976, 3, B-0027, in the Southern Oral History Program Collection #4007, Southern Historical Collection, Wilson Library, University of North Carolina at Chapel Hill.

87. Wiley Branton to Dr. W. G. Anderson, August 17, 1962, Lawson Papers (all quotes).

88. Penny Patch to Wiley Branton, December 8, 1962, Lawson Papers.

89. Carolyn Daniels, "We Just Kept Going," in *Hands on the Freedom Plow: Personal Accounts by Women in SNCC*, ed. Faith S. Holsaert, Martha Prescod Norman Noonan, Judy Richardson, Betty Garman Robinson, Jean Smith Young, and Dorothy M. Zellner (Urbana: University of Illinois Press, 2010), 154.

90. Jack Chatfield to SNCC Atlanta, December 24, 1962, Lawson Papers. See also Jack Chatfield to SNCC Atlanta, December 13, 1962, Lawson Papers.

91. Ralph Allen, Field Report, n.d., arrived at the VEP on April 6, 1963, Lawson Papers.

92. Ralph Allen, Field Report, n.d., arrived at the VEP on April 6, 1963, Lawson Papers.

93. Interview with Penelope Patch by David Cline, April 17, 2010, U-0453, in the Southern Oral History Program Collection #4007, Southern Historical Collection, Wilson Library, University of North Carolina at Chapel Hill.

94. Allen, Field Report, n.d., arrived at the VEP on April 6, 1963.

95. Janie Culbreth Rambeau, "Ripe for the Picking," in Holsaert et al., *Hands on the Freedom Plow*, 96.

96. Allen, Field Report, n.d., arrived at the VEP on April 6, 1963.

97. Chatfield to SNCC Atlanta, December 13, 1962.

98. Field Report, Charles Sherrod to Wiley Branton, February 3, 1963, Lawson Papers.

99. Allen, Field Report, n.d., arrived at the VEP on April 6, 1963.

100. Don Harris to VEP, March 3, 1964, Lawson Papers.

101. Don Harris to Wiley Branton, March 5, 1964, Reel 182 SRC Papers; Wiley Branton to James Forman, March 13, 1964, Reel 182, SRC Papers; Don Harris to Wiley Branton, March 21, 1964, Lawson Papers; and Randolph Blackwell to Wiley Branton, March 30, 1964, Reel 176, SRC Papers.

102. Don Harris, Field Report, March 27, 1964, Reel 182, SRC Papers.

103. George Bess to Don Harris and Worth Long, March 2–April 6, 1964, Lawson Papers.

104. Sammy Mahone and Sammy Rushin to Donald Harris and Wiley Branton, Field Report from Americus of two-week period ending August 5, 1964, Lawson Papers.

105. Sammy Mahone and Sammy Rushin to Donald Harris, received by VEP September 2, 1964, Lawson Papers.

106. Andrew Young to Wiley Branton, April 30, 1964, Reel 183, SRC Papers; Don Harris to VEP, July 12, 1964, Reel 182, SRC Papers; and Wiley Branton to James Forman, July 21, 1964, Reel 182, SRC Papers.

107. Randolph Blackwell to Wiley Branton, July 25, 1963, Reel 176, SRC Papers; and Democratic Coalition Newsletter 1, no. 9, August 13, 1963, Reel 181, SRC Papers. On the Democratic Coalition, see Max Krochmal, *Blue Texas: The Making of a Multiracial Democratic Coalition in the Civil Rights Era* (Chapel Hill: University of North Carolina Press, 2016), 318, 351–58; and Benjamin Márquez, *Democratizing Texas Politics: Race, Identity, and Mexican American Empowerment, 1945–2002* (Austin: University of Texas Press, 2014), 57–58. For his reflections on the rise of liberalism in Texas, see Interview with Lawrence C. Goodwyn by Jack Bass, November 18, 1974, A-0188, in the Southern Oral History Program Collection #4007, Southern Historical Collection, Wilson Library, University of North Carolina at Chapel Hill.

108. Nell Goodwyn to Wiley Branton, July 19, 1963, Reel 181, SRC Papers.

109. Jean Levine to Larry Goodwyn, August 13, 1963, Reel 181, SRC Papers; and Wiley Branton to Larry Goodwyn, August 21, 1963, Reel 181, SRC Papers.

110. Larry Goodwyn to Jack Minnis, September 6, 1963, Reel 181, SRC Papers.

111. Larry Goodwyn to Wiley Branton, September 1, 1963, Reel 181, SRC Papers.

112. Larry Goodwyn to Wiley A. Branton, October 21, 1963, Reel 181, SRC Papers.

113. Wiley Branton to Larry Goodwyn, September 28, 1963, Reel 181, SRC Papers.

114. Larry Goodwyn to Wiley Branton, October 25, 1963, Reel 181, SRC Papers. See also Wiley Branton to Larry Goodwyn, October 25, 1963, Reel 181, SRC Papers.

115. Dr. Martin Luther King, Jr. to Friend, November 3, 1963, Reel 181, SRC Papers (emphasis in original).

116. ". . . A Message for Official Block Captains," Democratic Coalition newsletter, n.d., Reel 181, SRC Papers (emphasis in original).

117. Maximilian Krochmal, "Labor, Civil Rights, and the Struggle for Democracy in Mid-Twentieth Century Texas" (PhD diss., Duke University, 2011), 514.

118. Wiley Branton to Larry Goodwyn, November 13, 1963, Reel 181, SRC Papers. See also Jack Minnis to Wiley Branton, November 11, 1963, Reel 181, SRC Papers; Larry Goodwyn to Wiley Branton, November 27, 1963, Reel 181, SRC Papers; Joseph A. Loftus, "Setback of Texas Liberals May Affect Kennedy," *New York Times*, November 11, 1963; and Márquez, *Democratizing Texas Politics*, 58.

119. Larry Goodwyn to Wiley Branton, December 17, 1963, Reel 181, SRC Papers.

120. Larry Goodwyn to Wiley Branton, June 8, 1964, Reel 181, SRC Papers. See also VEP Second Annual Report; Wiley Branton to Larry Goodwyn, December 26, 1963, Reel 181, SRC Papers; Larry Goodwyn to Wiley Branton, February 25, 1964, Reel 181, SRC Papers; Wiley Branton to Larry Goodwyn, February 25, 1964, Reel 181, SRC Papers; and Krochmal, "Labor, Civil Rights, and the Struggle," 519–544.

121. Wiley Branton to Marjorie Dammann, September 26, 1963; Wiley Branton to Marjorie Dammann, October 31, 1963; David R. Hunter to Wiley Branton, February 12, 1964; and Wiley Branton to David R. Hunter, February 25, 1964, all in Box 17, Folder 18, Stern Fund Records.

122. Leslie Dunbar to Maxwell Hahn, January 8, 1964, Box 2S438, Folder "SRC, Voter Registration, 1962–1965," Field Foundation Archives.

123. Maxwell Hahn to Leslie Dunbar, April 4, 1964, Box 2S438, Folder "SRC, Voter Registration, 1962–1965," Field Foundation Archives.

124. Leslie Dunbar to Stephen Currier, January 8, 1964, Folder "Southern Regional Council: Voter Education Project, 1963–1964," Taconic Foundation Records.

125. Stephen Currier to Leslie Dunbar, April 22, 1964; Wiley Branton to Stephen Currier, February 4, 1964; and Leslie Dunbar to Stephen Currier, February 10, 1964, Folder "Southern Regional Council: Voter Education Project, 1963–1964," Taconic Foundation Records. On September 28, 1964, the Taconic Foundation granted another $9,000 to the VEP. See Stephen Currier to Leslie Dunbar, September 28, 1964, Folder "Southern Regional Council: Voter Education Project, 1963–1964," Taconic Foundation Records.

126. VEP Report on NAACP Projects in 1962, n.d., Reel 172, SRC Papers.

127. Dunbar interview, December 18, 1978.

128. Branton interview, October 21, 1970. See also Watters and Cleghorn, *Climbing Jacob's Ladder*, 48.

129. Wiley Branton, Memorandum, Re: Talk with Martin Luther King Jr. Re: SCLC Voter Project, February 20, 1963, Lawson Papers.

130. Jack Minnis to Wiley Branton, February 12, 1963, Box 138, Folder 2, SCLC Papers, King Center.

131. Andrew Young to Jack Minnis, February 26, 1963, Box 138, Folder 2, SCLC Papers, King Center.

132. Andrew Young to Jack Minnis, February 26, 1963.

133. Dunbar interview, December 18, 1978.

134. Branton interview, October 21, 1970.

135. "Drive Opens with a Rush," *Charlotte Observer*, September 17, 1963.

136. Wiley Branton to Dr. Reginald A. Hawkins, September 6, 1963, Reel 182, SRC Papers; VEP Field Report, Dr. Reginald A. Hawkins to Wiley Branton, n.d., Reel 182, SRC Papers; Dr. Reginald A. Hawkins to Voter Education Project, Re: "Proposed Budget for February 1 to May 16, 1964," January 16, 1964, Reel 182, SRC Papers; and Wiley Branton to Dr. Reginald A. Hawkins, February 20, 1964, Reel 182, SRC Papers.

137. Hosea Williams to Wiley Branton, May 1, 1963, Lawson Papers (all quotes, emphasis in original). See also Watters and Cleghorn, *Climbing Jacob's Ladder*, 116.

138. VEP First Annual Report, 24–27.

139. CORE Field Report on Iberville Parish, Louisiana, Summer 1963, Lawson Papers.

140. William P. Mitchell to Wiley Branton, October 3, 1964, Lawson Papers.

141. Helen Hayes, Summary Report on Tennessee NAACP, November 2, 1964, Lawson Papers.

142. Narrative Report, Orlando, Florida, 1964, Lawson Papers.

143. Randolph Blackwell to Wiley Branton, February 25, 1964, Reel 176, SRC Papers.

144. Wiley Branton, Memorandum on Field Trips, May 31, 1963, Lawson Papers; and Jack Minnis, Memorandum on Birmingham Field Trip, June 20, 1963, Lawson Papers.

145. Branton testimony, *Hearings Before the United States Commission on Civil Rights*, Vol. I: Voting, Jackson, Mississippi, February 16–20, 1965, 177.

146. The most comprehensive study of voting statistics related to the VEP's work comes from Watters and Cleghorn, *Climbing Jacob's Ladder*, esp. 26–27, 49, 69, 245, and 376–77. See also VEP Second Annual Report, 4–18; Annual Report of the Executive Director of the Southern Regional Council, February 1964, 5–6, Box 12, Folder 15, Dunbar Papers; Annual Report of the Executive Director of the Southern Regional Council, April 1965, 1, Box 12, Folder 15, Dunbar Papers; Claude Sitton, "South Notes Rise in Negro Voters," *New York Times*, May 12, 1964; and Richard M. Valelly, *The Two Reconstructions: The Struggle for Black Enfranchisement* (Chicago: University of Chicago Press, 2004), 186.

147. SRC News Release, "What Happened in the South?" November 15, 1964, Reel 177, SRC Papers.

148. SRC Annual Meeting Minutes, November 20–21, 1964, Box 116, Folder 5, Brailsford R. Brazeal Papers, Robert W. Woodruff Library, Atlanta University Center. See also "What Happened in the South?" November 15, 1964.

149. SRC Executive Director's Annual Report, April 1965.

150. Leslie Dunbar in Watters and Cleghorn, *Climbing Jacob's Ladder*, xv–xvi.

Chapter Four

1. Bayard Rustin, "From Protest to Politics," *Commentary*, February 1965.

2. Leslie Dunbar, "The Changing Mind of the South: The Exposed Nerve," *The Journal of Politics* 26, no. 1 (February 1964): 20 (emphasis in original).

3. *The Negro Family: The Case for National Action* (Washington, DC: Office of Policy Planning and Research, U.S. Department of Labor, March 1965), 29.

4. To arrive at 403 as an approximation and an expenditure total of $580,065.73, I compared Maureen McLaughlin, "Voter Project Loses Grant," *Washington Post*, August 4, 1966; "VEP in Second Year; 50 Projects Funded," *VEP News* 1, no. 1 (June 1967); "VEP Programs Total 122 in '67; Busy Year Ahead," *VEP News* 2, no. 1 (January 1968); and Voter Education Projects, State-by-State Distribution, 1968, Box 43, Folder 4, Office Files, VEP Records.

5. Transcript, President Lyndon B. Johnson address to Congress, March 15, 1965, http://www.lbjlibrary.org/lyndon-baines-johnson/speeches-films/president -johnsons-special-message-to-the-congress-the-american-promise.

6. Leslie Dunbar to Stephen Currier, March 16, 1965, Folder "Southern Regional Council: Voter Education Project, 1965—June 1966," Taconic Foundation Records.

7. Confidential Report of the Southern Regional Council, by the Public Affairs Program of the Ford Foundation, May 7, 1965, Unpublished Reports, Series 010437, Office of the President, Office Files of Henry T. Heald, Ford Foundation Records.

8. Southern Regional Council, "Programming for Civic Education," September 1965, Folder "Southern Regional Council: Voter Education Project, 1965—June 1966," Taconic Foundation Records.

9. Dunbar interview, December 18, 1978.

10. Leslie Dunbar to Maxwell Hahn, May 16, 1965, Box 8, Folder 4, Dunbar Papers.

11. Leslie Dunbar to Stephen Currier, September 22, 1965, Folder "Southern Regional Council: Voter Education Project, 1965—June 1966," Taconic Foundation Records.

12. Dunbar interview, December 18, 1978; and "Atlantan Will Head Field Foundation," *Washington Post*, August 9, 1965.

13. Paul Anthony to Leslie Dunbar, December 7, 1965, Box 2S438, Folder "SRC, Voter Registration, 1962–1965," Field Foundation Archives. See also "Southern Reg. Council Picks New Director," *Pittsburgh Courier*, August 21, 1965; and Dunbar interview, December 18, 1978.

14. "A Proposal for Support of a Project in Citizenship Participation," December 1965, Box 2S438, Folder "SRC, Voter Registration, 1962–1965," Field Foundation Archives.

15. VEP Financial Report, as of July 15, 1966, Folder "Southern Regional Council: Voter Education Project, July—December 1966," Taconic Foundation Records.

16. Jordan, *Vernon Can Read!*, 24–25, 179; and Dunbar interview, December 18, 1978.

17. Jordan, *Vernon Can Read!*, 83.

18. Jordan, *Vernon Can Read!*, 68–125.

19. Jordan, *Vernon Can Read!*, 126–68.

20. Jordan, *Vernon Can Read!*, 43 (also 166–82). On Jordan's political ideology, see Interview with Vernon E. Jordan Jr. by Robert Penn Warren, March 17, 1964, Louie B. Nunn Center for Oral History, University of Kentucky.

21. Interview with Vernon E. Jordan Jr. by Evan Faulkenbury, July 19, 2013, in author's possession.

22. Alan Gartner to Paul Anthony, October 25, 1965, Box 62, Folder 14, Office Files, VEP Records.

23. Alan Gartner to Vernon Jordan, November 30, 1965, Box 62, Folder 14, Office Files, VEP Records.

24. Martin Luther King Jr. to Vernon Jordan, December 28, 1965, Box 22, Folder 40, MLK Papers, King Center.

25. John Morsell to Vernon Jordan, December 3, 1965, Box 2S438, Folder "SRC, Voter Registration, 1962–1965," Field Foundation Archives.

26. Vernon Jordan to Paul Anthony, December 29, 1965, Box 2S438, Folder "SRC, Voter Registration, 1962–1965," Field Foundation Archives.

27. Press Release, Southern Regional Council, February 18, 1966, Folder 7573, North Carolina Fund Records #4710, Southern Historical Collection, Louis Round Wilson Library, University of North Carolina at Chapel Hill (hereinafter NCF Records). See also "New Voter Drive Opened in South," *New York Times*, February 18, 1966; and Robert E. Baker, "Project That Registered 700,000 Again Seeks Negro Voters in South," *Washington Post*, February 18, 1966.

28. Address by Attorney General Nicholas Katzenbach to the Southern Regional Council, February 28, 1966, Box 2S438, Folder "SRC, Voter Registration, 1962–1965," Field Foundation Archives.

29. Address by Attorney General Nicholas Katzenbach to the Southern Regional Council, February 28, 1966.

30. John Herbers, "U.S. to Underplay Voter Drive Role," *New York Times*, March 1, 1966.

31. Remer Tyson, "It's Time to Let Votes Talk on Rights, Katzenbach Says," *Atlanta Constitution*, March 1, 1966. See also Robert E. Baker, "Katzenbach Advises Voter Education Drive," *Washington Post*, March 1, 1966; and Jack Nelson, "Katzenbach Speech Received Coolly by Rights Leaders," *Los Angeles Times*, March 1, 1966.

32. Jordan, *Vernon Can Read!*, 182.

33. Jordan, *Vernon Can Read!*, 184 (also, 182–85); Annual Report of the Executive Director of the Southern Regional Council for 1965, January 1966, Box 2S440, Folder "Southern Regional Council (State Councils), 1961," Field Foundation Archives; "VEP in Second Year; 50 Projects Funded," *VEP News* 1, no. 1 (June 1967); Interview with Thaddeus Olive by Susan Glisson, November 23, 2002, Southern Regional Council Oral History Collection, George A. Smathers Libraries, University of Florida; and Guidelines for Voter Education Project Grants, n.d., circa July 1966, Folder "Southern Regional Council: Voter Education Project, July–December 1966," Taconic Foundation Records.

34. Statistical Summary, Voter Education Project, January–October 1966, Box 2T25, Folder "SRC Inc. (VEP) Fall 1966," Field Foundation Archives; A Report on the Voter Education Project, October 19, 1967, Box 2T79, Folder "SRC (VEP) Fall 1967," Field Foundation Archives; Voter Education Projects, State-by-State Distribution, 1968, Box 43, Folder 4, Office Files, VEP Records. For 1969, no records exist listing each project, but the SRC Annual Report for 1969 counted ninety-eight projects for that year. See Annual Report of the Executive Director of the Southern Regional Council for 1969, January 1970, Box 2S415, Folder "SRC General 1971," Field Foundation Archives.

35. Grant Request, League of Women Voters of Alabama, Auburn, n.d., Reel 184, SRC Papers; Vernon Jordan to Mrs. Wallace Alston Jr., March 11, 1966, Reel 184, SRC Papers; R.E. Peters to Vernon Jordan, June 21, 1966, Reel 184, SRC Papers; Memorandum to VEP Advisory Committee, n.d., circa July 1966, Folder "Southern Regional Council: Voter Education Project, July–December 1966," Taconic Foundation Records; Vernon Jordan to Alice Alston, July 12, 1966, Reel 184, SRC Papers; and Annual Report of the Executive Director of the Southern Regional Council for 1966, January 1967, Box 2S440, Folder "Southern Regional Council (State Councils), 1961," Field Foundation Archives.

36. See Robert R. Korstad and James L. Leloudis, *To Right These Wrongs: The North Carolina Fund and the Battle to End Poverty and Inequality in 1960s America* (Chapel Hill: University of North Carolina Press, 2010).

37. "No Time Like the Present to Begin," *Durham Sun*, May 31, 1967. See also Minutes, North Carolina Voter Education Meeting, February 27, 1967, Folder 694, NCF Records; NCVEP Press Release, May 30, 1967, Folder 7573, NCF Records; Vernon Jordan to A. I. Dunlap, April 26, 1967, Folder 714, NCF Records; Day Piercy, "Leadership

Training and the NCVEP," August 26, 1968, 31, Folder 7497, NCF Records; and Minutes, Full Board Meeting of NCVEP, June 1, 1967, Folder 7566, NCF Records; and First Annual Report of the NCVEP, May 15, 1967–December 31, 1967, Folder 695, NCF Records.

38. Memorandum to the VEP Advisory Committee, n.d., Folder "SRC: VEP, July–December 1966," Taconic Foundation Records.

39. Glenn Robinson, "Registration Brisk in Charleston," *Charleston Evening Post*, n.d., reprinted in *VEP News* 2, no. 2 (February 1968). See also VEP Report, October 19, 1967.

40. Vernon Jordan to Floyd McKissick, March 30, 1967; Ruth Turner to Vernon Jordan, April 12, 1967; and Vernon Jordan to Ruth Turner, April 20, 1967, all in Box 62, Folder 14, Office Files, VEP Records.

41. Memorandum to Stephen Currier and Jane Lee Eddy, July 28, 1966, Folder "Southern Regional Council: Voter Education Project, July–December 1966," Taconic Foundation Records; and VEP Report, October 19, 1967.

42. John Morsell to Vernon Jordan, December 14, 1966, Box 2T78, Folder "SRC (VEP) Fall 1966," Field Foundation Archives.

43. "SCLC Disowns Pickets at VEP," *Afro-American*, May 10, 1969; Jordan, *Vernon Can Read!*, 193–94; "Civil Rights Group Pickets Another That Denied Help," *Wall Street Journal*, April 4, 1969; and Vernon Jordan to Hosea Williams, April 28, 1966, Box 22, Folder 40, MLK Papers, King Center.

44. Press Release, Voter Education Project, June 13, 1966, Reel 177, SRC Papers.

45. "The Effects of Federal Examiners and Organized Registration Campaigns on Negro Voter Registration," Voter Education Project Special Report, July 1966, Box 855, Folder 12, SCLC Papers, Emory University.

46. Voter Education Project, "Voter Registration in the South—Summer, 1966," Box 563, Folder 3, SCLC Papers, Stuart A. Rose Manuscript, Archives, and Rare Book Library, Emory University.

47. United States Commission on Civil Rights, *Political Participation* (Washington, DC: Government Printing Office, 1968).

48. Vernon Jordan, "Changing Rules in the Middle of the Game," *VEP News* 2, no. 5 (May 1968).

49. "How to Conduct a Registration Campaign," Voter Education Project, Patricia Collins, May 1967, Folder 1122, NCF Records.

50. "Know Your Georgia Government," Voter Education Project, 1967, Folder 1122, NCF Records.

51. Press Release, Southern Regional Council and Voter Education Project, "What Happened in the South, 1966," December 14, 1966, Folder 1120, NCF Records.

52. "Stephen Currier Missing on Flight," *New York Times*, January 19, 1967; "Heiress, Husband Missing on Plane Trip in Caribbean," *Los Angeles Times*, January 19, 1967; "Vanished Couple Feared Lost at Sea," *New York Amsterdam News*, February 11, 1967; Lankford, *The Last American Diplomat*, 347; and Fleming, *The Potomac Chronicle*, 169–72.

53. Gertrude Wilson, "Best of the Best," *New York Amsterdam News*, January 28, 1967.

54. Robert E. Baker, "Court Asked to Rule Curriers Legally Dead," *Washington Post*, February 2, 1967.

55. Whitney Young, "The Curriers Passed This Way and Made World a Better Place," *Philadelphia Tribune*, February 28, 1967. See also Edward P. Morgan, Radio Editorial on ABC Radio Network, February 3, 1967, Reel 27, SRC Papers; Reese Cleghorn, "A Vanished Plane, a Fortune, and a Story," unknown clipping, n.d., Reel 27, SRC Papers; and "800 Attend Rites for the Curriers," *New York Times*, February 16, 1967.

56. Paul Anthony to David Hunter, March 28, 1967, Box 17, Folder "VEP," Stern Fund Papers.

57. Vernon Jordan, "Martin King's Crusade Will Be Carried On," *VEP News* 2, no. 4 (April 1968). See also Leslie Dunbar to Paul Anthony, November 22, 1967, Box 64, Folder 13, Office Files, VEP Records; Leslie Dunbar to Paul Anthony, April 11, 1968, Box 64, Folder 13, Office Files, VEP Records; and Contributions to the VEP, n.d., received by Vernon Jordan on November 5, 1968, Box 65, Folder 20, Office Files, VEP Records.

58. A Statement of the Voter Education Project of the Southern Regional Council, Inc., June 14, 1969, Reel 170, SRC Papers.

59. Annual Report of the SRC Executive Director, January 1967.

60. Agenda, State Legislators Seminar, Voter Education Project, December 29–30, 1966, Box 2T39, Folder "SRC (VEP) miscellaneous Fall 1966," Field Foundation Archives.

61. Vernon Jordan to Leslie Dunbar, January 5, 1967, Box 2T39, Folder "SRC (VEP) miscellaneous Fall 1966," Field Foundation Archives.

62. Agenda, Local Government Seminar, Clark College, July 27–29, 1967, Folder "Southern Regional Council: Voter Education Project, 1967–1971," Taconic Foundation Records.

63. Cheryl Chisholm, "Officeholders Meet at Clark," *VEP News* 1, no. 3 (August 1967).

64. Cheryl Chisholm, "Officeholders Meet at Clark," *VEP News* 1, no. 3 (August 1967).

65. W. F. Minor, "Newly Elected Mississippians Told to Be on Guard," *New Orleans Times Picayune*, December 15, 1967.

66. Bayard Rustin, Speech to Institute for Mississippi Negro Elected Officials, Box 42, Folder 5, Office Files, VEP Records. See also Agenda, Institute for Mississippi Negro Elected Officials, December 14–15, 1967, Box 2S415, Folder "SRC: State Councils, Desegregation 1970," Field Foundation Archives; "Mississippi Negro Officials Meet, Conquer Bond Problem," *VEP News* 1, no. 7 (December 1967); and Vernon Jordan, "Jackson Meeting Historic Moment in Mississippi," *VEP News* 1, no. 7 (December 1967).

67. Marvin Wall to Vernon Jordan, January 26, 1968, Box 17, Folder "VEP," Stern Fund Papers. See also "Negro Candidates Make Strong Bid in Three States," *VEP News* 1, no. 5 (October 1967); "Negroes Win Major Races in Three Southern States," *VEP News* 1, no. 6 (November 1967); Vernon Jordan, "Candidates Fared Poorly? We Don't Agree," *VEP News* 1, no. 6 (November 1967); and Frederick Graves, "Black Political Power Now a Reality as Negroes Win Election," *Jet*, November 23, 1967, 6–7.

68. Vernon Jordan, Statement to the Associated Press Managing Editors Annual Convention, November 15, 1968, Box 2T79, Folder "VEP Fall 1967," Field Foundation Archives.

69. Janet Wells, "Over 100 Blacks Elected Nov. 5," *VEP News* 2, no. 11 (November 1968); and "Nov. 5 Winners Listed," *VEP News* 2, no. 11 (November 1968).

70. Vernon Jordan, ". . . A Rapidly Growing List . . ." Opening Remarks in the Conference Proceedings of the Southwide Conference of Black Elected Officials,

December 11, 1968, Box 2T71, Folder "SRC, Inc.," Field Foundation Archives. See also Harmon Perry, "Negro Politicians Watched, Voter Project Director Says," *Atlanta Journal*, December 12, 1968; and Annual Report of the Executive Director of the Southern Regional Council for 1968, January 1969, Box 2S415, Folder "SRC General 1971," Field Foundation Archives.

71. Vernon Jordan, ". . . A Rapidly Growing List . . ."

72. "Report of the Conference Coordinator," Southwide Conference of Black Elected Officials, n.d., Folder "Southern Regional Council: Conference of Black Elected Officials 1968," Taconic Foundation Records.

73. "Report of the Conference Coordinator," Southwide Conference of Black Elected Officials, n.d. See also Conference Proceedings of the Southwide Conference of Black Elected Officials, December 11–14, 1968, Box 2T71, Folder "SRC, Inc.," Field Foundation Archives.

74. Quoted in Janet Wells, "200 Black Elected Officials Attend First Southwide Meet," *VEP News* 2, no. 12 (December 1968).

75. Rep. Julian Bond, ". . . An Attack on All of Us . . ." in Conference Proceedings of the Southwide Conference of Black Elected Officials.

76. "The Use of Black Power," *Atlanta Constitution*, December 12, 1968. See also Ralph McGill, "Southerners at Their Best," *Atlanta Constitution*, December 12, 1968.

77. Lucius D. Amerson to Vernon Jordan, December 30, 1968, Folder "Southern Regional Council: Conference of Black Elected Officials 1968," Taconic Foundation Records.

78. Albert W. Thompson to Vernon Jordan, December 16, 1968, Folder "Southern Regional Council: Conference of Black Elected Officials 1968," Taconic Foundation Records.

79. Joseph A. Jordan Jr. to Vernon Jordan, December 19, 1968, Folder "Southern Regional Council: Conference of Black Elected Officials 1968," Taconic Foundation Records.

80. V. A. Edwards to Vernon Jordan, December 18, 1968, Folder "Southern Regional Council: Conference of Black Elected Officials 1968," Taconic Foundation Records. See also Steven F. Lawson, *In Pursuit of Power: Southern Blacks and Electoral Politics, 1965–1982.* New York: Columbia University Press, 1985.

81. Minutes to the Advisory Meeting of the VEP, June 21–23, 1968, Box 43, Folder 3, Office Files, VEP Records. See also Vernon Jordan to VEP Advisory Committee, June 21, 1968, Box 43, Folder 3, Office Files, VEP Records.

82. Leslie Dunbar to Vernon Jordan, November 27, 1968, Box 64, Folder 13, Office Files, VEP Records. See also Memorandum from the Field Foundation on VEP Grant Proposal, Fall 1968, Box 2T71, Folder "Southern Regional Council Miscellaneous (VEP) Fall 1968," Field Foundation Archives; and Memorandum from the Taconic Foundation on VEP Grant Proposal, November 26, 1968, Folder "Southern Regional Council: Voter Education Project, 1967–1971," Taconic Foundation Records.

83. "Voter Registration in the South—Summer, 1968," Folder 7607, NCF Records.

84. John Morsell to Vernon Jordan, March 31, 1969, Box 65, Folder 6, Office Files, VEP Records.

85. Jordan, *Vernon Can Read!*, 183.

86. Annual Report of the Executive Director of the Southern Regional Council for 1969, January 1970, Box 2S415, Folder "SRC General 1971," Field Foundation Archives.

Chapter Five

1. Statement of Hon. Wright Patman, *Hearings Before the Committee on Ways and Means*, House of Representatives, 91st Congress, First Session on the Subject of Tax Reform, Part 1, 15. See also Robert Sherrill, "'The Last of the Great Populists' Takes on the Foundations, the Banks, the Federal Reserve, the Treasury," *New York Times Magazine*, March 16, 1969.

2. On CORE, the Ford Foundation, and Carl Stokes, see Karen Ferguson, "Organizing the Ghetto: The Ford Foundation, CORE, and White Power in the Black Power Era, 1967–1969," *Journal of Urban History* 34, no. 1 (November 2007): 67–100; and Leonard M. Moore, *Carl B. Stokes and the Rise of Black Political Power* (Urbana: University of Illinois Press, 2002), 56.

3. On changes in conservative resistance to the civil rights movement after 1965, see Earl and Merle Black, *The Rise of Southern Republicans* (Cambridge, MA: Harvard University Press, 2002); Joshua D. Farrington, *Black Republicans and the Transformation of the GOP* (Philadelphia: University of Pennsylvania Press, 2016); Dean J. Kotlowski, *Nixon's Civil Rights: Politics, Principle, and Policy* (Cambridge, MA: Harvard University Press, 2002); Timothy N. Thurber, *Republicans and Race: The GOP's Frayed Relationship with African Americans, 1945–1974* (Lawrence: University Press of Kansas, 2013); and Kevin Yuill, *Richard Nixon and the Rise of Affirmative Action: The Pursuit of Racial Equality in an Era of Limits* (Lanham, MD: Rowman and Littlefield, 2006).

4. See Korstad and Leloudis, *To Right These Wrongs*, 328–35; and Zunz, *Philanthropy in America*, 228–31.

5. Annual Report of the Executive Director of the Southern Regional Council for 1969, January 1970, Box 2S415, Folder "SRC General 1971," Field Foundation Archives.

6. Francesta Farmer and Ruby Martin, "A Confidential Report on an Evaluation of the Voter Education Project," July 1984, Box 2T49, Folder "A Confidential Report on an Evaluation of the Voter Education Project," Field Foundation Archives.

7. Diane Galloway-May to Ozell Sutton, February 26, 1992, Reel 6389, Series OVP—Finance and Administration, Ford Foundation Records.

8. "Vote to Probe Red Influence in Foundations," *Chicago Daily Tribune*, April 5, 1952.

9. Walter White, "Cox Committee Tactics Threaten Good Works of Great Foundations," *Chicago Defender*, December 6, 1952. See also "Foundations Deny Knowledge of Supporting Subversives," *Washington Post*, December 4, 1952; "House Unit Criticizes Foundations for Aiding Some Reds but Generally Praises Projects," *Washington Post*, January 3, 1953; and Zunz, *Philanthropy in America*, 193–94.

10. Murrey Harder, "New Probe in Works: Reece Aims at Foundations Again," *Washington Post*, July 20, 1953.

11. "Probing Foundations," *Washington Post*, August 2, 1953.

12. See also Alice O'Connor, "The Politics of Rich and Rich: Postwar Investigations of Foundations and the Rise of the Philanthropic Right," in *American Capitalism: Social Thought and Political Economy in the Twentieth Century*, ed. Nelson Lichtenstein, 228–248

(Philadelphia: University of Pennsylvania Press, 2006); and Zunz, *Philanthropy in America*, 194–95.

13. "Personal Business," *Business Week*, May 7, 1960, 153–54.

14. "Tax-Exempt Foundations," *Washington Post*, March 29, 1968. See also Waldemar A. Nielsen, *The Big Foundations* (New York: Columbia University Press, 1972), 5–9; Thomas A. Troyer, "The 1969 Private Foundation Law: Historical Perspective on Its Origins and Underpinnings," *The Exempt Organization Tax Review* 27, no. 1 (January 2000): 55–59; Nancy Beck Young, *Wright Patman: Populism, Liberalism, and the American Dream* (Dallas: Southern Methodist University Press, 2000), 207–16; William H. Byrnes IV, "The Private Foundation's Topsy Turvy Road in the American Political Process," *Houston Business and Tax Law Journal* 4 (2004): 562; O'Connor, "The Politics of Rich and Rich," 243–44; Korstad and Leloudis, *To Right These Wrongs*, 328–29; and Zunz, *Philanthropy in America*, 202–6.

15. Douglas Robinson, "Ford Grant to Aid CORE in Cleveland," *New York Times*, July 14, 1967.

16. "$175,000 Ford Grant to Help Put Stokes in Office," *Afro-American*, August 5, 1967; and "CORE's Ford Grant Could Help Get Stokes Elected," *Chicago Defender*, August 12, 1967.

17. See Abe Zaidan, "Stokes Victory Shakes Cleveland Politicians," *Washington Post*, October 12, 1967; M. A. Farber, "Ford Fund Widens Reform Role and Draws Mounting Criticism," *New York Times*, December 23, 1968; Korstad and Leloudis, *To Right These Wrongs*, 333–34; and Zunz, *Philanthropy in America*, 220–23. On Carl Stokes, see Moore, *Carl B. Stokes and the Rise of Black Political Power*; and David and Richard Stradling, *Where the River Burned: Carl Stokes and the Struggle to Save Cleveland* (Ithaca, NY: Cornell University Press, 2015).

18. Fred M. Hechinger, "Ford Fund Pledges Drive against Racial Prejudice," *New York Times*, February 18, 1968; Fred M. Hechinger, "Now the Foundations Are on Trial for 'Activism,'" *New York Times*, February 2, 1969; "Ex-Kennedy Men Got $131,000 in Ford Grants, Panel Reports," *New York Times*, February 13, 1969; Nielsen, *The Big Foundations*, 9; Korstad and Leloudis, *To Right These Wrongs*, 329; and Molly C. Michelmore, *Tax and Spend: The Welfare State, Tax Politics, and the Limits of American Liberalism* (Philadelphia: University of Pennsylvania Press, 2012), 107–8.

19. Eileen Shanahan, "Foundations Face Tax Hearings Soon," *New York Times*, January 30, 1969.

20. Statement of Hon. Wright Patman, *Hearings Before the Committee on Ways and Means*, House of Representatives, 91st Congress, First Session on the Subject of Tax Reform, Part 1, 13. See also Rodney Crowther, "Patman Proposes Foundation Tax," *Baltimore Sun*, February 19, 1969.

21. R. Thomas Herman, "Tax-Exempt Foundations Feel the Heat," *Wall Street Journal*, February 18, 1969.

22. Herman, "Tax-Exempt Foundations Feel the Heat." See also Patman, *Hearings Before the Committee on Ways and Means*, 15; Hechinger, "Now the Foundations Are on Trial"; Louis Dombrowski, "Fairer Taxes Nixon's Goal, Kennedy Says," *Chicago Tribune*, February 8, 1969; Crowther, "Patman Proposes Foundation Tax"; Sherrill, "'The Last of the Great Populists'"; and Laurence Stern, "Tax Reformers to Scrutinize Foundations'

Exempt Status," *Washington Post*, February 12, 1969. On Wilbur D. Mills, see Julian E. Zelizer, *Taxing America: Wilbur D. Mills, Congress, and the State, 1945-1975* (Cambridge: Cambridge University Press, 1998).

23. Statement of Hon. John J. Rooney, *Hearings Before the Committee on Ways and Means*, House of Representatives, 91st Congress, First Session on the Subject of Tax Reform, Part 1, 213. See also Philip Warden, "[Rooney] Tells House How Election Rival Used Tax-Free Funds," *Chicago Tribune*, February 20, 1969.

24. Spencer Rich, "Political Use of Tax-Exempt Funds Charged," *Washington Post*, February 20, 1969; Rodney Crowther, "N.Y. Foundation Is Called Campaign Tactic," *Baltimore Sun*, February 20, 1969; "Head of Foundation Responds to Accuser," *New York Times*, February 21, 1969; and Kenneth R. Crawford, "The Rooney Reform," *Newsweek*, March 3, 1969.

25. Statement of McGeorge Bundy, *Hearings Before the Committee on Ways and Means*, House of Representatives, 91st Congress, First Session on the Subject of Tax Reform, Part 1, 363.

26. Bundy, *Hearings Before the Committee on Ways and Means*, 354–431; "House Unit Studying Tax Reform Grills Ford Foundation Chief on Exempt Status," *Wall Street Journal*, February 21, 1969; Eileen Shanahan, "Bundy Backs Ford Grants as within Limits of Law," *New York Times*, February 21, 1969; A. D. Horne, "Grants to RFK Aids Defended by Bundy," *Washington Post*, February 21, 1969; Nielsen, *The Big Foundations*, 11–12; Kai Bird, *The Color of Truth: McGeorge Bundy and William Bundy: Brothers in Arms* (New York: Simon and Schuster, 1998), 387–88; and Troyer, "The 1969 Private Foundation Law," 61.

27. "Text of President Nixon's Speech on Tax Reform," *New York Times*, April 22, 1969.

28. Allan C. Brownfeld, "The Financiers of Revolution," American Conservative Union, April 1969, 11. See also Marquis Childs, "Tax Reform Bill Bodes Ill for Future of Foundations," *Washington Post*, August 4, 1969; and Korstad and Leloudis, *To Right These Wrongs*, 330.

29. William Lambert, "The Justice . . . and the Stock Manipulator," *Life Magazine*, May 9, 1969. See also Fred P. Graham, "Life Said Fortas Received and Repaid a Wolfson Fee," *New York Times*, May 5, 1969; John P. MacKenzie, "Fortas Confirms Fee from Wolfson," *Washington Post*, May 5, 1969; and "Fortas' Letter to Warren on His Ties to Wolfson Foundation," *Washington Post*, May 16, 1969.

30. Whitney Young to President Richard M. Nixon, April 30, 1969, Series 9, Box 54, Folder 531, Office of the Vice-President of the Administration, Office Files of Arthur D. Trottenberg, Ford Foundation Records.

31. Murray Seeger, "Rights Setback Seen in Tax Reform Package," *Los Angeles Times*, May 8, 1969.

32. Press Release, Committee on Ways and Means, U.S. House, May 27, 1969, Series 9, Box 54, Folder 530, Trottenberg Files, Ford Foundation Records.

33. Anne Blaine Harrison and Vernon A. Eagle to Rep. Wilbur D. Mills, June 17, 1969, Box 65, Folder 16, Office Files, VEP Papers.

34. Ruth P. Field, Morris B. Abram, and Leslie Dunbar to Rep. Wilbur D. Mills, June 9, 1969, Box 65, Folder 16, Office Files, VEP Papers.

35. John W. Gardner, "A Whip That Can Cripple," *Washington Post*, June 8, 1969. See also Vernon Jordan to Rep. Wilbur D. Mills, June 19, 1969, Box 65, Folder 16, Office

Files, VEP Papers; "Shaking the Foundations," *Washington Post*, June 1, 1969; Don Oberdorfer, "Administration's Plans Peril Negro Strides in Politics," *Washington Post*, June 5, 1969; and "Foundation Attack Excessive," *Los Angeles Times*, June 18, 1969.

36. Draft Notes on Foundation Executives' Meeting, July 14, 1969, Series 6, Box 37, Folder 827, Office of the Vice-President of the Administration, Office Files of David Bell, Ford Foundation Records. See also Frank C. Porter, "Foundations Hit Plans for New Curbs," *Washington Post*, May 29, 1969; and "Shaking the Foundations," *Washington Post*, June 1, 1969.

37. Roy Wilkins, "Negro Voting Rights," Letter to the Editor, *New York Times*, August 8, 1969.

38. Wilkins, "Negro Voting Rights." See also "Tax Reform Bill OK'd by House Unit," *Chicago Tribune*, August 1, 1969; Childs, "Tax Reform Bill Bodes Ill"; "Preserving the Foundations," *New York Times*, August 6, 1969; "Tax Reform," *Congressional Quarterly*, August 8, 1969, 1423; "Tax-Exempt Organizations," *Congressional Quarterly*, August 8, 1969, 1427; and "Foundations Curbs Seen as Big Blow to Blacks," *Chicago Daily Defender*, August 16, 1969.

39. Part 1, *Hearings Before the Committee on Finance*, United States Senate, 91st Congress, First Session on H.R. 13270, September 4 and 5, 1969 (Washington: US Government Printing Office, 1969), 1.

40. Statement by the Southern Regional Council to the U.S. Senate Finance Committee, Re: HR 13270, September 11, 1969, Reel 170, SRC Papers.

41. John G. Simon to Senate Finance Committee, October 1, 1969, Folder "Southern Regional Council: Voter Education Project, 1967–1971," Taconic Foundation Records.

42. John G. Simon to Senate Finance Committee, October 1, 1969.

43. Michael Harrington, "From the Left," syndicated column, October 4/5, 1969, clipping in Box 3, Folder 4, Printed and Published Materials, VEP Records.

44. Part 6, *Hearings Before the Committee on Finance*, United States Senate, 91st Congress, First Session on H.R. 13270, October 3, 6, 7, 8, and 22, 1969, 5405.

45. Part 6, *Hearings Before the Committee on Finance*, 5405–6.

46. Part 6, *Hearings Before the Committee on Finance*, 5407.

47. Jan Nugent, "Foundation Curb Voted by Hill Unit," *Washington Post*, October 28, 1969.

48. VEP Press Release, October 30, 1969, Box 65, Folder 16, Office Files, VEP Papers. See also Meeting Notes by VEP staff, n.d., Box 65, Folder 16, Office Files, VEP Papers; and Vernon Jordan mass mail, October 28, 1969, Box 65, Folder 16, Office Files, VEP Papers.

49. Nate Welch to Senator Herman Talmadge, October 30, 1969, Box 65, Folder 16, Office Files, VEP Papers.

50. Wallace L. Young Jr. to Senator Russell Long, October 30, 1969, Box 65, Folder 16, Office Files, VEP Papers.

51. Vernon Jordan to "Friend," November 13, 1969, Box 65, Folder 16, Office Files, VEP Papers.

52. James T. Wooten, "Group Says Tax Vote Perils Black Vote," *New York Times*, November 19, 1969. See also "Voter Unit Hits Curb on Foundations," *Washington Post*, November 18, 1969; Reg Murphy, "Knives Sharpened for Registration," *Atlanta*

Constitution, November 19, 1969; David Sanford, "Rocking the Foundations: A Tax Reform that Clubs Reform," *The New Republic*, November 29, 1969, 17–20; and Roy Wilkins to Vernon Jordan, November 19, 1969, Box 65, Folder 16, Office Files, VEP Papers.

53. Eli N. Evans to Vernon Jordan, November 19, 1969, Box 65, Folder 16, Office Files, VEP Papers.

54. Press Release, Council on Foundations, Inc., November 22, 1969, Box 65, Folder 16, Office Files, VEP Papers. For information about penalties, see David F. Rock, "V.E.P. and the 1969 Tax Reform Act," 1970, Box 44, Folder 8, VEP Papers; Homer C. Wadsworth, "Private Foundations and the Tax Reform Act of 1969," *Law and Contemporary Problems* 39, no. 4 (Autumn 1975): 261; "Punishing the Foundations," *New York Times*, November 3, 1969; and General Explanation of the Tax Reform Act of 1969, H.R. 13270, 91st Congress, Public Law 91-172, Prepared by the Staff of the Joint Committee on Internal Revenue Taxation, December 3, 1970 (Washington: U.S. Government Printing Office, 1970).

55. Senator Ralph W. Yarborough and Senator Hugh Scott to "Senator," November 26, 1969, Box 65, Folder 16, Office Files, VEP Papers. See also Vernon Jordan to all U.S. Senators, December 2, 1969, Box 65, Folder 16, Office Files, VEP Papers; and Senate Press Release, "Yarborough Scott to Introduce Amendment on Tax Exempt Foundations," November 26, 1969, Box 65, Folder 16, Office Files, VEP Papers.

56. Duane Riner, "Foundation Aid to Vote Registration Backed," *Atlanta Constitution*, December 5, 1969.

57. Mrs. John A. Campbell to Vernon Jordan, December 10, 1969, Box 65, Folder 16, Office Files, VEP Papers. See also Riner, "Foundation Aid to Vote Registration Backed"; "Private Foundations and the Tax Reform Bill of 1969," Research Report by Maurer, Fleisher, Zon and Associates, Inc., ca. 1971, Series 1, Box 4, Folder 37, Council on Foundations, Inc. Records, Rockefeller Archive Center.

58. David E. Rosenbaum, "14 Conferees to Iron Out Tax Bill Details in Private," *New York Times*, December 12, 1969.

59. Rosenbaum, "14 Conferees to Iron Out Tax Bill." For an explanation of conference committee rules, see Elizabeth Rybicki, "Conference Committee and Related Procedures: An Introduction," Congressional Research Service Report, March 9, 2015.

60. Senator Herman Talmadge to Vernon Jordan, December 15, 1969, Box 67, Folder 11, Office Files, VEP Papers.

61. David F. Rock, "VEP and the 1969 Tax Reform Act," 1970, Box 44, Folder 8, VEP Publications, VEP Papers.

62. Eileen Shanahan, "Tax Bill Signed; President Vows Balanced Budget," *New York Times*, December 31, 1969.

63. McGeorge Bundy to Ford Foundation Trustees, December 24, 1969, Series 2, Box 19, Folder 240, Office of the President, Office Files of McGeorge Bundy, Ford Foundation Records. See also "Foundations and the Tax Reform Act of 1969," Proceedings of Conferences Held on February 17 and 23, 1970 (New York: The Foundation Center, 1970).

64. Paul Anthony to Supporting Foundations, February 27, 1970, Folder "Southern Regional Council: General Program, 1958–1964," Taconic Foundation Records.

65. Paul Anthony to Supporting Foundations, February 27, 1970.

66. Dunbar interview, December 18, 1978 (all quotes).

67. Minutes, VEP, Inc. Board of Directors meeting, March 21, 1970, Reel 177, SRC Papers; and IRS letters to VEP, Inc., May 14, 1970, Box 2T94, Folder "VEP 2nd fall 1969," Field Foundation Archives. See also "The New VEP," *Atlanta Constitution*, June 6, 1970; "South's Voter Education Project Becomes an Independent Force," *New York Times*, June 7, 1970; "Voter Education, Southern Council Split," *Pittsburgh Courier*, June 20, 1970; and Interview with Hodding Carter III by Evan Faulkenbury, December 8, 2015, U-1121, in the Southern Oral History Program #4007, Southern Historical Collection, Wilson Library, University of North Carolina at Chapel Hill.

68. Vernon Jordan to Leslie Dunbar, February 23, 1970, Box 2T71, Folder "SRC, Inc. (VEP) fall 1968," Field Foundation Archives; and "Jordan Takes UNCF Post; Lewis New VEP Director," *VEP News* 4, no. 1 and 2 (February 1970).

69. Lewis interview, November 20, 1973; Archie E. Allen, "John Lewis: Keeper of the Dream," *New South* 26, no. 2 (Spring 1971): 15–25; and Lewis, *Walking with the Wind*, 17–70.

70. Lewis interview, November 20, 1973; Interview with John Lewis by Vicki Daitch, March 19, 2004, John F. Kennedy Library Oral History Program; and Lewis, *Walking with the Wind*, 71–434.

71. Basil J. Whiting to John Lewis, June 16, 1970, Reel 177, SRC Papers.

72. Leslie Dunbar to Paul Anthony, March 3, 1970, Box 2T94, Folder "VEP 2nd fall 1969," Field Foundation Archives.

73. Lawyers at Paul and Weiss to Leslie Dunbar, June 18, 1970, Box 2T94, Folder "VEP 2nd fall 1969," Field Foundation Archives.

74. William H. Nims to McGeorge Bundy, July 23, 1970, Reel 4959, Record Group: Grants, Series: OVP—Finance and Administration, Sub Series: Rights and Social Justice Programs, Ford Foundation Records.

75. Leslie Dunbar to John Lewis, June 19, 1970, Reel 177, SRC Papers.

76. Thomas W. Wahman to Dana S. Creel, August 27, 1970, Record Group 3.1, Box 1078, Folder 6578, Rockefeller Brothers Fund Records, Rockefeller Archive Center.

77. John Lewis to Paul Anthony, n.d., Reel 177, SRC Papers; and VEP Financial Statement, August 1970, Box 2T25, Folder "SRC Inc. (VEP) fall 1966," Field Foundation Archives. See also Carter interview, December 8, 2015, U-1121.

78. Interview with John Lewis by Evan Faulkenbury, July 18, 2013, in author's possession.

79. VEP Fundraising Letter, n.d., Reel 28, Series 200 U.S., Record Group "General Correspondence," Rockefeller Foundation Records, Rockefeller Archive Center.

80. Report of the VEP Executive Committee Meeting, July 24–26, 1970, Box 34, Folder 10, Office Files, VEP Records.

81. VEP Press Release, "What Happened in the South, 1970," November 1970, Reel 177, SRC Papers; and VEP Annual Report, 1970.

82. Summary of Auditors Report of VEP, Inc., 1970, by Alexander Grant and Company, submitted on December 31, 1970, Box 2, Folder 3, Financial Records, VEP Records.

83. The 1973 VEP Annual Report did not include a full tally of projects. See VEP Annual Report, 1970; VEP Annual Report, 1971, Reel 177, SRC Papers; VEP Annual

Report, 1972, Box 855, Folder 12, SCLC Papers, Emory University; VEP Annual Report, 1973, Box 2S409, Folder "Voter Education Project: 75-19, Fall 1974," Field Foundation Archives; VEP Annual Report, 1974, Record Group 3.1, Box 1079, Folder 6584, Rockefeller Brothers Fund Records; VEP Annual Report, 1975, Record Group 3.1, Box 1079, Folder 6585, Rockefeller Brothers Fund Records; and VEP Annual Report, 1976, Box 2S409, Folder "VEP 76-42," Field Foundation Archives.

84. VEP Press Release, Archie E. Allen, "Thomas County, Georgia: Profile of a Black Voter Registration Drive," June 22, 1972, Record Group 3.1, Box 1078, Folder 6581, Rockefeller Brothers Fund Records.

85. Allen, "Thomas County, Georgia."

86. Allen, "Thomas County, Georgia."

87. VEP Fundraising Letter, n.d., Rockefeller Foundation Records.

88. Summary of the Voter Education Project's Direct Mail Experience, 1971–1975, Box 2S466, Folder "Voter Education Project, 1976," Field Foundation Archives; and Harry J. Wexler to R. Harcourt Dodds, April 6, 1977, Series 1, Box 30, Folder 6, National Affairs Division, Vice-President, Office Files of Mitchell Sviridoff, Ford Foundation Records. On Jesse Helms and direct mail, see William A. Link, *Righteous Warrior: Jesse Helms and the Rise of Modern Conservatism* (New York: St. Martin's Press, 2008), 144–48.

89. VEP Press Release, May 31, 1974, Folder "Voter Education Project, Inc. 1973–1974," Taconic Foundation Records.

90. See VEP Annual Report, 1975; VEP Annual Report, 1976; and Wexler to Dodds, April 6, 1977.

91. R. W. Apple Jr., "The States Ratify Full Vote at 18," *New York Times*, July 1, 1971.

92. Lewis, *Walking with the Wind*, 434–35.

93. VEP Press Release, October 28, 1976, Record Group 3.1, Box 1079, Folder 6585, Rockefeller Brothers Fund Records; and Wexler to Dodds, April 6, 1977.

94. VEP Annual Report, 1973.

95. VEP Annual Report, 1971, Reel 177, SRC Papers. See also VEP Press Release, "John Lewis and Julian Bond to Make Voting Rights Tour of Fifteen Mississippi Counties," June 11, 1971, Box 855, Folder 14, SCLC Papers, Emory University; and *VEP News* 5, no. 1 (April–June 1971).

96. Wells, "Voting Rights in 1975." See also VEP Annual Reports, for 1972, 1974, and 1975; VEP Press Release, August 26, 1972, Record Group 3.1, Box 1078, Folder 6581, Rockefeller Brothers Fund Records; VEP Press Release, September 25, 1972, Record Group 3.1, Box 1078, Folder 6581, Rockefeller Brothers Fund Records; VEP Press Release, October 17, 1974, Box 2S409, Folder "Voter Education Project: 75-19, Fall 1974," Field Foundation Archives; and Interview with Julian Bond by Evan Faulkenbury, November 19, 2013, U-1120, in the Southern Oral History Program Collection #4007, Southern Historical Collection, Wilson Library, University of North Carolina at Chapel Hill.

97. VEP Press Release, February 12, 1973, Record Group 3.1 — Grants, Box 1079, Folder 6582, Rockefeller Brothers Fund Records.

98. Report of the Executive Director to the Board of Directors meeting, November 16, 1970, Box 34, Folder 10, Office Files, VEP Records.

99. "Interim Report to the Carnegie Corporation on the Operation of the VEP-Sponsored College Service Centers for Elected Officials," September 10, 1971, Box 1078, Folder 6580, Series 3.1 Grants, Rockefeller Brothers Fund Records.

100. Interview with Taunya Banks by Evan Faulkenbury via Skype, March 28, 2017, in author's possession.

101. Banks interview, March 28, 2017. See also "Interim Report to the Carnegie Corporation," September 10, 1971; VEP Annual Report, 1971; and VEP Annual Report, 1972; Eli Evans to Vernon Jordan, March 28, 1969, Box 2T79, Folder "VEP Fall 1967," Field Foundation Archives; "Services Set Up for Officeholders," *VEP News 2*, no. 7 (July 1968); "Service Centers at Five Colleges for Black Officials," *VEP News 3*, no. 1 (January 1969); and Walter Rugaber, "Blacks in Office: 'One of the Miracles of the Democratic Process,'" *New York Times*, December 15, 1968.

102. VEP Press Release, July 12, 1976, Box 2S409, Folder "VEP 76-42," Field Foundation Archives.

103. William Greider, "Hispanic-Americans Learn the Game of Politics," *Washington Post*, April 3, 1977. See also Ed Stanfield to Paul Anthony, December 4, 1967, Box 2T79, Folder "VEP Fall 1967," Field Foundation Archives; Articles of Incorporation, Southwest Voter Registration Education Project (SVREP), Box 14, Folder 1, Wiley Branton Papers, Moorland-Spingarn Research Center, Howard University (hereinafter Branton Papers); SVREP Board Meeting Minutes, January 17, 1975, Box 14, Folder 1, Branton Papers; SVREP Quarterly Report, March 1, 1977, Box 14, Folder 2, Branton Papers; and VEP Annual Reports for 1970, 1972, and 1974. On Willie Velásquez, see Juan A. Sepúlveda Jr., *The Life and Times of Willie Velásquez: Su Voto es Su Voz* (Houston: Arte Público Press, 2003).

104. Ford Foundation Review Team Meeting, May 3, 1971, Box 47, Folder 13, Office Files, VEP Records.

105. B. Drummond Ayres, "Black Clubbed in Selma Assails Blacks Aiding Wallace," *New York Times*, April 24, 1974.

106. Hugh Price to Harry Dodds, May 28, 1974, Series 1, Box 30, Folder 6, National Affairs Division, Vice-President, Office Files of Mitchell Sviridoff, Ford Foundation Records. See also John Lewis to Harcourt Dobbs, May 31, 1974, Series 1, Box 30, Folder 6, Sviridoff Files, Ford Foundation Records; and R. Harcourt Dodds to Howard R. Dressner, July 9, 1974, Series 1, Box 30, Folder 6, Sviridoff Files, Ford Foundation Records.

107. John Lewis to Leslie Dunbar, December 4, 1974, Box 2S409, Folder "Voter Education Project: 75-19, Fall 1974," Field Foundation Archives.

108. Paul West, "Recession Seen as Rights Peril," *Atlanta Constitution*, November 14, 1974.

109. Paul West, "Hard Times Drying Up Funding for Civil Rights," *Atlanta Constitution*, December 9, 1974. See also Lewis to Dunbar, December 4, 1974; VEP Annual Report, 1974; and John Lewis to Wiley Branton, December 4, 1974, Box 6, Folder 20, Branton Papers.

110. Testimony from John Lewis before the Civil and Constitutional Rights Subcommittee on the House Committee of the Judiciary, March 3, 1975, Box 6, Folder 20, Branton Papers.

111. Testimony from John Lewis before the Civil and Constitutional Rights Subcommittee on the House Committee of the Judiciary, March 3, 1975.

112. VEP Press Release, April 9, 1975, Box 2S409, Folder "Voter Education Project: 75-19, Fall 1974," Field Foundation Archives. See also Janet Wells, "Voting Rights in 1975: Why Minorities Still Need Federal Protection," *Civil Rights Digest* (Summer 1975), 13–15; and VEP Annual Report, 1975.

113. VEP Press Release, April 9, 1975, Box 2S409, Folder "Voter Education Project: 75-19, Fall 1974," Field Foundation Archives.

114. VEP Fundraising Letter from Vivian Malone Jones to Wiley Branton, November 10, 1977, Box 5, Folder 44, Branton Papers.

115. Peter Scott, "Report Criticizes Strategy, Spending of Voter Project," *Atlanta Constitution*, May 3, 1985.

116. Tonya Lewis, "Voter Registration and Education Projects: A Profile of Ford Foundation Grantees," August 29, 1986, Unpublished Reports, #013830, Ford Foundation Records. See also R. Harcourt Dodds to National Affairs Division of the Ford Foundation, February 27, 1979, Series 1, Box 30, Folder 6, Sviridoff Files, Ford Foundation Records; Farmer and Martin, "A Confidential Report on an Evaluation of the Voter Education Project"; and Billy Cutler, "Planting Seeds: The Voter Education Project," *Southern Exposure* 12, no. 1 (1984): 41–45.

117. Lorri Denise Booker, "At 25, Black Voter Project Has Same Goals," *Atlanta Constitution*, May 8, 1987.

118. Galloway-May to Sutton, February 26, 1992. See also Ford Foundation Précis, Request No. USIAP-116, n.d., Reel 6389, Series OVP—Finance and Administration, Ford Foundation Records; "Voter Education Project Set to Close," *Washington Post*, February 15, 1992; and William Raspberry, "End of the Voter Education Project," *Washington Post*, March 2, 1992.

Epilogue

1. Memorandum from the Southern Regional Council, for discussion, August 23, 1961.

2. Kousser, *Colorblind Injustice*, 1.

3. Jordan interview, July 19, 2013.

Bibliography

Manuscript Collections

Atlanta, Georgia
   Archives Research Center, Robert W. Woodruff Library, Atlanta University
      Center
      Brailsford R. Brazeal Papers
      Voter Education Project (VEP) Organizational Records
   Stuart A. Rose Manuscript, Archives, and Rare Book Library, Emory University
      Constance Curry Papers
      Leslie W. Dunbar Papers
      Southern Christian Leadership Conference (SCLC) Papers
   Martin Luther King Jr. Center for Nonviolent Social Change, Inc.
      Martin Luther King Jr. Papers
      Southern Christian Leadership Conference (SCLC) Papers
Austin, Texas
   Dolph Briscoe Center for American History, University of Texas at Austin
      Field Foundation Archives
Boston, Massachusetts
   Boston University Howard Gotlieb Archival Research Center
      Dr. Martin Luther King Jr. Archive
   John F. Kennedy Presidential Library
      Robert F. Kennedy Attorney General Papers
      Burke Marshall Personal Papers
      Harris Wofford Papers
Cambridge, Massachusetts
   Harvard Law School Historical and Special Collections
      Lloyd K. Garrison Papers
Chapel Hill, North Carolina
   Southern Historical Collection, Louis Round Wilson Special Collections Library,
      University of North Carolina at Chapel Hill
      Taylor Branch Papers
      North Carolina Fund Papers
      Daniel Pollitt Papers
Madison, Wisconsin
   Wisconsin Historical Society
      Carl and Ann Braden Papers
      Congress of Racial Equality (CORE) Records, 1941–1967
      Congress of Racial Equality (CORE), Southern Regional Office Records

Congress of Racial Equality (CORE), Monroe Chapter (LA) Records
Stern Fund Records
United Packinghouse, Food, and Allied Workers Records, 1937–1968
The Plains, Virginia
Currier Family Archive
Sleepy Hollow, New York
Rockefeller Archive Center
Council on Foundations, Inc. Records
Ford Foundation Records
Rockefeller Brothers Fund Records
Rockefeller Foundation Records
Taconic Foundation Records [Note: I looked through this collection before final processing, thanks to archivist Mary Ann Quinn. Sources referenced throughout this book can now be found in "Series 1: Grants" in Boxes 32, 139, 141, 142, 161, 162, and 163.]
Washington, DC
Library of Congress
Rosa Parks Papers—Digital Collection
Moorland-Spingarn Research Center, Howard University
Wiley Branton Papers

Accessed via ProQuest History Vault

Chicago Historical Society
Claude A. Barnett Papers
Martin Luther King Jr. Center for Nonviolent Social Change, Inc.
Southern Christian Leadership Conference (SCLC) Papers
Library of Congress
National Association for the Advancement of Colored People (NAACP) Papers
A. Philip Randolph Papers
A. Philip Randolph Institute
Bayard Rustin Papers
Harry S. Truman Presidential Library
President's Committee on Civil Rights Files

In Author's Possession

Steven Lawson Research Papers on the Voter Education Project

Microfilm Collections

Civil Rights during the Kennedy Administration, 1961–1963, edited by Carl M. Brauer. Frederick, MD: University Publications of America, 1986.
Congress of Racial Equality (CORE) Papers, consulting editors August Meier and Elliott Rudwick. Frederick, MD: University Publications of America, 1983.

Southern Regional Council (SRC) Papers, 1944–1968. Ann Arbor, MI: University Microfilms International, 1983.

Published Papers, Edited Source Collections, Court Rulings, Legislation, and Government Publications

Allan C. Brownfeld. "The Financiers of Revolution," American Conservative Union, April 1969.

Brown v. Board of Education, 349 U.S. 294 (1955).

Carson, Clayborne, senior ed. *The Papers of Martin Luther King Jr.*, Volumes 4 and 7. Berkeley: University of California Press.

Civil Rights Act of 1957, 85th Congress, H.R. 6127, Public Law 85-315, September 9, 1957.

Fleming, Harold C. *The Potomac Institute Incorporated, 1961–1971*, report published by the Potomac Institute, 1972.

"Foundations and the Tax Reform Act of 1969," proceedings of conferences held on February 17, 1970, at Kansas City and February 23, 1970, at New York City. New York: The Foundation Center, 1970.

General Explanation of the Tax Reform Act of 1969, H.R. 13270, 91st Congress, Public Law 91-172, prepared by the Staff of the Joint Committee on Internal Revenue Taxation, December 3, 1970. Washington, DC: U.S. Government Printing Office, 1970.

Hearings Before the Committee on Ways and Means, House of Representatives, 91st Congress. Washington, DC: U.S. Government Printing Office, 1969.

Hearings Before the Committee on Finance, United States Senate, 91st Congress, First Session on H.R. 13270. Washington, DC: U.S. Government Printing Office, 1969.

The Negro Family: The Case for National Action. Washington, DC: Office of Policy Planning and Research, U.S. Department of Labor, March 1965.

President Lyndon B. Johnson address to Congress, March 15, 1965. http://www .lbjlibrary.org/lyndon-baines-johnson/speeches-films/president-johnsons -special-message-to-the-congress-the-american-promise.

Price, Margaret. *The Negro Voter in the South*. Atlanta: Southern Regional Council, 1957.

———. *The Negro and the Ballot in the South*. Atlanta: Southern Regional Council, 1959.

Revenue Act of 1934, Section 511, Article 13, Regulations 79 Relating to Gift Tax under the Revenue Act of 1932, as Amended and Supplemented by the Revenue Acts of 1934 and 1935, U.S. Treasury Department, Bureau of Internal Revenue. Washington, DC: Government Printing Office, 1936.

The Stern Fund: The Story of a Progressive Family Foundation. New York: Institute for Media Analysis, 1992.

Testimony of Wiley A. Branton, Director, Voter Education Project, Southern Regional Council before the United States Commission on Civil Rights, February 16–20, 1965, in Jackson, Mississippi, Volume I: Voting.

Taconic Foundation: Twenty-Five Years, June 1985.

United States Commission on Civil Rights, *Political Participation*. Washington, DC: Government Printing Office, 1968.

Oral Histories

In Author's Possession

Taunya Banks— March 28, 2017

Vernon Jordan—July 19, 2013

John Lewis—July 18, 2013

Columbia Center for Oral History, Columbia University

Wiley A. Branton—October 21, 1970

Field Foundation Archives, Dolph Briscoe Center for American History, University of Texas at Austin

Maxwell Hahn—November 12, 1979

Henry Hampton Collection, Film and Media Archive, Washington University Libraries

John Doar —November 15, 1985

John F. Kennedy Library Oral History Program

Robert F. Kennedy and Burke Marshall— December 4, 1964

John Lewis—March 19, 2004

Burke Marshall—May 29, 1964

John Seigenthaler— July 22, 1964

John Seigenthaler— February 22, 1966

Moorland-Spingarn Research Center, Howard University

Ella Baker—June 19, 1968

Louie B. Nunn Center for Oral History, University of Kentucky

Wiley A. Branton— March 17, 1964

Vernon E. Jordan Jr. — March 17, 1964

Civil Rights History Project, Smithsonian Institution's National Museum of African American History and Culture and the Library of Congress

Charles Sherrod—June 4, 2011

Southern Oral History Program, Southern Historical Collection, University of North Carolina at Chapel Hill

Ella Baker— September 4, 1974
Julian Bond— November 19, 2013
Hodding Carter III— December 8, 2015

Leslie W. Dunbar— December 18, 1978
Lawrence C. Goodwyn— November 18, 1974
John Lewis— November 20, 1973

Penelope Patch— April 17, 2010
Laurie Pritchett— April 23, 1976
Wyatt Tee Walker— March 15, 2013

Southern Regional Council Oral History Collection, George A. Smathers Libraries, University of Florida

Leslie W. Dunbar— Thaddeus Olive—
May 10, 2002 November 23, 2002

Southern Rural Poverty Collection, DeWitt Wallace Center for Media and Democracy, Sanford School of Public Policy, Duke University

Leslie W. Dunbar—February 5, 1992

Taylor Branch Papers, Southern Historical Collection, University of North Carolina at Chapel Hill

Harry Belafonte— Charles Jones— Louis Martin—June 10,
March 6–7, 1985 November 24, 1986 1985
John Doar—May 12, 1986 Burke Marshall— Charles Sherrod—
Timothy Jenkins— September 26, 1984 October 7, 1985
March 11, 1986

Memoirs

Cobb, Charles E., Jr. *This Nonviolent Stuff'll Get You Killed: How Guns Made the Civil Rights Movement Possible*. New York: Basic, 2014.

Forman, James. *The Making of Black Revolutionaries*. Seattle: University of Washington Press, 1972, 1997.

Fleming, Harold C., with Virginia Fleming. *The Potomac Chronicle: Public Policy and Civil Rights from Kennedy to Reagan*. Athens: University of Georgia Press, 1996.

Holsaert, Faith S., Martha Prescod Norman Noonan, Judy Richardson, Betty Garman Robinson, Jean Smith Young, and Dorothy M. Zellner, eds. *Hands on the Freedom Plow: Personal Accounts by Women in SNCC*. Urbana: University of Illinois Press, 2010.

Jordan, Vernon E., Jr., with Annette Gordon-Reed. *Vernon Can Read! A Memoir*. New York: PublicAffairs, 2001.

King, Martin Luther, Jr. *Stride toward Freedom: The Montgomery Story*. New York: Harper and Brothers, 1958; reprint by Beacon Press, 2010.

Lafayette, Bernard, Jr., and Kathryn Lee Johnson. *In Peace and Freedom: My Journey in Selma*. Lexington: University Press of Kentucky, 2013.

Lewis, John, with Michael D'Orso. *Walking with the Wind: A Memoir of the Movement*. New York: Simon and Schuster, 1998.

Wofford, Harris. *Of Kennedys and Kings: Making Sense of the Sixties*. New York: Farrar, Straus, and Giroux, 1980.

Wofford, Harris and Clare. *India Afire*. New York: J. Day, 1951.

Digital Collections

SNCC Digital Gateway—https://snccdigital.org/

Periodicals and Newspapers

Afro-American
Atlanta Constitution
Atlanta Daily World
Atlanta Journal
Augusta Courier
Baltimore Sun
Business Week
Charleston Evening Post
Charlotte Observer
Chicago Defender
Chicago Daily Tribune
Civil Rights Digest
Commentary
Congressional Research
   Service Report
Congressional Quarterly
Delta Democrat-Times

Durham Sun
Editorial Research Reports
Harper's Magazine
Jet
Legal Times
Life
Los Angeles Times
The Nation
New Orleans Times-
   Picayune
Pittsburgh Courier
New South
Newsweek
New York Amsterdam News
New York Journal-
   American
New York Times

New York Times Magazine
News and Courier
   (Charleston, SC)
Philadelphia Tribune
Rock Hill Evening Herald
Selma Times Journal
Southern Exposure
The State (Columbia, SC)
U.S. News and World
   Report
VEP News
Virginian-Pilot
Wall Street Journal
Washington Post

Theses and Dissertations

Hickmott, Alec Fazackerley. "Randolph Blackwell and the Economics of Civil Rights." MPhil thesis, University of Sussex, 2010.

Hinson, William Jefferson, Jr. "A History of the Voter Education Project, 1962–1975." Senior thesis, Emory University, 1977.

Jones, Rhonda D. "Tithe, Time and Talent: An Analysis of Fundraising Activity for the Southern Christian Leadership Conference (SCLC), 1957–1964." PhD dissertation, Howard University, 2003.

Krochmal, Maximilian. "Labor, Civil Rights, and the Struggle for Democracy in Mid-Twentieth Century Texas." PhD diss., Duke University, 2011.

McDonough, Julia Anne. "Men and Women of Good Will: A History of the Commission on Interracial Cooperation and the Southern Regional Council, 1919–1954." PhD diss., University of Virginia, 1993.

Secondary Sources

Anderson, Karen. Little Rock: Race and Resistance at Central High School. Princeton, NJ: Princeton University Press, 2010.

Andrews, Kenneth T. Freedom Is a Constant Struggle: The Mississippi Civil Rights Movement and Its Legacy. Chicago: University of Chicago Press, 2004.

Arsenault, Raymond. *Freedom Riders: 1961 and the Struggle for Racial Justice*. New York: Oxford University Press, 2006.

Asch, Christopher Myers. *The Senator and the Sharecropper: The Freedom Struggles of James O. Eastland and Fannie Lou Hamer*. New York: The New Press, 2008.

Becker, Stephen. *Marshall Field III*. New York: Simon and Schuster, 1964.

Behrend, Justin. *Reconstructing Democracy: Grassroots Black Politics in the Deep South after the Civil War*. Athens: University of Georgia Press, 2015.

Berman, Ari. *Give Us the Ballot: The Modern Struggle for Voting Rights in America*. New York: Picador, 2015.

Bird, Kai. *The Color of Truth: McGeorge Bundy and William Bundy; Brothers in Arms*. New York: Simon and Schuster, 1998.

Black, Earl, and Merle Black. *The Rise of Southern Republicans*. Cambridge, MA: Belknap Press of Harvard University Press, 2002.

Blakey, Roy G., and Gladys C. Blakey. "The Revenue Act of 1934." *American Economic Review* 24, no. 3 (September 1934): 450–61.

Branch, Taylor. *Parting the Waters: America in the King Years, 1954–1963*. New York: Simon and Schuster, 1988.

Brauer, Carl M. *John F. Kennedy and the Second Reconstruction*. New York: Columbia University Press, 1977.

Bryant, Nick. *The Bystander: John F. Kennedy and the Struggle for Black Equality*. New York: Basic Books, 2006.

Byrnes, William H., IV. "The Private Foundation's Topsy Turvy Road in the American Political Process." *Houston Business and Tax Law Journal* 4 (2004): 496–593.

Cannadine, David. *Mellon: An American Life*. New York: Alfred A. Knopf, 2006.

Carson, Clayborne. *In Struggle: SNCC and the Black Awakening of the 1960s*. Cambridge, MA: Harvard University Press, 1981, 1995.

Carter, David C. *The Music Has Gone Out of the Movement: Civil Rights and the Johnson Administration, 1965–1968*. Chapel Hill: University of North Carolina Press, 2009.

Carter, Dan T. *The Politics of Rage: George Wallace, the Origins of the New Conservatism, and the Transformation of American Politics*. New York: Simon and Schuster, 1995.

Catsam, Derek. *Freedom's Main Line: The Journey of Reconciliation and the Freedom Rides*. Lexington: University Press of Kentucky, 2009.

Cha-Jua, Sundiata Keita, and Clarence Lang. "The 'Long Movement' as Vampire: Temporal and Spatial Fallacies in Recent Black Freedom Studies." *Journal of African American History* 92, no. 2 (Spring 2007): 265–88.

Chappell, David L. *Inside Agitators: White Southerners in the Civil Rights Movement*. Baltimore: The John Hopkins University Press, 1994.

Charron, Katherine Mellen. *Freedom's Teacher: The Life of Septima Clark*. Chapel Hill: University of North Carolina Press, 2009.

Chernow, Ron. *The Warburgs: The Twentieth-Century Odyssey of a Remarkable Jewish Family*. New York: Vintage, 1994.

Crespino, Joseph. *In Search of Another Country: Mississippi and the Conservative Counterrevolution*. Princeton, NJ: Princeton University Press, 2007.

Crosby, Emilye, ed. *Civil Rights History from the Ground Up: Local Struggles, a National Movement*. Athens: University of Georgia Press, 2011.

Deutsch, Stephanie. *You Need a Schoolhouse: Booker T. Washington, Julius Rosenwald, and the Building of Schools for the Segregated South*. Evanston, IL: Northwestern University Press, 2011.

Dickerson, Dennis C. *Militant Mediator: Whitney M. Young, Jr.* Lexington: University Press of Kentucky, 1998.

Dittmer, John. *Local People: The Struggle for Rights in Mississippi*. Urbana: University of Illinois Press, 1994.

Dobson, Sean. "Freedom Funders: Philanthropy and the Civil Rights Movement, 1955–1965." Commissioned by the National Committee for Responsive Philanthropy, June 2014.

Dudziak, Mary L. *Cold War Civil Rights: Race and the Image of American Democracy*. Princeton, NJ: Princeton University Press, 2000.

Dunbar, Leslie W. "The Changing Mind of the South: The Exposed Nerve." *Journal of Politics* 26, no. 1 (February 1964): 3–21.

Eagles, Charles W. "Toward New Histories of the Civil Rights Era." *Journal of Southern History* 66, no. 4 (November 2000): 815–48.

Egerton, John. *Speak Now against the Day: The Generation before the Civil Rights Movement in the South*. Chapel Hill: University of North Carolina Press, 1995.

Emberton, Carole. *Beyond Redemption: Race, Violence, and the American South after the Civil War*. Chicago: University of Chicago Press, 2014.

Eskew, Glenn T. *But for Birmingham: The Local and National Movements in the Civil Rights Struggle*. Chapel Hill: University of North Carolina Press, 1997.

Fairclough, Adam. *Race and Democracy: The Civil Rights Struggle in Louisiana, 1915–1972*. Athens: University of Georgia Press, 1995.

———. *To Redeem the Soul of America: The Southern Christian Leadership Conference and Martin Luther King Jr*. Athens: University of Georgia Press, 1987.

Farrington, Joshua D. *Black Republicans and the Transformation of the GOP*. Philadelphia: University of Pennsylvania Press, 2016.

Faulkenbury, Evan. "'Monroe Is Hell': Voter Purges, Registration Drives, and the Civil Rights Movement in Ouachita Parish, Louisiana." *Louisiana History* 59, no. 1 (Winter 2018): 40–66.

Ferguson, Karen. "Organizing the Ghetto: The Ford Foundation, CORE, and White Power in the Black Power Era, 1967–1969." *Journal of Urban History* 34, no. 1 (November 2007): 67–100.

———. *Top Down: The Ford Foundation, Black Power, and the Reinvention of Racial Liberalism*. Philadelphia: University of Pennsylvania Press, 2013.

Finley, Keith M. *Delaying the Dream: Southern Senators and the Fight against Civil Rights, 1938–1965*. Baton Rouge: Louisiana State University Press, 2008.

Foner, Eric. *Reconstruction: America's Unfinished Revolution, 1863–1877*. New York: Harper and Row, 1988.

Friedman, Lawrence J., and Mark D. McGarvie, eds. *Charity, Philanthropy, and Civility in American History*. New York: Cambridge University Press, 2003.

Garrow, David J. *Bearing the Cross: Martin Luther King Jr. and the Southern Christian Leadership Conference*. New York: William Morrow, 1986.

———. "Philanthropy and the Civil Rights Movement." Working paper for the Center for the Study of Philanthropy, the Graduate Center at the City University of New York, October 1987.

Haines, Herbert H. "Black Radicalization and the Funding of Civil Rights: 1957–1970." *Social Problems* 32, no. 1 (October 1984): 31–43.

Hall, Jacquelyn Dowd. "The Long Civil Rights Movement and the Political Uses of the Past." *Journal of American History* 91, no. 4 (March 2005): 1233–63.

———. *Revolt against Chivalry: Jesse Daniel Ames and the Women's Campaign against Lynching*. New York: Columbia University Press, 1993.

Hamlin, Françoise N. *Crossroads at Clarksdale: The Black Freedom Struggle in the Mississippi Delta after World War II*. Chapel Hill: University of North Carolina Press, 2012.

Harriss, C. Lowell. "Philanthropy and Federal Tax Exemption." *Journal of Political Economy* 47, no. 4 (August 1939): 526–41.

Hersh, Burton. *The Mellon Family: A Fortune in History*. New York: William Morrow, 1978.

Hine, Darlene Clark. *Black Victory: The Rise and Fall of the White Primary in Texas*. Columbia: University of Missouri Press, 1979, 2003.

Hogan, Wesley C. *Many Minds, One Heart: SNCC's Dream for a New America*. Chapel Hill: University of North Carolina Press, 2007.

Jackson, Thomas F. *From Civil Rights to Human Rights: Martin Luther King Jr. and the Struggle for Economic Justice*. Philadelphia: University of Pennsylvania Press, 2007.

Jacoway, Elizabeth. *Turn Away Thy Son: Little Rock, the Crisis That Shocked the Nation*. New York: The Free Press, 2007.

Jenkins, J. Craig, and Craig M. Eckert. "Channeling Black Insurgency: Elite Patronage and Professional Social Movement Organizations in the Development of the Black Movement." *American Sociological Review* 51, no. 6 (December 1986): 812–29.

Jones, William P. *The March on Washington: Jobs, Freedom, and the Forgotten History of Civil Rights*. New York: W. W. Norton, 2013.

Joseph, Peniel E. "The Black Power Movement: A State of the Field." *Journal of American History* 96, no. 3 (December 2009): 751–76.

Katagiri, Yasuhiro. *Black Freedom, White Resistance, and Red Menace: Civil Rights and Anticommunism in the Jim Crow South*. Baton Rouge: Louisiana State University Press, 2014.

Keyssar, Alexander. *The Right to Vote: The Contested History of Democracy in the United States*. New York: Basic Books, 2000.

Kilpatrick, Judith. *There When We Needed Him: Wiley Austin Branton, Civil Rights Warrior*. Fayetteville: University of Arkansas Press, 2007.

Korstad, Robert R. *Civil Rights Unionism: Tobacco Workers and the Struggle for Democracy in the Mid-Twentieth Century South*. Chapel Hill: University of North Carolina Press, 2003.

Korstad, Robert R., and James L. Leloudis. *To Right These Wrongs: The North Carolina Fund and the Battle to End Poverty and Inequality in 1960s America*. Chapel Hill: University of North Carolina Press, 2010.

Koskoff, David E. *The Mellons: The Chronicle of America's Richest Family*. New York: Thomas Y. Crowell, 1978.

Kotlowski, Dean J. *Nixon's Civil Rights: Politics, Principle, and Policy*. Cambridge, MA: Harvard University Press, 2002.

Kousser, J. Morgan. *Colorblind Injustice: Minority Voting Rights and the Undoing of the Second Reconstruction*. Chapel Hill: University of North Carolina Press, 1999.

Krochmal, Max. *Blue Texas: The Making of a Multiracial Democratic Coalition in the Civil Rights Era*. Chapel Hill: University of North Carolina Press, 2016.

Kruse, Kevin. *White Flight: Atlanta and the Making of Modern Conservatism*. Princeton, NJ: Princeton University Press, 2005.

Lagemann, Ellen Condliffe, ed. *Philanthropic Foundations: New Scholarship, New Possibilities*. Bloomington: Indiana University Press, 1999.

Lankford, Nelson D. *The Last American Diplomat: The Biography of David K. E. Bruce, 1898-1977*. Boston: Little, Brown and Company, 1996.

Lassiter, Matthew D. *The Silent Majority: Suburban Politics in the Sunbelt South*. Princeton, NJ: Princeton University Press, 2006.

Lau, Peter F. *Democracy Rising: South Carolina and the Fight for Black Equality since 1865*. Lexington: University Press of Kentucky, 2006.

Lawson, Steven F. *Black Ballots: Voting Rights in the South, 1944-1969*. New York: Columbia University Press, 1976.

———. *In Pursuit of Power: Southern Blacks and Electoral Politics, 1965-1982*. New York: Columbia University Press, 1985.

Lawson, Steven F., and Charles Payne. *Debating the Civil Rights Movement, 1945-1968*. Lanham, MD: Rowman and Littlefield, 1998, 2006.

Lee, Chana Kai. *For Freedom's Sake: The Life of Fannie Lou Hamer*. Urbana: University of Illinois Press, 1999.

Lewis, George. *The White South and the Red Menace: Segregationists, Anticommunism, and Massive Resistance, 1945-1965*. Gainesville: University Press of Florida, 2004.

Lichtenstein, Nelson, ed. *American Capitalism: Social Thought and Political Economy in the Twentieth Century*. Philadelphia: University of Pennsylvania Press, 2006.

Link, William A. *Righteous Warrior: Jesse Helms and the Rise of Modern Conservatism*. New York: St. Martin's Press, 2008.

Litwack, Leon. *Been in the Storm So Long: The Aftermath of Slavery*. New York: Alfred A. Knopf, 1979.

Lucander, David. *Winning the War for Democracy: The March on Washington Movement, 1941-1946*. Urbana: University of Illinois Press, 2014.

Márquez, Benjamin. *Democratizing Texas Politics: Race, Identity, and Mexican American Empowerment, 1945-2002*. Austin: University of Texas Press, 2014.

May, Gary. *Bending toward Justice: The Voting Rights Act and the Transformation of American Democracy*. New York: Basic Books, 2013.

McAdam, Doug. *Political Process and the Development of Black Insurgency, 1930-1970*. Chicago: University of Chicago Press, 1982, 1999.

Meier, August, and Elliot Rudwick. *CORE: A Study in the Civil Rights Movement, 1942-1968*. New York: Oxford University Press, 1973.

Michelmore, Molly C. *Tax and Spend: The Welfare State, Tax Politics, and the Limits of American Liberalism*. Philadelphia: University of Pennsylvania Press, 2012.

Miller, Steven P. *Billy Graham and the Rise of the Republican South*. Philadelphia: University of Pennsylvania Press, 2009.

Mills, Kay. *This Little Light of Mine: The Life of Fannie Lou Hamer*. Lexington: University Press of Kentucky, 2007.

Minchin, Timothy J., and John A. Salmond. *After the Dream: Black and White Southerners since 1965*. Lexington: University Press of Kentucky, 2011.

Moon, Henry Lee. *Balance of Power: The Negro Vote*. New York: Doubleday, 1948.

Moore, Leonard M. *Carl B. Stokes and the Rise of Black Political Power*. Urbana: University of Illinois Press, 2002.

Moore, Winfred B., Jr., and Orville Vernon Burton, eds. *Toward the Meeting of the Waters: Currents in the Civil Rights Movement of South Carolina during the Twentieth Century*. Columbia: University of South Carolina Press, 2008.

Morris, Aldon D. *The Origins of the Civil Rights Movement: Black Communities Organizing for Change*. New York: The Free Press, 1984.

Morris, Tiyi Makeda. *Womanpower Unlimited and the Black Freedom Struggle in Mississippi*. Athens: University of Georgia Press, 2015.

Moye, J. Todd. *Let the People Decide: Black Freedom and White Resistance Movements in Sunflower County, Mississippi, 1945–1986*. Chapel Hill: University of North Carolina Press, 2004.

Nelson, Stanley. *Devils Walking: Klan Murders along the Mississippi in the 1960s*. Baton Rouge: Louisiana State University Press, 2016.

Nielsen, Waldemar A. *The Big Foundations*. New York: Columbia University Press, 1972.

Niven, David. *The Politics of Injustice: The Kennedys, the Freedom Rides, and the Electoral Consequences of a Moral Compromise*. Knoxville: University of Tennessee Press, 2003.

Ortiz, Paul. *Emancipation Betrayed: The Hidden History of Black Organizing and White Violence in Florida from Reconstruction to the Bloody Election of 1920*. Berkeley: University of California Press, 2005.

Paget, Karen M. *Patriotic Betrayal: The Inside Story of the CIA's Secret Campaign to Enroll American Students in the Crusade Against Communism*. New Haven, CT: Yale University Press, 2015.

Parris, Guichard, and Lester Brooks. *Blacks in the City: A History of the National Urban League*. Boston: Little, Brown and Company, 1971.

Payne, Charles M. *I've Got the Light of Freedom: The Organizing Tradition and the Mississippi Freedom Struggle*. Berkeley: University of California Press, 1995, 2007.

Phillips-Fein, Kim. "Conservatism: A State of the Field." *Journal of American History* 98, no. 3 (December 2011): 723–43.

Phillips, Kimberly L. *War! What Is It Good For?: Black Freedom Struggles and the U.S. Military from World War II to Iraq*. Chapel Hill: University of North Carolina Press, 2012.

Ransby, Barbara. *Ella Baker and the Black Freedom Movement: A Radical Democratic Vision*. Chapel Hill: University of North Carolina Press, 2003.

Riser, Volney R. *Defying Disfranchisement: Black Voting Rights Activism in the Jim Crow South, 1890–1908*. Baton Rouge: Louisiana State University Press, 2010.

Ryan, Yvonne. *Roy Wilkins: The Quiet Revolutionary and the NAACP*. Lexington: University Press of Kentucky, 2014.

Schlesinger, Arthur M., Jr. *A Thousand Days: John F. Kennedy in the White House*. Boston: Houghton Mifflin, 1965.

Sepúlveda, Juan A., Jr. *The Life and Times of Willie Velásquez: Su Voto es Su Voz*. Houston: Arte Público Press, 2003.

Singh, Nikhil Pal, ed. *Climbin' Jacob's Ladder: The Black Freedom Movement Writings of Jack O'Dell*. Berkeley: University of California Press, 2010.

Sitkoff, Harvard. *The Struggle for Black Equality*. New York: Hill and Wang, 1981, 1993, 2008.

Sokol, Jason. *There Goes My Everything: White Southerners in the Age of Civil Rights, 1945–1975*. New York: Alfred A. Knopf, 2006.

Sosna, Morton. *In Search of the Silent South: Southern Liberals and the Race Issue*. New York: Columbia University Press, 1977.

Stern, Mark. *Calculating Visions: Kennedy, Johnson, and Civil Rights*. New Brunswick, NJ: Rutgers University Press, 1992.

Storrs, Landon R. Y. *The Second Red Scare and the Unmaking of the New Deal Left*. Princeton, NJ: Princeton University Press, 2013.

Stradling, David and Richard. *Where the River Burned: Carl Stokes and the Struggle to Save Cleveland*. Ithaca, NY: Cornell University Press, 2015.

Sullivan, Patricia. *Days of Hope: Race and Democracy during the New Deal Era*. Chapel Hill: University of North Carolina Press, 1996.

Thurber, Timothy N. *Republicans and Race: The GOP's Frayed Relationship with African Americans, 1945–1974*. Lawrence: University Press of Kansas, 2013.

Troyer, Thomas A. "The 1969 Private Foundation Law: Historical Perspective on Its Origins and Underpinnings." *The Exempt Organization Tax Review* 27, no. 1 (January 2000): 52–65.

Tyson, Timothy B. *Radio Free Dixie: Robert F. Williams and the Roots of Black Power*. Chapel Hill: University of North Carolina Press, 1999.

Umoja, Akinyele Omowale. *We Will Shoot Back: Armed Resistance in the Mississippi Freedom Movement*. New York: New York University Press, 2013.

Valelly, Richard M. *The Two Reconstructions: The Struggle for Black Enfranchisement*. Chicago: University of Chicago Press, 2004.

Visser-Maessen, Laura. *Robert Parris Moses: A Life in Civil Rights and Leadership at the Grassroots*. Chapel Hill: University of North Carolina Press, 2016.

Wadsworth, Homer C. "Private Foundations and the Tax Reform Act of 1969." *Law and Contemporary Problems* 39, no. 4 (Autumn 1975): 255–62.

Waite, Maurice, ed. *Pocket Oxford English Dictionary*, 11th ed. Oxford: Oxford University Press, 2013.

Ward, Jason Morgan. *Defending White Democracy: The Making of a Segregationist Movement and the Remaking of Racial Politics, 1936–1965*. Chapel Hill: University of North Carolina Press, 2011.

Watters, Pat, and Reese Cleghorn. *Climbing Jacob's Ladder: The Arrival of Negroes in Southern Politics*. New York: Harcourt, Brace and World, 1967.

Weiss, Nancy J. *The National Urban League, 1910-1940*. New York: Oxford University Press, 1974.

Woods, Jeff. *Black Struggle, Red Scare: Segregation and Anti-Communism in the South, 1948-1968*. Baton Rouge: Louisiana State University Press, 2004.

Wright, Gavin. *Sharing the Prize: The Economics of the Civil Rights Revolution in the American South*. Cambridge, MA: Belknap Press of Harvard University Press, 2013.

Young, Nancy Beck. *Wright Patman: Populism, Liberalism, and the American Dream*. Dallas: Southern Methodist University Press, 2000.

Yuill, Kevin. *Richard Nixon and the Rise of Affirmative Action: The Pursuit of Racial Equality in an Era of Limits*. Lanham, MD: Rowman and Littlefield, 2006.

Zelden, Charles L. *The Battle for the Black Ballot:* Smith v. Allwright *and the Defeat of the Texas All-White Primary*. Lawrence: University Press of Kansas, 2004.

Zelizer, Julian E. *Taxing America: Wilbur D. Mills, Congress, and the State, 1945-1975*. Cambridge: Cambridge University Press, 1998.

Zunz, Olivier. *Philanthropy in America: A History*. Princeton, NJ: Princeton University Press, 2012.

Index

Abelard Foundation, 104
Abernathy, Ralph, 19, 21, 26
Alabama Council on Human Relations, 16–17
Alabama State Coordinating Association for Registration and Voting (ASCARV), 57–58
Albany Movement (GA), 59, 71–75
Alexander, Will, 12
All-Citizens Registration Committee (Atlanta, GA), 64
All Citizens Voters League of Laurens County (GA), 15–16
Allen, Ralph, 73–74
Alston, Alice, 98
American Baptist Seminary, 57
American Conservative Union, 116
American Federation of Labor and Congress of Industrial Organizations (AFL-CIO), 76–78
American Friends Service Committee (AFSC), 3, 34, 64–65
Amerson, Lucius, 103, 108
Ames, Jesse Daniel, 12–13
Anderson, W. G., 72
Anthony, Paul, 93–95, 104, 105, 109, 119, 123–25
anticommunism, effect on black voting rights, 12–15, 19–20, 22, 25, 34, 112–13
Auburn (AL) League of Women Voters, 98

Bailey, Herman "Kofi," 129
Baker, Ella, 23–27, 45
Banks, Taunya, 130–31
Beasely, Mildred, 73–74
Belafonte, Harry, 44

Benson, Lucy, 119
Berry, Marion, 71
Blackwell, Randolph, 1, 65, 68–69, 74–75
Bond, Julian, 107–8, 112, 128–30, 132
Boyd, William, 45–46
Boynton, Amelia, 57–58
Boynton v. Virginia (1960), 42
Branton, Wiley A., 4–5, 58; background of, 59–61; and the first VEP, 62–63, 66–83, 94
Brazeal, Brailsford R., 15–16
Brooks, John, 49, 52
Brown, Ed, 134
Brownfeld, Allan, 116
Brown v. Board of Education (1954 & 1955), 8, 14–15, 20, 27, 38, 60, 124
Bruce, David K. E., 31
Bundy, McGeorge, 114–16, 123

Caddo Parish (LA) VEP, 98
Calhoun County (SC) Voters League, 98
Caplin, Mortimer, 54–55, 61–62
Carnegie Corporation, 34, 113, 115, 121, 130
Charleston County (SC) Voter Registration Project, 99–100
Chatfield, Jack, 72–73
Chatham County Crusade for Voters (GA), 80–81
Chisholm, Shirley, 107–8, 127
Christopher Reynolds Foundation, 34
Citizens Committee of Charleston (SC), 99–100
Citizens Committee of Wilson and Wilson County (NC), 82
Citizens Coordinating Committee of Daytona Beach (FL), 126–27

Civil Rights Act of 1957, 17–18, 21–22,
    26, 27, 39
Civil Rights Act of 1964, 81, 90
Clark, Septima, 19–20, 42–43
Cleghorn, Reese, 83
Cobb, Charlie, 67
Coleman, Clarence, 134
Collins, Patricia, 102
Commission on Interracial Coopera-
    tion, 12–13
Congress of Industrial Organizations, 12
Congress of Racial Equality (CORE),
    29–30, 41, 43; and forming the VEP,
    47–56; and the first VEP, 59, 63–65,
    68, 81; and the second VEP, 95, 100;
    and the Tax Reform Act of 1969,
    110–11, 114
Cook, Eugene, 14
Council of Federated Organizations
    (COFO), 65–71
Council on Foundations, 117–18, 121
Courts, Gus, 9
Cox, Edward, 112–13
Crusade for Citizenship (1958), 9,
    22–28, 30
Current, Gloster, 52
Currier, Audrey, 31–34, 103–4
Currier, Stephen, 30–37, 40; and launch-
    ing the VEP, 47–56; and the first VEP,
    61–63, 78–79; and the second VEP,
    92–93, 103–4

Dahmer, Vernon, 101
Dallas County Voters League (AL), 57–58
Democratic Party, 30, 39–40, 61–62, 70,
    82–83, 90–91, 96, 102
DeWind, Adrian, 54–56
Diggs, Charles, 26
Doar, John, 39–40, 69–70
Dougherty City Voter Education League
    (GA), 65
Due, John, 58
Dunbar, Leslie W., 37, 95, 125; back-
    ground of, 45–47; and launching the
    VEP, 47–56; and the first VEP, 59,

61–62, 74, 78–79, 83; and the second
    VEP, 90–94, 104, 109; and the Tax
    Reform Act of 1969, 117, 123–25, 132
Durham Committee on Negro Affairs
    (NC), 64

Eisenhower, Dwight, 18, 21, 60
Engelhardt, Sam, 10
Evers, Medgar, 66

Fair Employment Practices Committee, 18
Farmer, James, 41, 47–49, 51, 63–64
Field, Marshall, III
Field, Ruth, 63
Field Foundation, 26–27, 32, 34, 42–43,
    47, 125; and the first VEP, 62–63,
    78–79; and the second VEP, 92–94,
    104, 109; and the Tax Reform Act of
    1969, 112, 117, 125, 131, 133–34
Finance Committee (U.S. Senate),
    118–23Fleming, Harold, 31, 34–35,
    37–40, 43, 46–47, 50, 56
Ford Foundation, 14, 34, 46, 92, 94, 104,
    109; and the Tax Reform Act of 1969,
    110–12, 114–16, 118, 123, 125–27,
    132, 134
Fortas, Abe, 116
Fort Valley (GA) Citizens Education
    Commission, 98
Freedom Rides, 29–30, 41–42, 55, 57,
    61, 70, 124
Fund for the Republic, 14–15

Garrison, Lloyd K., 32–33, 47, 50, 54
Goldwater, Barry, 82
Goodwyn, Larry, 75–78
Goodwyn, Nell, 75
Graham, Billy, 18, 22
Granger, Lester, 47, 49
Greater Little Rock Voter Registration
    Movement (AR), 65
Greenwood movement (MS), 59, 68–71

Hamer, Fannie Lou, 67, 128
Harrington, Michael, 119

Harris, Don, 74–75
Harris, Roy, 13–14
Hawkins, Dee, 9
Hawkins, Reginald, 80, 107
Henry, Aaron, 65–66, 70–71
Highlander Folk School, 42–43, 45
Hollowell, Don, 94–95
Holmes, Hamilton, 94–95
Horton, Myles, 42
Humphrey, Hubert, 94, 107
Hunter, Charlayne, 94–95
Hurley, Ruby, 95

Internal Revenue Service (IRS), 4–5, 16, 43, 54–56, 62, 72; and the Tax Reform Act of 1969, 110, 123–25, 131
Interstate Commerce Commission, 42, 55

Jackson, Mahalia, 20
Javits, Jacob, 20, 128–29
Jefferson County Voter Registration Campaign (AL), 65
Jenkins, Timothy, 43–44, 47, 51
Johnson, Guy B., 13
Johnson, Lyndon B., 82–83, 90–92, 111, 114
Jones, Charles, 29, 44
Jones, Vivian Malone, 133
Jordan, Barbara, 103, 105
Jordan, Vernon E., Jr., 4, 91; background of, 94–95; and the second VEP, 95–109; and the Tax Reform Act of 1969, 111–12, 117–24

Katzenbach, Nicholas, 95–97
Kennedy, Edward, 128–29
Kennedy, John F., 29, 35, 37–40, 68
Kennedy, Robert F., 29–30, 39–44, 55, 68–70, 114
King, Martin Luther, Jr., 16–17, 35, 94, 124; and the Prayer Pilgrimage for Freedom, 18–21; and the Crusade for Citizenship, 22–28; and launching the VEP, 40–43, 47–56; and the first VEP,

72, 77, 79; and the second VEP, 95, 97, 100, 104
Knox, Kathleen, 7

Lafayette, Bernard and Colia, 57–58
Lawson, Jim, 57, 124–25
Lee, George Washington, 9
Lee County (AL) Voters League, 98
Legal Defense Fund (NAACP), 60, 94
Levine, Jean, 61
Levison, Stanley, 23, 41
Lewis, John, 58, 61, 112; background of, 124–25; and VEP, Inc., 125–33
Lincoln County (TN) Voter Registration Project, 98
literacy tests, 10–11, 15
Little Rock Nine (AR), 60–61
Lomax, Louis, 52–53, 62
Long, Russell, 6, 111, 118–23
Long, Worth, 74
Lucky, Mae, 10–11
Lynchburg (VA), Voters League, 98

Madison County Coordinating Committee (AL), 81
March on Washington Movement, 18–19
Marion Ascoli Fund, 94
Marshall, Burke, 40–44, 47, 51, 54–55, 62, 70
Marshall, Thurgood, 47, 60–61
Mary Reynolds Babcock Foundation, 104
Mays, Benjamin, 13–14
McDew, Charles, 29, 47, 50–51
McLaurin, Charles, 67
McNair, Landy, 67
McPherson, James, 1, 3–4, 7
Mellon family, 31–34
Miller, Helen Hill, 63
Mills, Wilbur, 114–18
Minnis, Jack, 57, 65–66, 80–81
Mississippi Freedom Democratic Party, 81, 107
Mitchell, George S., 13–14, 46
Mitchell, James, 21

Montgomery Improvement Association (MIA), 16–17
Moon, Henry Lee, 6, 51–52
Moore, Amzie, 44
Morsell, John, 79, 95, 100, 109
Moses, Bob, 44–45, 66–71

Nabrit, James M., Jr., 28
Nash, Diane, 29–30
National Association for the Advancement of Colored People (NAACP), 11–12, 14, 60–61, 94–95, 127; relationship with SCLC, 17–18, 24, 43, 50; and forming the VEP, 47–56; and the first VEP, 59, 63–65, 68, 71–72, 79, 81–82; and the second VEP, 95, 98, 100, 109
National Student Association, 47–48, 64
National Urban League (NUL), 18; and forming the VEP, 47–56; and the first VEP, 59, 63–65
New World Foundation, 34, 47, 104, 117
New York Foundation, 104
Nixon, Richard, 21–22, 38–39, 111, 116, 123
Non-Partisan Voters Registration Coordinating Committee (Charlotte, NC), 80
Northampton County (NC) Voters Movement, 98
North Carolina Fund, 98–99, 104
North Carolina Voter Education Project, 98–99

Odum, Howard, 13
Olive, Thaddeus, 97, 126
Orangeburg (SC) movement, 1–4, 7

Parks, Rosa, 19
Patch, Penny, 72–73
Patman, Wright, 110–11, 113–15
Patton, W. C., 49
Pensacola Improvement Association (FL), 98

philanthropic foundations: pre-VEP voting rights interest, 5–6, 26–27, 29–30, 34; federal tax exemption requirements, 4–5, 16, 35–37, 48, 54–56; and the Tax Reform Act of 1969, 110–34
Pierce, James, 17
Pollitt, Daniel, 37–38
poll tax, 10, 15, 75–78
Potomac Institute, 35, 37, 56
Powell, Adam Clayton, 20, 24–25
Prayer Pilgrimage for Freedom (1957), 9, 17–21
Price, Margaret, 15, 27–28
Pritchett, Laurie, 72
Progressive Democratic Party (SC), 12

Rambeau, Janie Culbreth, 73
Randolph, A. Philip, 9, 18–21, 22
Reconstruction era, memory of, 91, 93, 104–8
Reece, B. Carroll, 113
registrars, denying voting rights, 10–11, 15, 16, 58, 80–81
Republican Party, 40, 61, 77, 82–83, 96, 102
Revenue Act of 1934, 36
Rich, Marvin, 63
Rittleton, John, 56
Rockefeller Brothers Fund, 37, 46, 94, 104, 126, 131
Rockefeller Foundation, 34
Rogovin, Mitchell, 54
Rooney, John, 115
Roosevelt, Franklin D., 18
Rosenwald (Julius) Fund, 32, 63
Rougeau, Weldon, 97
Rustin, Bayard, 19, 23, 90–91, 96, 105–8

San Patricio and Bee County Voter Registration Council (TX), 127
Scott, Hugh, 121–22
Screven County (GA) VEP, 98
Seigenthaler, John, 41, 55

Senate (U.S.) Finance Committee, 118–23
Sherrod, Charles, 29–30, 71–75
Shuttlesworth, Fred, 25
Simon, John, 119
Smith, Lamar, 8–9
Smith v. Allwright (1944), 11, 15
Southern Christian Leadership Conference (SCLC), 17; and the Prayer Pilgrimage for Freedom, 18–21; and the Crusade for Citizenship, 22–28; and forming the VEP, 42–43, 47–56; and the first VEP, 59, 63–65, 68, 70, 72, 75, 79–80; and the second VEP, 95, 98, 100
Southern Conference for Human Welfare, 12
Southern Negro Youth Congress, 12
Southern Regional Council (SRC), 4, 9, 125; origins of, 12–13; disfranchisement research, 13–16, 27–28; federal tax exemption implications, 16, 43, 48, 51, 54, 61–62; and forming the VEP, 34–35, 37–41, 43–56; and the first VEP, 61–63, 78, 82–83; and the second VEP, 90–97, 107–8; and the Tax Reform Act of 1969, 112, 119–25
Southwest Georgia Voter Education Project, 127
Southwest Voter Registration Education Project (SVREP), 131
Southwide Conference for Black Elected Officials (1968), 107–8, 130
Stern Family Fund, 62–63, 78–79, 92, 104
Stokes, Carl, 110, 114
Storey, Moorfield, 11
Student Nonviolent Coordinating Committee (SNCC), 29–30, 41–42, 100, 124–25; and voter registration, 43–45, 57–58; and forming the VEP, 47–56; and the first VEP, 59, 63–75
Sunflower County (MS) VEP, 98

Taconic Foundation, 33–37, 47, 50–56; and the first VEP, 61–62, 78–79; and the second VEP, 92–94, 103–4, 119
Talmadge, Herman, 6, 14, 61–62, 111, 120–23
Tax Reform Act of 1969, 5–6; deliberations on, 110–23; impact of, 123–34
Texas Democratic Coalition, 75–78
Thomas, Charles, Jr., 2–3
Thompson, Geraldine, 133–34
Thurmond, Strom, 21
Till, Emmett, 124
Travis, Jimmy, 68–69
Tuskegee Civic Association, (AL), 81

United Church of Christ, 42–43
U.S. Commission on Civil Rights, 21, 24, 39, 71, 101–2
U.S. Department of Justice (DOJ), 4, 21, 29–30; and black voting rights, 39–44; and launching the VEP, 47–56; and the first VEP, 62, 69–71; and the second VEP, 93, 95–97, 101
U.S. Department of the Treasury, 54, 113–14

Velásquez, Willie, 131
Vietnam War, 81, 90–91, 111, 114
violence, for attempting to register, 8–9, 27, 58, 64, 68–69, 71–72, 100–101
Voter Education Project (VEP): purposes of, 1–7; grants to independent registration campaigns, 2–3, 57–58, 64–65, 80–82, 98–100; grants to the Big Five, 63–65, 79–82, 98, 100; federal tax-exemption implications, 54–56, 61–62, 68, 75–77, 108–9, 117–34; and philanthropic foundations, 62–63, 65, 71–72, 78–79, 93–94, 103–4, 120–21, 125–26; and impact on national politics, 82–83, 103, 105–7; and VEP, Inc. (post-1969), 123–34
voter purges, 11, 15–16
Voters of Texas Enlist (VOTE), 59, 75–78

Voting Rights Act of 1965, 4, 83, 91–93, 95–97, 100–102, 108–9, 133

Walker, Wyatt Tee, 29, 42–43, 47–48, 50–51, 64
Wall, Marvin, 97, 100–101, 106, 126
Wallace, George, 111, 132
Wallace, Henry A., 12
Warburg family, 30–31
Washington, Booker T., 59–60
Watters, Pat, 83
Ways and Means Committee (U.S. House of Representatives), 54, 110–11, 114–18
Weatherford, Willis, 12
Wheeler, John, 83

White, Ella Lee, 11
White, Walter, 113
White citizens' councils, 11, 14–15, 57–58
Wilkins, Roy, 9, 19–20, 47–49, 51–56, 79, 117–18, 120
Williams, Hosea, 80–81, 100, 127, 132
Wofford, Harris, 38–41, 47, 51, 55, 62
Wolfson Foundation, 116
Womanpower Unlimited (MS), 65

Yarborough, Ralph, 121–22
Young, Andrew, 75
Young, Whitney, 47–48, 51, 104, 116, 119–20